Attachment-Focused Family Therapy

WORKBOOK

A Norton Professional Book

Attachment-Focused Family Therapy

WORKBOOK

Daniel A. Hughes, PhD

W. W. Norton & Company

New York London

For information about permission to reproduce selections from this book, write to
Permissions, W. W. Norton & Company, Inc., 500 Fifth Avenue, New York, NY 10110

For information about special discounts for bulk purchases, please contact W. W. Norton
Special Sales at specialsales@wwnorton.com or 800-233-4830

Manufacturing by Hamilton Printing
Book design by Carol Desnoes
Production manager: Leeann Graham

Library of Congress Cataloging-in-Publication Data
Hughes, Daniel A.
    Attachment-focused family therapy workbook / Daniel A. Hughes.
        p. cm. – (A Norton professional book)
    Includes bibliographical references and index.
    ISBN 978-0-393-70649-9 (pbk.)
    1. Family therapy–Problems, exercises, etc. 2. Attachment behavior–Problems, exercises, etc. I. Title.
    RC488.5.H8272 2011
    616.89'1560076–dc22   2010043550

W. W. Norton & Company, Inc., 500 Fifth Avenue, New York, N.Y. 10110
www.wwnorton.com
W. W. Norton & Company Ltd., Castle House, 75/76 Wells Street, London W1T 3QT

3 4 5 6 7 8 9 0

I dedicate this book to my three daughters:

Megan, Kristin, and Madeline.

Three hearts and minds endowed with strength, joy, wisdom, and compassion,

each unique and wonderful.

Contents

Acknowledgments

I wish to acknowledge Allan Schore and Dan Siegel for their continuing influence on my professional development. The breadth and depth of their insights and integrative knowledge continue to inspire my own development.

I also wish to acknowledge the wealth of knowledge regarding infant intersubjectivity given to us by Colwyn Trevarthen. His insights into emotional and cultural development within the young child are the wellspring of many of my clinical principles and interventions. All three of these individuals have been very gracious and willing to share their knowledge with someone who hoped to apply their wisdom to the treatment of families.

Diana Fosha and Sue Johnson, whose work I greatly admire, find complementary to my own, and which has influenced my own, also receive my gratitude.

I am deeply indebted to many colleagues, friends, and families whom I have treated over the years who have each uniquely contributed to my application of attachment and intersubjectivity theories to therapy. Their names are too numerous to mention, but each has brought a unique perspective to the development of the individual and family.

I also am deeply indebted to the following individuals who have been and continue to be instrumental in the ongoing development of AFFT and DDP. All are certified as therapists and consultants in this model of treatment: Art Becker-Weidman, Mick Borgeson, Geraldine Casswell, Kim Golding, Julie Hudson, Alison Keith, Pamela McCloskey, Pam Tower, Deb Shell, and Robert Spottswood.

I am especially grateful for the assistance of the following individuals who reviewed one or more chapters of this workbook: Pamela McCloskey, Kim Golding, Deb Shell, Julie Hudson, Robert Spottswood, and Art Becker-Weidman. The evolution of DDP and AFFT have been greatly influenced over the years by their insights, experience, and thoughtful suggestions.

Attachment-Focused Family Therapy

WORKBOOK

Introduction

Attachment-focused family therapy (AFFT) is a model of treatment that has developed over the past 15 years and is now being practiced by therapists throughout the United States, United Kingdom, Canada, Ireland, and Australia as well as by a few therapists in other European countries and Taiwan. AFFT was originally developed to provide treatment to foster and adoptive families with children who manifest signs of developmental trauma and attachment disturbances. It was known as dyadic developmental psychotherapy (DDP) and still is referred to as DDP when it is applied to this specific population. The basic principles and interventions of AFFT, when applied to foster, adoptive, biological—to all families—remain the same.

Attachment-Focused Family Therapy Workbook, along *with Attachment-Focused Family Therapy* (2007) and *Attachment-Focused Parenting* (2009), are intended to assist therapists in learning this model of treatment so that they can apply it with skill and positive results. They are not intended to stand alone, but to be one part of a comprehensive training program that includes a minimum of 8 days of training combined with the extensive utilization of this model of treatment. The therapist also receives consultations on selected videos of treatment sessions by skilled therapists who are certified in the use of this model.

This workbook was difficult to write because of the inherent nature of the intersubjective process applied in AFFT, known as affective-reflective dialogue (A-R dialogue). One cannot say that a therapist should approach a specific problem with a sequence of five interventions. Even if it were possible to recommend the first intervention for a specific problem, the second one would be determined by the family's unique response to the first one. The third intervention would be determined by the family's unique response to the second one, and so on.

The core process of AFFT is A-R dialogue. The primary way in which the therapist becomes engaged in the dialogue is with the attitude of PACE, which stands for playfulness, acceptance, curiosity, and empathy. PACE corresponds to the attitude that one might most closely identify with the conversation—without words—that occurs routinely between a parent and infant.

During AFFT the therapist facilitates intersubjective communication between parent and child. Examples of this dialogue may be found frequently throughout the workbook. I frequently stop the dialogue and comment on what is occurring. Therapists are encouraged to study these dialogues and comments in detail to get a sense of the moment-to-moment attachment-focused communications and interventions that represent AFFT. These are moment-to-moment interventions that cannot be prepared in advance. Such preparation would distort A-R dialogue and the intersubjective process itself. The family members—parent and child—need to influence the therapist and this influence refers especially to here-and-now interventions that are meant to influence them. Studying these examples in depth will provide an awareness of the nature of the therapy itself. A more comprehensive understanding for the therapist can only come through observing therapists who are well qualified in the use of this treatment model, utilizing the model in treatment sessions and receiving feedback regarding its application. Learning AFFT, as in learning any skill, requires much repetition, while being open to the successes and failings of one's efforts, while being mentored by someone who is proficient in the activity. The workbook is meant to facilitate this experiential learning process, not to replace it.

While important aspects of the therapeutic dialogue are conveyed in the workbook by presenting examples, equally important aspects are much more difficult to teach in written form. I am referring to the nonverbal communication that is continuously occurring. The voice prosody, facial expressions, movements, gestures, timing, and intensity each contribute greatly to the meaning of the dialogue. While it is possible to write about what vocal or facial expressions are present, what is being conveyed through writing is much less than if one could actually see the facial expression or hear the vocal rhythms or inflections. For this reason, a DVD of part of a treatment session is included as part of the workbook. This will enable the therapist to have a more complete understanding of an actual A-R dialogue.

AFFT is a method of treatment that requires the full range of clinical skills that are common to excellent clinicians from a variety of backgrounds and orientations. Central to AFFT are skills that are crucial in building the therapeutic relationship, such as acceptance, curiosity, and empathy. Related skills involve the ability to facilitate the joint exploration of the lives of the members of the family. The focus is on the events that they have experienced together as well as those which have a large impact on one member of the family, thus making it important to the others in the family. The events explored are not restricted to individual or family problems. Rather, AFFT focuses on helping family members get to know each other from a basic stance of acceptance, rather than evaluation. This understanding includes their strengths and vulnerabilities as well as the impact that they are having on each other, for better or worse.

The following books serve as companion readings for this workbook:

Hughes, D. (2007). *Attachment-focused family therapy.* New York: Norton.

Hughes, D. (2009). *Attachment-focused parenting.* New York: Norton.

ATTACHMENT-FOCUSED FAMILY THERAPY

AFFT is a model of therapeutic change that is based on the theories and research of attachment and intersubjectivity. At its core, this treatment involves facilitating the development of specific patterns of communication and relationship among family members. These patterns provide safety and learning for all members of the family without relying on fear, shame, or force.

In this manner of relating, each family member maintains an openness to the inner life of the other while communicating his or her own inner life, including thoughts, emotions, and intentions. All are safe to give expression to their own experiences. The experience of one has an effect on the experience of the other. And it is reciprocal. In so doing, joint meanings are created and a cooperative stance emerges. In such families where safety and intersubjective exploration are lived realities, what is best for one is most often best for all.

Applying attachment theory and research to psychological treatment is still a fairly new endeavor. Since effective family and individual therapy must create safety for those engaged in treatment and since safety is at the core of attachment theory, this theory most certainly has much to contribute to providing effective treatment. Without having a sense of safety, the individual—child or adult—is not receptive to new learning. Not being safe, the individual relies on old learning—past events that may or may not be similar—as well as the more basic parts of the brain involving precognitive reactions that provide an immediate response to a new, sudden, and possibly threatening stimulus. Learning the subtleties of family and community life, the patterns, rhythms, and meanings of nonverbal and verbal communication, requires a sense of safety that is necessary to activate, in an integrated manner, all parts of the brain and body.

Intersubjectivity theory is closely aligned with attachment theory and is also crucial in the development of the individual within the family. Whereas attachment describes the role of safety, intersubjectivity describes the manner in which infants learn about the self, the family, and the larger community and culture. It describes how the experience—the meanings given to the objects and events of one's life—of the parents are passed down to the children. It also describes how the experiences of the children often influence the continuing development of the parents.

Research indicates that attachment security facilitates the development of the individual's ability to regulate both emotional states and their affect expressions. Attachment security also facilitates reflective functioning. Given its interwoven presence with attachment, it is reasonable to believe that intersubjectivity also facilitates these crucial areas of development. The core process of AFFT, A-R dialogue, works toward developing these skills, their integration, and the attachment relationships and intersubjective experiences that will enable them to continue long after treatment stops. Therapeutic principles and interventions beneficial for the coregulation of affect—including affect matching and lead-ing—as well as reflective functioning are discussed in great detail throughout the book. Now I briefly summarize the nature of these two broad treatment goals.

Affect Regulation

Children who develop secure attachment relationships with their parents or caregivers are likely to be better able to regulate their emotional states and their affective expressions of these states than are children who are not securely attached to their parents, especially children who do not have organized attachment patterns. The parent assists the infant in learning to regulate affect and any underlying emotions by matching the affect expression of these emotions and remaining regulated himself. The infant's affective state is coregu-lated with the parent's active participation long before the infant or young child develops the ability to self-regulate affect. In fact, when parents are not available for such repetitive experiences of coregulation—as is the case in situations of neglect—the infant and young child is at great risk of not being able to adequately develop the ability to self-regulate. Such a child is then likely to manifest very unpredictable and labile affective states, rage outbursts, pervasive anxiety, or intense fears, as well as difficulty managing excitement or attaining calm after becoming agitated.

Attunement—defined by Dan Stern (1985) as the intersubjective sharing of affect—is at the heart of the infant's development of affect regulation skills. Within the attuned interac-tions between parent and infant, the parent is coregulating the affective states as they emerge from within the infant. When the infant is regulated, the parent's attuned response matches the affect and deepens the experience for both infant and parent. When the infant is becoming dysregulated, the parent matches the affect and leads the infant into a regulated state. This is done in an intuitive, primarily nonverbal, manner.

Reflective Functioning

Children who manifest attachment security with the primary attachment figures are also likely to manifest superior reflective functioning skills compared to children who do not experience such attachment security. Reflective functioning refers to the child's ability to be aware of his inner life, that is, his thoughts, emotions, intentions, wishes, values, beliefs, perceptions, and memories as well as the inner lives of others. The child who reflects well is able to make sense of his own behavior and the behaviors of others. He is also able to notice and make sense of nonverbal expressions of others.

Just as a child does not develop autoregulation of affect without first experiencing coregulation, so too is the child unable to develop reflective functioning on her own. The infant learns such skills by experiencing her parent very frequently making sense of her expressions and behaviors, being sensitive to the meaning of her expressions and then responding in a contingent manner to those expressions. The parent and child then develop an elaborate system of nonverbal communication. They each note the expression of the other, guess its meaning, communicate their guess, and fine-tune their understanding and activity based on the response of the other to this guess. The parent's high priority of getting to know his child, to communicate his awareness and then to be guided by the child's response, enables the child to become aware of and successfully communicate her inner life to her parent, while at the same time learning to make sense of how her parent's behaviors reflect her inner life.

Therapy attempts to help clients to make sense of their thoughts, feelings, and intentions and then successfully communicate them to others. Therapy also attempts to help clients be able to accurately make sense of the thoughts, feelings, and emotions of others so as to better communicate and cooperate. When a client already possesses good reflective functioning, the therapist can be nondirective and the client is likely to utilize the therapeutic hour fairly successfully. When a client has not developed reflective skills well, he will benefit most from a therapist who is quite actively and openly curious about his inner life, makes guesses about the meanings of nonverbal expressions and behaviors, and fine-tunes his guesses based on the responses of the client. This process is very similar to that of the parent and young child during which the parent is facilitating the development of the child's reflective functioning. The parent is not nondirective nor ambiguous in these interactions. It is an actual, reciprocal process of mutual discovery about the meanings of the young child's behavior. The same process can greatly facilitate the development of reflective functioning in therapy.

This workbook first presents a summary of attachment and intersubjectivity, which represent the basic theories being applied. Chapter 2, "Intersubjectivity," is presented in greater depth to convey the manner in which its three central components permeate the treatment sessions.

A-R dialogue and PACE represent the primary, moment-to-moment process of the treatment. The process of the dialogue and the attitude of PACE enable the content that is being regulated and explored to unfold and move toward greater depth of experience and integration into the narratives of the family members. Sequential aspects of this process are described in a separate chapter as well as relationship repair, which is crucial to maintain the safety of the dialogue and the relationship itself.

Chapter 7, "The Parent as Attachment Figure," describes the basic manner in which the therapist first works with the parents, building a safe working alliance with them, to ensure that they are able to join the therapist in ensuring attachment security for the child.

Finally, Chapter 8 discusses DDP, the application of AFFT to foster and adoptive families. The therapist needs to understand the unique features of this population and the treatment modifications that may be needed.

1 Attachment

Attachment is much more than a theory. It reflects a body of research that both extends from infancy to old age and also influences the development and functioning of most areas of human activity (Cassidy & Shaver, 2008). It is relevant to our understanding of human development and to the interwoven areas of mental health, health, education, infancy, early childhood, parenting, social services, and aging (Cicchetti, Toth, & Lynch, 1995; Sroufe, Egeland, Carlson, & Collins, 2005). In this work, its relevance for psychotherapy, and family therapy in particular, will hopefully be made clear.

ATTACHMENT THEORY AND RESEARCH: CORE PRINCIPLES, COMPONENTS, AND IMPLICATIONS FOR TREATMENT

1. **An innate motivating factor in our human species is to turn to our attachment figures for safety.** This is most evident during infancy because the infant is very dependent upon the parents—or other caregivers—during the first several years of development. Safety begins with the child's physical well-being, involving food, water, shelter, clothing, and protection from physical dangers. Safety also involves the child's psychological well-being. The child depends upon the parents for the experiences of social and emotional engagement that are crucial for neuropsychobiological development.

    Attachment-focused family therapy (AFFT) begins by facilitating safety for the parents with the therapist and then having the parents and therapist facilitate safety for the child. A central goal of treatment is to help the parents to become more aware of their child's safety needs and ways to ensure that the child lives with a habitual sense of safety in his relationship with them. At the same time, the parents are helped to be more aware of their own needs for safety with each other, as parents, and within their lives generally.

2. **Recent neurological research offers much support and validation for attachment theory and research.** The brain and mind work best in relationship with others. Some theorists have described the human brain as being essentially a "dyadic brain," developing best and functioning best in concert with individuals with whom we are safe and

interested in joint explorations (Fosha, Siegel, & Solomon, 2009; Schore, 2001; Siegel, 2001). The development of the young child's brain with regard to social-emotional-cultural learning (as well as much of cognitive, physiological, and sensory-motor learning) is dependent upon safety and ongoing contact with attachment figures.

AFFT works to facilitate the neuropsychological development of members of the family by facilitating their readiness and ability to become engaged with each other in reciprocal, attuned, affective, and reflective interactions.

3. **The young child's relationship with his parent becomes a secure base from which he begins to explore.** As he explores, he comes across the unexpected, including events and objects that elicit fear and uncertainty. When this happens, he quickly returns to his parents for safety—they are his safe haven. This has been called the circle of security (Marvin, Cooper, Hoffman, & Powell, 2002) as the safety of the secure base leads to exploration, which generates associated fears and leads to a return to this base, now experienced as a safe haven.

   In AFFT the therapist helps the parents to see that at all ages, their child benefits from turning to them for comfort and support when under stress. There is no time when a child needs to be independent and manage things on her own. The child needs to develop the ability to find safety within herself and within her relationships with her parents and be able to determine which is preferable in a given situation. It is helpful to remember that toddlers often turn to their parents for comfort after being disciplined by their parents. AFFT encourages parents to see discipline as being more helpful when the parent initiates a repair of the relationship with the child following the discipline.

4. **The young child especially begins to explore his social and emotional world**. He develops patterns of engagement with his attachment figures. These patterns are reciprocal and contingent processes of nonverbal and verbal communication. They are essentially intersubjective experiences, which will be considered in great detail in a subsequent chapter and throughout this work.

   In AFFT the therapist actively utilizes these same intersubjective patterns to facilitate the social and emotional development of the members of the family. In such reciprocal communication patterns, parental authority is not compromised while the parent-child relationships deepen and all members of the family remain safe to develop their autonomy. The process of A-R dialogue, the central activity of AFFT, is essentially this intersubjective pattern or relating and communicating.

5. **In one pattern of engagement in relationships characterized by attachment security, there is a balance between the child relying on her attachment figure and learning to rely on her own developing skills.** With attachment security, neither independence nor dependence is valued over the other. In various circumstances, reliance on another is indicated while at other times, self-reliance is the better choice. With maturation, self-reliance occurs more and more frequently but reliance on another remains relevant

and completely valued throughout life. Interdependence as a way of life is far superior to constant independence or dependence.

Conflicts between the individual and the family unit, the child's autonomy, and parental beliefs as to what is best for the child represent the frequent themes of AFFT. By differentiating behavior from the experience of family members, evaluating only behavior, and responding with PACE to both behavior and experience, the AFFT therapist is able to facilitate the integration of both self and relationships within the family. One need not be sacrificed for the other.

6. **A second pattern of a child's interpersonal engagements is characterized by minimizing the importance of the attachment figure and attempting to avoid attachment relationships.** When a child cannot rely on the attachment figure, she too quickly and too strongly tries to rely on herself. Lacking necessary skills that have not yet developed, she attempts to control most situations, not engaging in reciprocal activities, and eventually moving into rigid intimidation and avoidance patterns. She tends to reduce the value of her emotions and attempts to rely on a cognitive approach to making decisions and guiding her life.

In AFFT the therapist explores the possible roots of these avoidance patterns in the attachment history of the parents. He then explores with parent and child together the thoughts, emotions and wishes that have led to these patterns while facilitating the safe experience of deeper emotional intimacy, without sacrificing the ability to be self-reliant.

7. **A third pattern of engagement for a child is characterized by minimizing the importance of his own self-reliance skills and anxious clinging to the attachment figure.** Being preoccupied with his attachment figure, he does not develop self-reliance abilities. He is anxious because the attachment figure is not consistently available and responsive and as a result, he is not able to move into the balance of security. Such children have been described as being too attached, though that is not accurate. They are anxiously attached.

In AFFT the therapist explores the possible roots of these anxious patterns in the attachment history of the parents. He then explores with parent and child the thoughts, emotions, and wishes that have led to these patterns while facilitating the safe experience of individuation and self-reliance, without sacrificing the ability to be emotionally intimate.

8. **A fourth group of children are unable to develop a consistent pattern that is either balanced, or overreliant on the self, or overreliant on the parent.** These children are at risk to become very disorganized and dysregulated in their functioning in response to any stress. They try to cope with stress with an extreme need to control all aspects of their environment. Stresses that cannot be controlled are often experienced as traumas that lead to pervasive dysfunctioning. These children are at risk to develop mental health problems of both externalization and internalization.

In AFFT, the therapist engages the family in a slow and deliberate process to attempt to generate safety for the parent and then for parent and child together. Disorganized attachment patterns in children are often associated with their parents being frightening to or being frightened by their child when the child's attachment behaviors are the most intense. Thus the parental response to the child's terror, rage, despair, or shame will be explored, often leading to aspects of the parents' attachment histories. Since the child's self-reliance skills are poorly developed, it will take longer to reduce his symptoms and since his other-reliance skills are disorganized, the development of trust and ability to rely on an attachment figure for development will also be a gradual process. Parents are also likely to need an extended period of safe exploration of their interactions with their child's challenges.

9. **These attachment patterns develop over time as inner working models of self and others.** These models become basic assumptions and perceptions that influence our inner lives, including our thoughts, feelings, and even memories. These models involve our sense of self-worth, competence, lovability, and value. They guide our emotional awareness and expression as well as the emphasis and boundaries of our reflective abilities. These inner working models become the source of strengths and confidence and an open, flexible approach to self and relationship development or the source of a rigid or chaotic stance that anticipates barriers and avoids opportunities for development.

   In AFFT the therapist utilizes A-R dialogue to safely explore the inner working models of parent and child. The unique qualities of the inner working models are accepted and seen as the source of the rich contributions that each member brings to the family, rather than being seen as a threat to the family.

10. **Attachment security is based on having parents who are available, sensitive, and responsive on a consistent basis and especially when the child's attachment behaviors are activated.** Attachment security develops when parents provide comfort and support when the child is frightened and vulnerable. When children do not receive comfort in response to vulnerability, they tend to reduce the impact of emotions by becoming overly rational (avoidant pattern), or they become ruled by their emotions (anxious). When the failure of attachment figures to provide comfort and support is too chronic or when the stresses are too severe, the child is at risk to rely on neither herself nor her attachment figure in a consistent manner (disorganized).

    In AFFT the therapist explores the child's responses to distress, normalizes these responses in the context of the history of attachment patterns within the family, and explores possibilities for responding to stress in a more adaptive manner. The parents' responses to distress are also explored to determine ways to enable them to have a more flexible and available response to their child's distress.

11. **Secure attachment relationships are ideally suited to assist individuals in understanding and resolving stressful and dysregulating emotions such as fear, anxiety, despair, anger, shame, and grief.** Within an attachment relationship, individuals are

often able to regulate such emotions whereas they might fail to do so when dealing with them alone. The comfort provided frequently within an attachment relationship of security is crucial for managing and integrating the stresses of life. Negative emotions become smaller within attachment relationships.

In AFFT the therapist attempts to activate psychoneurological attachment and caregiving behaviors in the child-parent dyad. When he is able to initiate and maintain A-R dialogue during the treatment, with the absence of the habitual angry, defensive, and avoidant patterns, these natural patterns are able to emerge.

12. **Secure attachment relationships are also ideally suited to deepen and enhance positive emotions such as joy, excitement, pride, and satisfaction.** Sharing these emotions with an attachment figure enables them to be experienced more fully and comprehensively. Without attachment relationships, such emotions are likely to be less evident and have less meaning in a person's life. Positive emotions become larger and better regulated within attachment relationships.

In AFFT the therapist explores strengths as much as vulnerabilities. In doing so the family become more aware of their thoughts, emotions, and wishes that lie apart from the problems and are able to address them from greater emotional strengths, which in turn increases their reciprocal joy and pride.

13. **Attachment relationships are also ideally suited to facilitate the development of reflective functioning.** Within safe relationships, individuals are free to become aware of, explore, and communicate their inner lives of thoughts, feelings, intentions, and other features. When a parent is deeply interested in the inner life of her child, the child becomes interested in it as well and is motivated to communicate central aspects of who she is to her parent. With such safety, the child also becomes openly interested in what her parents think and feel and intend to do. With such open, emotional, and thoughtful communication, the place that each has in the mind and heart of the other is clear and secure.

In AFFT the therapist's development of A-R dialogue increases the family members' reflective functioning, which in turn increases their abilities to resolve the problems that led the family to treatment.

14. **Attachment security is based on interactive repair whenever there is a break in the relationship due to separations, conflicts, misattunements and misunderstandings, or differing goals.** All attachment relationships have such breaks, and many attachment relationships become insecure or even disorganized when interactive repair is not present in a very predictable manner. Such repairs make it clear to the child that the relationship is very important, no separation will be final, and no conflict will end the relationship. The relationship is safe and its permanence is ensured regardless of the current situation. Relationship repair is the responsibility of the parent, regardless of the source of the break; otherwise the parent is communicating that the relationship is not more important than the conflict.

In AFFT the therapist models and utilizes relationship repair throughout the sessions. A commitment to repair and means of engaging in successful repair is made clear and its role in maintaining attachment security is established.

15. **When conflicts or withdrawal are common in a family, too often the primary focus is on the behavior between members of the family, with each having negative assumptions about the meaning of the other's behavior.** An attachment perspective focuses instead on the meaning of the behavior, bringing a nonjudgmental curiosity about the behavior, seeking to understand its meaning, including what it may or may not represent with regard to attachment.

    Within AFFT, the therapist utilizes A-R dialogue to differentiate the experience of the family members from their behaviors. The former are not evaluated but met with PACE. Behavioral differences are then much easier to understand and resolve.

16. **Attachment security is facilitated by experiencing unconditional acceptance, being prized for who you are.** Children who are securely attached to their parents are more likely to have parents who are able to accept a much greater range of their child's inner life of thoughts, feelings, and wishes than are children who manifest insecure or disorganized patterns.

    Within AFFT, the therapist facilitates the parents' ability to accept the full range of their child's thoughts, feelings, and intentions, while restricting their discipline to the child's behaviors.

17. **Attachment theory suggests that a parent's greatest influence over her child's behavior involves the nature of the attachment patterns and related intersubjective interactions.** This contrasts with behavioral theory's focus on a parent influencing her child's behavior through linking consequences to the behavior, attempting to reinforce or extinguish the behavior itself. From the perspective of attachment theory, successful family treatment endeavors to establish attachment safety and open, intersubjective communication, which will provide the flexible foundation and framework from which past and future behaviors are able to be addressed.

    In AFFT the therapist's primary goal is to facilitate attachment security in the parent-child relationship. When the relationship is strengthened, the behavioral problems tend to dissipate or to be much more receptive to interventions focused on addressing them.

18. **Attachment theory extends from infancy through old age.** Safety within attachment relationships is crucial at all ages for maintaining psychological functioning and well-being. Establishing and maintaining a coherent autobiographical narrative is greatly aided by having one's narrative interwoven with the coherent narratives of others who are important to us.

    Within AFFT, the therapist attends to the attachment narratives of all members of the family. As she helps the parents to establish more coherent autobiographical narratives, she is increasing their ability to facilitate the coherence of their children's narratives.

19. **Secure attachment in children is described as autonomous attachment in adults.** Avoidant attachment in childhood is called dismissive attachment in adults, while anxious attachment in childhood is called preoccupied attachment in adults. Finally, disorganized attachment in childhood is described as unresolved attachment in adulthood. These adult patterns of attachment are important when adults—as parents—attempt to facilitate attachment security within their child. The act of parenting activates—brings alive again—the attachment experiences of one's own childhood. Autonomously attached adults are much more successful in raising children who are securely attached than are adults who fall within the other three classifications.

    For this reason, AFFT needs to begin by determining the attachment classification of the parent to facilitate resolution of the parent's attachment history if necessary. Even when the parent's attachment history is autonomous and resolved, aspects of her history still may be activated by her child's behaviors and it is helpful for the therapist to help the parent to be aware of the connections.

EXERCISES

True/False Exercise

Answer *true* or *false* to each statement.

1. Safety and attachment:
   A. The most basic function of attachment is to provide safety for the child. _____
   B. Safety is no longer an important factor in adult attachment relationships. _____
   C. Safety has no noticeable impact on neurological functioning. _____
   D. With regard to attachment, safety refers to both biological and psychological features._____

2. Circle of security refers to:
   A. A child becoming too attached and overly dependent upon the parent._____
   B. The part of the cycle where safety is stressed rather than exploration. _____
   C. The dual features of secure base and safe haven in attachment. _____
   D. The complete cycle of safety and exploration. _____

3. Attachment security:
   A. Is important for preschool children but after that it creates a danger of dependence. _____
   B. Is positively associated with many aspects of accomplishment and development. _____
   C. Facilitates integration and balance between self-reliance and other-reliance. _____
   D. Needs to be gently discouraged during the development of adolescent independence. _____

4. An avoidant attachment pattern:
   A. Places great reliance on self, and minimizes the importance of attachment. _____
   B. Emphasizes emotions over cognitions in making decisions. _____
   C. Stresses control rather than reciprocal activities. _____
   D. Is a necessary stage between dependence and independence. _____

5. An anxious attachment pattern:
   A. Places equal reliance on self and other. _____
   B. Emphasizes emotions over cognitions in making decisions. _____
   C. Is often incorrectly described as a child being too attached to a parent. _____
   D. Represents a lack of a coherent attachment pattern. _____

6. A disorganized attachment pattern:

A. Is considered to be a risk factor for the development of mental health problems. _____

B. Is correlated with problems of externalization, but not internalization. _____

C. Impairs the development of both self-reliance and reliance on others. _____

D. Is the classification that is associated with the greatest need to control everything. _____

7. Relationship repair:
   A. Is central to attachment security. _____
   B. Is only necessary when the parent has made a parenting mistake. _____
   C. Is the responsibility of the parent to ensure that it happens. _____
   D. Conveys that the relationship is more important than the source of the break. _____

8. Secure attachments facilitate:
   A. The regulation of negative emotions. _____
   B. The regulation of positive emotions. _____
   C. Reflective functioning. _____
   D. A positive inner working model. _____

9. A parent's attachment history:
   A. Has no bearing on the attachment classification of the child. _____
   B. Needs to be resolved to optimize the likelihood of the child's attachment security. _____
   C. Is no longer of importance once the child moves beyond infancy. _____
   D. Is activated through the acts of parenting. _____

10. From an attachment perspective:
    A. The parent needs to focus most on providing consequences for behavior. _____
    B. The parent needs to focus on the meanings of behavior. _____
    C. The parent's primary influence on the child is the relationship. _____
    D. Discipline is unrelated to the attachment relationship. _____

Experiential Exercises

1. Recall past times when you were in distress and you sought comfort from an attachment figure.
   A. Recall a time when the attachment figure dismissed your distress.
   B. Recall a time when the attachment figure gave you advice rather than comfort.
   C. Recall a time when the attachment figure provided comfort.
   D. Compare the experiences noted above. What were the differing effects of the three experiences of the distress?

2. Recall past times when you faced distress alone.
   A. Did you try to manage the distress differently?
   B. Did you think of an attachment figure at the time and if so, were the thoughts helpful?
   C. Were there differences in your ability to reduce distress in the absence of an attachment figure?

3. Recall past times of pride or joy.
   A. How did it affect the positive emotion when you shared it with an attachment figure?
   B. How did it affect the positive emotion when you experienced it alone?
   C. When you shared the positive emotion with an attachment figure, what was the response? How did that affect the experience?

4. What was the nature of relationship repair when you were a child? How did that affect the nature of your attachments with your parents? How did that affect the nature of conflicts within the home? How did that affect your sense of emotional closeness with your parents?

5. Did you share your thoughts, feelings, and wishes with your parents often? Did that help you to be more aware of your inner life? Did that affect your relationship with your parent? Did your parent share his or her inner life with you? Did that affect your relationship with your parent?

ANSWERS TO TRUE/FALSE EXERCISE

1. A. T	3. A. F	5. A. F	7. A. T	9. A. F
B. F	B. T	B. T	B. F	B. T
C. F	C. T	C. T	C. T	C. F
D. T	D. F	D. F	D. T	D. T
2. A. F	4. A. T	6. A. T	8. A. T	10. A. F
B. F	B. F	B. F	B. T	B. T
C. T	C. T	C. T	C. T	C. T
D. T	D. F	D. T	D. T	D. F

2 Intersubjectivity

Intersubjective communications involve the sharing of experiences where each one is open to both influencing and being influenced by the experience of the other. Conveying information, while important, is not the heart of these communications. It is through the sharing of one's inner life with the other that one becomes open to the other's experience of one's inner life, and where the other is also able to be impacted by one's own experience of that person. It is this reciprocal sharing of experience that enables individuals to thrive within intimate relationships without losing their uniqueness. In fact, within intersubjective experiences, each member of the dyad is more able to discover his or her uniqueness. When families lose touch with the magic of intersubjective experiences, they lose touch with their mission to foster the development of each member. When families communicate intersubjectively, they are able to develop the uniqueness of the individual family member, while at the same time deepening the safety, joy, and companionship that can emerge within attachment security. When a family struggles and is not able to meet the needs of all of its members, an attachment-focused family therapy can do no better than bring the gift of intersubjective experience into that family.

Intersubjectivity can be seen most clearly in the parent-infant relationship. This process, in which the parent and infant are gazing into each other's eyes, keeping their expressions and gestures in synchrony, using their voices as if they were musicians playing a duet, has been studied in detail by a psychologist who has done much in helping us to understand its qualities as well as its central role in emotional, social, and cultural development. Colwyn Trevarthen (2001), from the University of Edinburgh in Scotland, refers to this parent-infant time as one of "joyful dialogic companionship." Trevarthen describes this drive for such companionship as an equal complement to the drive toward attachment. It is through these moments that the—hopefully coherent and organized—experience of the parent is shared with the infant and enables the infant to begin to organize his own experience into a coherent sense of self along with a meaningful sense of the events and objects of the world. While doing so the parent is also impacted by the infant's emerging experience of the parent as parent.

Through intersubjective experiences, the subjective experiences of one contribute to the development of the subjective experiences of the others, and vice versa. It is a reciprocal process. Because of its inherent reciprocal nature, it has often been overlooked as a potentially powerful therapeutic stance. Many have thought that the therapist needs to be detached from the client. The therapist has often been given the goal of being "objective." The therapist has been asked to be wary of the possibility that the client might have an influence on him. If there were such a reciprocal influence, it would be assumed that the therapist had lost his professional boundaries.

Yet, just as infants and older children would be disempowered if they did not have the capacity to have a positive impact on their parents, so too is a client disempowered when she gives expression to what one might view as courage or honesty or compassion or love and the therapist does not experience those qualities in the client or, if he does, he conceals it from the client. This chapter contrasts the intersubjective stance with the traditional therapeutic stance and presents the three central features of intersubjective experiences.

IN THIS CHAPTER

I. The Intersubjective Therapeutic Stance

II. The Intersubjective Versus the Traditional Therapeutic Stance

III. The Three Central Components of Intersubjective Experience

    A. The Coregulation of Affect

        1. When the client manifests an emotion through the bodily affective expression of that emotion, the therapist is able to convey empathy and understanding of the client's experience by matching this affective expression.

        2. When the therapist conveys through matched affect that she gets the general purpose of the client's affective expression—to communicate what the client is feeling and how strongly he is feeling it—the affect often quickly decreases and the person then may focus on communicating about the underlying factors associated with that emotion.

        3. When the client conveys his emotion through its affective expression and the therapist does not match his affect—and thus does not convey that she gets it—the client is at risk to either escalate his affective expression or else to withdraw from the dialogue, at least emotionally.

        4. When the therapist matches the affective expression of the client's emotion, the client's emotion is more likely to remain regulated—the therapist is coregulating the client's affect and its underlying emotion.

        5. With the affect and its underlying emotion remaining regulated, the client is often able to reflect on an event and reexperience that event.

        6. The coregulation of affect creates safety, and then facilitates exploration through enhanced reflective functioning.

B. Joint Focus of Attention:
   1. Difficulties in Maintaining Joint Attention
   2. Addressing Difficulties in Joint Attention
      a. When the client has difficulty attending to a particular theme because of the emergence of dysregulating emotions associated with that theme, the therapist matches the affective expressions of the client to assist the client in reestablishing emotional regulation and in jointly focusing on that theme.
      b. When the client is becoming emotionally disengaged from the dialogue and beginning to daydream or show that he is distracted, the therapist can intensify her own affective experience of the event being explored to facilitate the client's experiencing the event more fully, including its emotional components.
      c. When the client is not entering into the intersubjective dialogue, the therapist might also simply bring the reluctance or difficulty to his attention and then maintain joint attention on his immediate functioning.
      d. When there is reluctance to engage in joint attention over a theme, especially in the treatment of children, it is wise for the therapist to let the child go first, with the therapist going second.
      e. When it is evident that the therapist is not able to elicit an engagement in a theme in an intersubjective manner, it is wise to take a break from the theme and from the effort to explore it.
C. Complementary Intentions
   1. Difficulties in Maintaining Complementary Intentions and Addressing These Difficulties
      a. The client makes it clear that he does not want to continue with the dialogue.
      b. The therapist and client are engaged in a dialogue, but their intentions for doing so are different.
      c. The client is clear that he does not want to engage in the therapeutic relationship or dialogue at all.
IV. A Final Example

Many of our clients have too seldom experienced others experiencing their strengths and conveying how they value who they are. Yet, if the key figures in their lives do not experience those traits within their expressions of self, they are much less likely to experience themselves as manifesting those traits. In AFFT, the therapist's central goal is to assist the members of the family to see within each other the unique qualities of strengths and vulnerabilities that characterize each one. The therapist then assists the members of the family to respond to the strengths that they perceive in each other with pride and enjoyment, while responding to the vulnerabilities in each other with compassion and an offer of guidance and support.

The therapist's goal is to reactivate the intersubjective experiences that most likely were present when the adults were getting to know each other, when the parents were getting to know their infants, and when the infants were getting to know their parents. The therapist works to reacquaint the members of the family with the very qualities that exist within each of them that they used to cherish and enjoy. The therapist does so by experiencing these qualities himself and then communicating his experiences of the family members intersubjectively so that they can experience them again through the eyes of the therapist. The therapist searches for and discovers these qualities and then shares them with the others. But he does more than share them. He helps each family member to discover these same qualities in the others so that they can begin to see him differently and become engaged with him differently. When intersubjective experiences return to the day-to-day life of the family, the primary purpose of family therapy has been completed.

I. THE INTERSUBJECTIVE THERAPEUTIC STANCE

The therapeutic relationship is considered to be a central agent of change and is probably the most important "evidence-based" component of effective psychotherapy. Too often therapist training programs assume that such a relationship is easily achieved and requires little understanding or training. Such programs then focus primarily on specific techniques that do not contribute as much to change as does the relationship itself and which require an effective therapeutic relationship to be effective.

Attaining a successful therapeutic relationship is more difficult than is often thought, in part because many clients have particular relationship vulnerabilities, especially in a relationship that addresses very important personal and interpersonal factors that are often difficult to resolve cognitively, in isolation from others. Such factors tend to be easier to address and resolve when the experience of the therapeutic relationship itself contains qualities of an attachment relationship that is characterized by security. Thousands of studies have now demonstrated that attachment security facilitates many areas of cognitive, social, emotional, psychological, and behavioral functioning. Individuals with attachment disorganization—where patterns of attachment are not evident in managing environmental challenges and distress—are at risk for manifesting psychopathology in areas of both internalization and externalization. Developing a therapeutic relationship around principles of attachment security and intersubjectivity may well be a highly productive means for ensuring increased therapeutic effectiveness.

II. THE INTERSUBJECTIVE VERSUS THE TRADITIONAL THERAPEUTIC STANCE

A frequent therapeutic stance is one in which the therapist remains neutral in response to the client's story with the intention of not influencing how the client is experiencing the events of his life that he is discussing during the course of treatment. The therapist strives to help the client feel safe enough to express any of his thoughts and feelings about an event without implying in any manner what the client should think or feel. The therapist conveys a nonjudgmental attitude. The therapist strives to remain ambiguous about what she might think or feel about what the client is telling her. Through maintaining a neutral stance, the therapist hopes to provide the client with a safe space where the client is confident that no matter what he says, the therapist will remain constant—predictable in her lack of a specific response, in maintaining a nonjudgmental tone. However, her ambiguous stance regarding the client's experiences tends to create anxiety that may well reduce safety.

In contrast to the traditional neutral stance, within the intersubjective therapeutic stance, the therapist is very clear about her experience of the events that the client is discussing as well as her experience of the client's expressed experience of those events. The clarity of the therapist's communications within the intersubjective stance is facilitated best through A-R dialogue, which will be discussed in great depth in the next chapter. Such dialogue is characterized by a story-telling quality to the communication rather than by a serious, rational discussion.

Because of the nature of intersubjectivity, this therapeutic stance is likely to influence the client's experience of the event, and in fact an important therapeutic goal is to actually have such an influence. The influence is not to create a specific way to reexperience the event, but rather to develop the openness and readiness to reexperience the event based on all aspects of the client's autobiographical narrative, including his current intersubjective experiences with the therapist and other attachment figures.

By conveying her clear experience of the client's experience of the event and the event itself, the therapist is supporting the act of actively experiencing the event, deepening that experience and helping it to become more comprehensive and coherent. By actively joining the client in his experience of an event, the therapist is creating an opening whereby the client is more able to reexperience the event and to cocreate new meanings of the event.

Within the intersubjective stance, the therapist still maintains the nonjudgmental attitude that is present in the neutral stance. In fact, this nonjudgmental attitude is even more evident since the therapist is very clear about this experience of the client's experience as well as the nature of the therapeutic relationship. The therapist highly values the client's autonomy. When the therapist and client have a different experience of an event, the therapist makes that explicit with a total acceptance of any difference. When the client disagrees with the therapist, the therapist makes clear her delight in the client's disagreement and the courage and honesty that it represents, as well as the crucial importance of the client giving priority to his experience over the therapist's experience.

Within the intersubjective stance, the therapist very actively enables the client to cocreate a new experience of the event while coregulating any emotion associated with the event. If the client is alone in the experience, he is at risk of dysregulation of his emotional state, which is likely to interfere with his reflective focus on the event, or to be rigidly focused on controlling or avoiding his emotion, which is also likely to interfere with reflecting on the event.

Within the intersubjective stance, the therapist genuinely likes the client and experiences Carl Rogers's "unconditional positive regard" for his client. It is the therapist's responsibility to get to know the client deeply enough to be able to discover the unique person lying under the symptoms and defenses. With that depth of knowledge it is relatively easy for the therapist to like the client. This is crucial, because if the therapist does not like the client, the client will know it regardless of how neutral and ambiguous a stance the therapist holds.

Within the intersubjective stance, the therapist joins her experience of the event with the client's experience, creating two perspectives of the event. This enables the client to implicitly know that his experience is not an objective reality—it is a perspective and can be flexible and modified. An experience can evolve, based on new experiences that bring a new perspective. The therapist's perspective, given within an attitude of complete acceptance of whatever the client is experiencing, greatly enhances the likelihood that the experience can be created anew.

With the neutral stance, safety is enhanced by the therapist's nonjudgmental stance, though the therapist's ambiguity might make this stance less certain for the client. Also, exploration is enhanced through the therapist's nonjudgmental presence as well as her reflective comments. With the intersubjective stance, both safety and exploration are further enhanced. The therapist's intersubjective presence enables any emotion associated with an event to be coregulated, and any thoughts about the event to be enhanced by the presence of the therapist's perspective, with any similarities and differences clarified and accepted.

III. THE THREE CENTRAL COMPONENTS OF INTERSUBJECTIVE EXPERIENCE

Three factors need to be present for intersubjectivity to exist in the present within the relationship. These factors represent the joining of the minds of the individuals who are engaged with each other in a reciprocal relationship. The relationship needs to be reciprocal—both individuals are impacted by the active engagement with the other—or the interactions cannot be considered to be intersubjective. This does not mean that the content of the dialogue needs to be focused on the lives of both members of the dyad. In therapy, the therapist's life is not the focus of the dialogue, but the dialogue about the life of his client is actively impacting him and has a place within his own narrative. The three factors—the joining of the minds of those intersubjectively present—involve their affect regulation, joined awareness, and complementary intentions.

A. The Coregulation of Affect

Affect is defined here as the nonverbal or bodily expression of either a specific emotion or a milder, more general sense of content or discontent. Affects are conveyed—following what Dan Stern refers to as "vitality affects" through the intensity, rhythm, beat, duration, contour, and shape of the bodily expressions, which include facial expressions, voice prosody, gestures, and movements. Attunement represents the sharing of affect intersubjectively, which leads to its coregulation.

1. When the client manifests an emotion through the bodily affective expression of that emotion, the therapist is able to convey empathy and understanding of the client's experience by matching this affective expression. For the client, her affect is an expression of the underlying emotion. For the therapist, his affect is an expression of his understanding and empathy for the client's underlying emotional attunement.

EXAMPLES

Child is angry:

CHILD: She never listens to me! Never!

THERAPIST: Never! No wonder you get angry if she never listens to you. How hard that would be if your own mom never listens to you!

Child is sad:

CHILD: He doesn't like me. . . . He doesn't. [Slow, quiet, subdued tone.]

THERAPIST: Ah. . . . That would be so, so hard . . . if it seems that he does not like you. . . . So hard.

Child is frightened:

CHILD: And he screamed! And said it was my fault! And it wasn't! And he said that he was going to beat me!

THERAPIST: Oh, my! He screamed at you and said that he was going to beat you! Oh, how scary that must have been. How scary!

Child is excited:

CHILD: She said that I can go! I can go! She said that I tried hard and I can go!

THERAPIST: She did! You can go! Great! Great! I know how hard you tried and how much you want to go. Great!

Comment: In these examples, the therapist responds to the child's expressions with the same intensity, rhythm, and pitch in his voice, along with similar facial expressions and gestures or posture. This nonverbal matching enables the child to experience an emotional bond with the therapist, having confidence that he understands. When affect is matched, the child feels understood—the therapist gets how strong the child's emotion is about something. Matching affect does not require that you have the same emotion as the other. In the above examples the therapist became excited but did not become angry. The therapist's excitement is in response to the child's excitement. The therapist experiences the child's anger but is not angry himself. Here the matched affect represents the therapist's empathy for the child's anger, but the therapist is not angry.

2. When the therapist conveys through matched affect that she gets the general purpose of the affective expression—to communicate what the client is feeling and how strongly he is feeling it—the affect often quickly decreases and the person then may focus on communicating about the underlyling factors associated with that emotion.

EXAMPLES
Child is angry:
CHILD: She never listens to me! Never!

THERAPIST: Never! No wonder you get angry, if she never listens to you! How hard that would be if your own mom never listens to you.

CHILD: I tell her something and it doesn't seem to matter! Like she doesn't even hear me!

THERAPIST: Oh, my! So it seems that what you are saying doesn't even matter to your mom. How upsetting that would be if it doesn't matter to her!

CHILD: Sometimes I think that my mom only pretends that she is listening because she doesn't change at all after I tell her my side.

THERAPIST: I get it. It seems to you that if she were listening, sometimes she would change her decision about something. And it seems to you that she never does.

CHILD: Well, hardly ever. Like she has to be right and doesn't want to be wrong.

THERAPIST: I see. So maybe she is listening but you think that she might have a hard time admitting it if she made a mistake.

CHILD: Yeah. She doesn't like to say that I'm right about something.

THERAPIST: Okay. I have a better sense now about what's bothering you. And I think that your mom does too. Why don't you tell her what you think.

Comment: While the therapist matches the child's affective expression about his anger that his mother does not appear to listen to him, the child continues to elaborate until the therapist asks him to tell his mother about it in greater detail. The reasons under his anger then are more likely to be expressed.

Child is sad:
CHILD: He doesn't like me. . . . He doesn't. [Slow, quiet, subdued tone.]

THERAPIST: Ah. . . . That would be so, so hard . . . if it seems that he does not like you. . . . So hard. [Almost the same slow, quiet, and subdued tone, but without the hopelessness that the child's expressions are conveying.]

CHILD: He doesn't. . . . He really doesn't. . . . He never wants to play with me.

THERAPIST: Ah, I get it. . . . You ask your dad to play . . .

CHILD: And he says "not now" or "I'm busy now."

THERAPIST: Ah . . . so you think, "If he liked me he'd want to play with me."

CHILD: Yeah. . . . He used to want to play with me. But he never does anymore.

THERAPIST: Ah . . . that might be confusing for you. . . . Like, why did he used to play with you and then stop playing with you? . . . Like, what happened? . . . Like, "What did I do?"

Comment: While matching affect, empathy for the experience is being expressed. At the same time the therapist is also able to be curious, while still matching the affect. These questions are much less likely to be experienced as being intrusive when the therapist uses the same tone when he is being curious. Curiosity then leads to elaboration and greater reflection.

CHILD: I think sometimes that he wishes that I were different. I don't like sports and he does. I think he'd like me if I played sports.

THERAPIST: So that's how you've made sense of his not playing with you like he used to. You think that he would if you liked sports . . . if you had different interests.

CHILD: Yeah, like I'm not the boy he always wanted.

THERAPIST: I can see how you might think that. Does your dad know that you think that?

CHILD: No. . . . I can't tell him. He really wouldn't like me then.

THERAPIST: So you think that you'd be taking a big chance if you told him that. Things might get even worse than they are now between you.

CHILD: Do you think that he'd be mad if I told him that?

THERAPIST: From what he has said to me, I don't think he'd get mad.

CHILD: What did he say to you?

THERAPIST: He said that he feels sad because he thinks that you two are not as close as you used to be.

CHILD: He said that!

THERAPIST: Yeah, he said that he thinks he's not a very good dad . . . that he should be able to figure out a way to be closer to his son, but he doesn't know how.

CHILD: Why doesn't he know how?

THERAPIST: His dad never played with him, so it doesn't come easily for him.

CHILD: His dad never did?

THERAPIST: No. So it's hard for him to know how to be a dad. But he wants to learn.

CHILD: He does!

THERAPIST: And I think that I can teach him. Would you like me to?

CHILD: Yeah.

Comment: In this example one might think that the therapist could have told the boy immediately that his dad did like him and then suggest that they work on building the relationship. However, by matching the child's affect first, the therapist demonstrated that he really got the depth of the child's discouragement. Being with the child in his experience of the relationship distance from his dad, the therapist conveyed that he really understood and had empathy for the child's experience. If reassurance or information comes too soon, the child will feel that the therapist is simply rescuing him from the experience—that the therapist is simply saying that to make the child feel better. The child will also not have the sense that the therapist really understands him, so he is likely to have less confidence in the therapist's thoughts.

3. When the client conveys his emotion through its affective expression and the therapist does not match his affect—and thus does not convey that she gets it—the client is at risk to either escalate his affective expression or else to withdraw from the dialogue, at least emotionally.

EXAMPLE

TEENAGER: You really don't care about me at all! You sit there, making big money, and all I am to you is a paycheck! What a fucking joke this is! [Loud anger, ridicule, contempt.]

THERAPIST: You think that I'm only seeing you because I get paid and that makes you angry. [Said in a matter-of-fact, serious tone.]

TEENAGER: Isn't that what I just said? You are really an idiot! You don't deserve your big money!

THERAPIST: So you are more angry with me now because I showed that I was listening to what you told me. Why does that make you more angry? Don't you want me to listen?

TEENAGER: Yeah, you listened! And you figured out that I'm case number 84 in that big book on your desk! So, genius, what are you supposed to do to fix case number 84?

THERAPIST: I'm supposed to keep listening to you and not be upset over your anger at me.

TEENAGER: Maybe you'll get upset when I walk out the door! [He gets up and leaves.]

Comment: If the therapist had matched the affective expression of his anger, the teenager would have been more likely to enter into an intersubjective dialogue than was the case in the above example.

TEENAGER: You really don't care about me at all! You sit there, making big money, and all I am to you is a paycheck! What a fucking joke this is! [Loud anger, ridicule, contempt.]

THERAPIST: It seems to you that you're just a paycheck to me! No wonder you're angry about being here! No wonder you see no value in talking with me!

TEENAGER: Yeah! Go ahead and deny it! That's what you have to say! That's what the book told you to say when someone tells you that you just want the money!

THERAPIST: So you have no confidence in anything I say! You think that I find things to say so that I can manipulate you. So that I can trick you into thinking I care about you!

TEENAGER: That's about right! I'd trust the biggest jerk at school before I'd trust you!

THERAPIST: And I am getting paid! This is how I make my income! So it's like there's no way that you would ever believe that I really cared about what happens to you!

TEENAGER: That's about right too! You're on a roll . . . two in a row! Aren't you sharp!

THERAPIST: I don't feel very sharp right now! I have no idea how I can tell you that I do care, I am getting paid, and I'm not manipulating you . . . and have you believe me.

TEENAGER: So don't bother.

THERAPIST: Yeah, that would help! You'd really trust me then . . . like I'm only going to try to get to know someone who makes it easy for me. . . . Like you're too hard . . . Like you're not worth the money . . . so I'll find someone easier.

TEENAGER: Why don't you? There are a lot of "good boys" out there.

THERAPIST: Because I like your honesty. I like your passion! I like you for protecting yourself from someone that you think is likely to bail out on you or sell you down the river.

TEENAGER: And your saying that is supposed to get me to trust you?

THERAPIST: I have no idea if that will help you to decide to trust me or not. I do know that you deserve my honesty too! You deserve to know that I have some passion too, to work hard to earn your trust so maybe I can make some difference in your life.

TEENAGER: Why would you want to do that?

THERAPIST: You mean besides liking your honesty, passion, and smarts . . . okay, more honestly . . . because of how quickly I've come to respect and like you.

TEENAGER: Yeah, right. [Quietly, uncertain.]

THERAPIST: Yeah, that's right. [Calm and matter-of-fact.]

TEENAGER: And because you're making money. [Smiles.]

THERAPIST: That too. [Smiles.]

4. When the therapist matches the affective expression of the client's emotion, the client's emotion is more likely to remain regulated—the therapist is coregulating the client's affect and its underlying emotion. Anger is less likely to lead to rage, fear is less likely to lead to terror, and sadness is less likely to lead to despair.

5. With the affect and its underlying emotion remaining regulated, the client is often able to reflect on an event and reexperience that event. With the associated emotions remaining regulated, events that had been very stressful, disorganizing, or avoided are now able to be explored and understood in a reflective manner.

6. The coregulation of affect creates safety, and then facilitates exploration through enhanced reflective functioning.

B. Joint Focus of Attention

For individuals to be intersubjectively present, they need to be focused on the same content, whether it is something in the present being experienced together, something from the past being shared by one person that the other had not experienced, or something that is being remembered together.

When two individuals are focusing on an event, they are bringing two perspectives to that event, raising the possibility that one or both may now be experiencing that event differently. When the individuals are aware that they have two different perspectives of the event, they then realize that their individual perspective is not the same as the event itself. This realization leads to discovering the possibility that their perspective—their experience of the event—is able to be changed since it is not the event itself.

It is evident in treating clients who have experienced trauma that the memory of the trauma is often experienced as being the same as the trauma. This may lead to intense emotional dysregulation and the client may experience the memory as retraumatizing. When the client becomes aware that the therapist is having another experience of that event, she also discovers that the traumatic event can now be safely remembered because the memory of the event is an experience of it, not the event in itself. And the experience can be changed, often being influenced by the therapist's experience of it, which is created by intersubjectivity.

This same reality is true in exploring many less stressful events that occur within the family. Through joint attention to the event, along with the developing awareness that there are two different—but equally valid—experiences of the event, the possibility of change is created. The belief "if I am right, then you must be wrong" is no longer necessary. The defensive stance that leads one family member to protect the self by criticizing the other is no longer necessary. Within the intersubjective stance, all experiences are equal. As each is explored and understood, the reasons for the differing experiences become clear. The differences then are likely to become smaller, with the similarities assuming the central place in the experiences. Or the diffferences remain but be more likely to be accepted rather than being a source of unresolved conflict.

1. Difficulties in Maintaining Joint Attention

When both the client and therapist are motivated to focus on the same event and when the emotions associated with the event remain regulated, then this joint focus on the event is fairly easy to initiate and maintain. This is common within a nondirective stance when the client has the motivation and ability to explore difficult themes.

However, often clients have developed patterns of avoidance regarding attending to events that are experienced as stressful. For example, if a boy stole money from his father, efforts by the therapist to explore that event may evoke experiences of shame and related attachment themes of rejection and devaluing the relationship. When the boy resists such explorations, the risk is that this will lead to an angry lecture from the father (or a more rational lecture from the therapist). Such lectures will break the intersubjective connection that is needed to be able to openly explore with the boy his experiences related to taking the money and the subsequent relationship consequences resulting from that act. If the therapist believes that it will not be therapeutic to take a nondirective stance and explore the event when the boy is ready, then the therapist must initiate the discussion of that event. Such initiation is the easy part. The skill involves maintaining the joint focus on the event so that the intersubjective experiences of it can be explored. This is the therapist's responsibility: The exploration must remain intersubjective if it is to be therapeutic. If it drifts into becoming defensive exchanges in which the therapist becomes the judge, then the dialogue is not likely to be beneficial to anyone. It will lead either to further conflict or to a dominant/submissive stance where the experience of one member of the family goes underground and any hope for a true resolution is lost.

2. Addressing Difficulties in Joint Attention

The therapist needs to closely monitor the client's response when she initiates a focus on a stressful theme to ensure that the intersubjective quality of the dialogue remains present. She needs to note whether or not the joint discussion is leading the family member toward expressions of dysregulated affect or toward distancing from the dialogue through distractions or diminished affective engagement. The therapist needs to either successfully address either response to her initiatives or discontinue directing her attention to that theme.

a. When the client has difficulty attending to a particular theme because of the emergence of dysregulating emotions associated with that theme, the therapist matches the affective expressions of the client to assist the client in reestablishing emotional regulation and in jointly focusing on that theme. The client may begin to become agitated, avoid eye contact, show changes in his discourse (such as sentence structure, speech pressure, moving into a monologue), or show changes in breathing patterns. When this is apparent, the therapist actively joins the dialogue with very similar affective expressions and observes whether or not the child (or parent) is able to remain regulated.

b. When the client is becoming emotionally disengaged from the dialogue and beginning to daydream or show that he is distracted, the therapist can intensify her own affective experience of the event being explored to facilitate the client's experiencing the event more fully. In this instance, rather than matching the client's affect, the therapist is leading the client into an affective experience of an event that the client may be avoiding. The client may follow the lead quite easily and fully experience the event. However, he may also find the emerging affect to be too stressful and he may work harder to disengage from the dialogue. When this occurs, the therapist needs to accept the clear intention of the client to not focus on that event.

EXAMPLE

THERAPIST: Wait, wait! I really want to know. What did you say to your mom when she said that you would have to wait for your brother?

ADOLESCENT: I said that I want time to have my own life too!

THERAPIST: Ah! So sometimes being the older brother gets a bit much for you and you don't want to have to watch him.

ADOLESCENT: I don't mind. It's just, not so much.

EXAMPLE

THERAPIST: Before we set this aside, I was wondering. I was wondering, what makes it so hard when your dad asks you to help him with a chore that would only take about 10 minutes?

CHILD: It seems that is the only time he talks with me! When he wants me to do something for him!

THERAPIST: The only time! Ah, if it seems to you that your dad only wants to talk with you when he has a chore for you, I can see how that would be hard for you. I can see that!

c. When the client is not entering into the intersubjective dialogue, the therapist might also simply bring the reluctance or difficulty to his attention and then maintain joint attention on his immediate functioning. This must be done with complete acceptance, along with gentle curiosity about its source and empathy for any evidence of distress.

EXAMPLE

THERAPIST: I noticed that when you mentioned how your father yelled and then walked out of the room, you pulled back and looked away.

ADOLESCENT: Why won't he just listen?

THERAPIST: Ah! So that really bothered you and maybe you were a bit reluctant to show how much.

ADOLESCENT: It does bother me! Can't I have a voice too?

THERAPIST: Ah! You want to talk with your dad and be heard. Have you ever told your dad that? Have you ever said, "Dad, when we disagree, I just wish that we could talk to each other and really listen to each other. And work it out."

EXAMPLE

THERAPIST: Our discussion seems to be really hard for you. Could you tell me what makes it so hard or would you rather take a break from it?

CHILD: I don't know! Sometimes everything is just too hard.

THERAPIST: Everything! Ah! No wonder it is hard talking about these hard things. Seems like there are just so many hard things!

CHILD: Yeah! I just want to be a regular kid! Other kids don't have to think about all this stuff.

d. When there is reluctance to engage in joint attention over a theme, especially in the treatment of children, it is wise to let the child go first with the therapist going second.

When it is the therapist's turn, if the child resists, then in a playful manner the therapist can easily say, "That's not fair!" Most children will smile and grumble a bit and then join the therapist in exploring that theme.

EXAMPLE

THERAPIST: I have been wondering about what you said earlier about not being able to spend much time with your mom lately.

SARAH: The teacher let us watch a neat movie today. It's called *Up*!

THERAPIST: Up! What's that?

SARAH: It's animated! About a boy and an old man floating up in the air in his house! It was attached to thousands of balloons!

THERAPIST: And these balloons lifted the whole house?

SARAH: Yeah, and the boy wasn't supposed to be there but he was doing a good deed, and they went to a strange place where there were hundreds of dogs . . . [Another 5 minutes of discussion follows until the movie has been described.]

THERAPIST: Wow! That sounds like one neat movie. What were we talking about before you remembered the movie?

SARAH: I don't know. But next week at school . . .

THERAPIST: Wait a minute. . . . Wait a minute. . . . What was it? . . . Oh, yeah! About you and your mom!

SARAH: The teacher said . . .

THERAPIST: Wait a minute! My turn! We talked about Up and now I'd like to talk about you and your mom.

SARAH: But I want to tell you about school next week.

THERAPIST: That's not fair! My turn. After we talk about you and your mom, then we can talk about school next week.

SARAH: She's just always busy now. Like hanging out with me is the last thing that she wants to do.

EXAMPLE

THERAPIST: I wonder if we could talk about how you both seem to really want different rules around the TV and it causes an argument almost every day that just won't go away.

SUSAN: Can we go to the mall after we get out of here?

THERAPIST: Susan, I think this is the third time I brought up the TV arguments and it seems to me that you really don't want to talk about them. What's that about?

SUSAN: We'll never agree! It will just cause a fight here and we won't get to the mall!

THERAPIST: Ah, I get it. Why talk about something if the talking only makes it worse!

SUSAN: Yeah, it's been going on forever and it's not going to stop!

THERAPIST: So, you're really discouraged about that! Seems kind of hopeless to you.

SUSAN: Well, we've never agreed yet. Why would it be different now? It would just be a waste of time.

THERAPIST: Thanks for telling me why you did not want to discuss the TV. I couldn't figure it out before since it is such an big issue for you and your parents and I want to help with it. But you're saying it won't do much—if any—good.

SUSAN: It won't.

THERAPIST: Would you be willing to go along with me a bit and see if I can earn my money? If I can help you all with this issue, I think that a number of other ones will fall into place.

SUSAN: Go for it.

THERAPIST: Thanks for that. I know I'm pushing you a bit about it. Thanks for giving me a chance to help you guys with this.

EXAMPLE

THERAPIST: I notice that we did not finish the story about the conflict at the park.

CLIENT: Nothing really to say. We just stopped talking about it. That's what usually happens. We just know that our disagreement isn't getting anywhere so we drop it.

THERAPIST: Does that linger at all? Where you don't feel close to each other?

CLIENT: Yeah, I guess. But it goes away and what else is there to do when you don't agree?

THERAPIST: Good question. And I wonder if when you can't agree to disagree, that is hard to let go of and leaves you both isolated. Be great to figure something out that would address that.

CLIENT: Like what?

THERAPIST: Thanks for asking! I have lots of ways to help to repair a relationship.

e. When it is evident that the therapist is not able to elicit engagement in a theme in an intersubjective manner, it is wise to take a break from the theme and from the effort to explore it. Acknowledge the strength of the person's wish not to explore it, accept that wish, and move onto another, less stressful, theme without any frustration.

EXAMPLE

THERAPIST: So why do you think it is hard to talk about your friend not wanting you to come over to his house with the other kids?

JOHN: I said that I didn't want to talk about it!

THERAPIST: Yeah, I heard you and am fine if we don't. I just wondered why you don't want to talk about it.

JOHN: I just don't!

THERAPIST: Can you help me to get the reason?

JOHN: The reason is that I don't!

THERAPIST: I hear you now! Maybe I wasn't listening right the last times you said that. Maybe the point that you're making is that you don't want to talk about it at all, including why you don't want to talk about it. And I kept jabbering on! I can see why you were getting impatient!

JOHN: I'm glad that you can.

THERAPIST: And thanks for your persistence! It might have seemed like I was trying to bully you into something. I'm sorry if that's how it felt to you.

JOHN: It's okay.

THERAPIST: Thanks. Do you have any plans for this weekend?

C. Complementary Intentions

For individuals to be intersubjectively present, they need to want the same things from their time together. They need to have complementary intentions, that is, to talk and listen, teach and learn, understand and be understood, as well as simply play, work, or share dinner together. These intentions are reciprocal and may be interchangeable as the dialogue progresses. Cooperation can be defined as being engaged in activities where the individuals involved hold complementary intentions.

The intention of the therapist in AFFT is often to simply get to know the inner lives of the members of the family and to do so in an enjoyable and safe manner. A related, immediate goal is often to initiate and maintain intersubjective experiences with each family member while also facilitating similar intersubjective experiences among the members of the family themselves. The therapist's goal is often to maintain the momentum of the ongoing engagement in the session where he—and the members of the family—are open to the experiences of one other, without judgment or defensiveness so that they truly understand one another and value what is unique about each other.

In AFFT, the therapist makes his intentions very clear. His experiences of the family members are very clear. He is not ambiguous or understated in sharing his experience. This manner of acceptance and openness facilitates within the family members the safety to discover and express their own inner lives, while modeling for them how they can learn to be with each other.

This open and direct sharing of experience is not to be equated with the therapist telling others what he "feels" when that leads to harsh criticisms and even cruel and hurtful observations. If the therapist has a negative experience in response to a client's behavior, he is not likely to give expression to his negative experience. It is best for the therapist to get to know the person more deeply until he discovers the strengths, motives, and vulnerabilities that underlie a client's behaviors. If he is able to better walk in the shoes of the client, he is not likely to have a negative experience regarding the motives for a behavior, even when he sets a boundary regarding that behavior in therapy.

The therapist is wise not to maintain the intention to "fix" a family or a member of the family. While that might be the parents' intention, the therapist is wise to hold tightly to the intention to simply get to know the inner lives of the family members. When it is clear that there is no intention to fix anyone, all members of the family begin to feel safer, though there might be anxiety about how the simple intention to relate to each other with PACE will achieve the therapeutic changes that are desired by the various family members.

1. Difficulties in Maintaining Complementary Intentions and Addressing These Difficulties

Dialogue is not intersubjective when the individuals have different motives for engaging in it or when one wants to engage in a conversation with the other who resists or refuses. In these cases, it is important for the therapist to suspend further discussion about that theme or to address the therapeutic process itself before continuing. If the process is able to be maintained and all become comfortable with it, the theme that is presently being avoided will come up again, and the next time family members are likely to be more willing to address it.

a. The client makes it clear that he does not want to continue with the dialogue. When this occurs, the therapist needs to respect that decision and end the discussion without any resistance. She might comment that they might discuss it another time, or she might casually wonder why the client does not want to discuss a theme, but she needs to convey total acceptance of the client's decision. If the therapist believes that it is an important theme and it is in the client's interest to explore it further, she should make her reason clear and present it openly to the client. The important factor for the therapist to remember is that the process of engaging in an intersubjective dialogue is more important than the particular content.

EXAMPLE

THERAPIST: I hear you clearly that you do not want to talk more about your disagreement with your dad about the use of the car. Would you be okay with me telling you why I think that it would be important for you both if we could understand that situation better? Then if you still want to leave it alone, I won't fuss about it at all.

JAKE: Yeah, go ahead.

THERAPIST: Thanks, Jake. My sense is that the use of the car is only part of a bigger picture for you both. Jake, It seems to me that the car represents your saying to your dad, "Dad, I'm not a kid anymore, I can handle the responsibility! Sometimes I think that you don't trust my judgment at all and at other times I think that you don't want me to grow up!"

[To the father.] And Dad, I think with the car you are saying to your son, something like, "I love you son and know that you want to—and need to—spread your wings and become more independent. Sometimes I get scared that you might not see any value in my guidance any more—that your independence will leave no room for me in your life."

If that makes sense, Jake, would you be willing to continue with the discussion further about the car in terms of what it might represent for you both?

JAKE: Okay, I'll try that.

Comment: In this example the therapist gives the child a preview of how the intersubjective discussion might go, so that he is more able to make a decision about whether or not to engage in it. This is often helpful in changing the client's mind because he becomes aware of a way of communication that most likely does not occur within the family. He also is aware that the conversation is embedded with PACE and will not lead to trying to change his mind or behavior. Of course, if he still does not want to continue with that theme in the dialogue, the therapist needs to completely accept the decision. Further efforts to explore it would only be experienced as being motivated by an effort to change his mind.

b. The therapist and client are engaged in a dialogue, but their intentions for doing so are different.

EXAMPLE

THERAPIST: So, John, I think that you're saying that it is really hard for you when your mom says that you can't spend the night at your friend's house.

JOHN: Yeah, other kids can spend the night with their friends. She doesn't get it!

THERAPIST: So, if other kids can do it, you are wondering why you can't too!

JOHN: Yeah, she doesn't trust me or something.

THERAPIST: So if your mom says no because she doesn't trust you—I wonder if that makes it even harder for you.

JOHN: So tell her to let me go! I'm old enough and I won't get into trouble!

THERAPIST: Oh, wait, John, wait a second! Are you hoping that from talking about this with me, I'll come to agree with you and tell your mom that she should let you do it?

JOHN: Yeah, isn't that what this is for? You decide which one of us is right?

THERAPIST: I'm so sorry, John, that I wasn't more clear about what this is for. I see why you seem to be getting frustrated. You thought that I was the judge about this argument that you two were having.

JOHN: Yeah, why can't I spend the night?

THERAPIST: I'm sorry again, John. I don't decide who is right. I don't know if there is a right and wrong. What I'm doing is trying to understand how you both understand this argument, what you think and feel and want about it, and hopefully to help you both understand each other better.

JOHN: How is that supposed to help?

Comment: The therapist may have told the family members that he is not the judge as to who is right, but they often need to actually experience his refusal to pick a winner before they understand that therapy is about something else. If the therapist does believe that the parents' decision regarding their child might be making the situation worse, the therapist tells the parent that in private and accepts their decision as to whether they will change their prior decision or not. Questioning their decision in front of the child is likely to reduce the parents' sense of safety and increase the conflict between them and their child.

THERAPIST: Because I think that you are both good, bright people who love each other a lot. If I can help you two to speak about your thoughts, feelings, and reasons, then I think that you'll both agree on a solution or be able to understand and accept better why you don't agree and how to stay close with each other even if you do disagree. Make any sense, John?

JOHN: I guess so, but I just think that she doesn't trust me.

THERAPIST: Thanks for that, John. Let's explore that further about what it would mean if you are right that she doesn't trust you. And then hear from your mom about what she says her reasons are and what she thinks about your thoughts about it.

JOHN: Okay. So I go first?

THERAPIST: You go first, and I'll jump in when I need to ask questions and wonder about what you mean so that I—and hopefully your mom—can understand you better.

c. The client is clear that he does not want to engage in the therapeutic relationship or dialogue at all.

EXAMPLE

THERAPIST: Well, Judy, I wonder what you think about what I just said to your dad.

JUDY: When are we done?

THERAPIST: About 30 more minutes. Is that important to you?

JUDY: Yeah!

THERAPIST: Thanks for telling me. What makes it important?

JUDY: What do you think? This is such a waste of time!

THERAPIST: Now I get it! It's a waste of time to you so the shorter time here the better.

JUDY: Duh!

THERAPIST: Thanks for making that clear! What makes it a waste of time for you?

JUDY: What do you think?

THERAPIST: Okay, I can guess, but I might be wrong. If you told me, you might say, "Because you don't get it! And my parents don't get it! They just want to tell me what to do and they don't care at all what I want! And since you work for them, you're just going to tell me what to do too! You won't listen to me so I'm not listening to you! Now do you get it—why this is a waste of time?" Is that about right?

JUDY: You got that right, shrink!

Comment: While Judy says that she does not want to engage in the session, she actually is engaging in it through her continuing dialogue with the therapist, regardless of the content. (Of course, pointing that out to her will only end the dialogue.) By guessing how negative her thoughts and feelings are about the therapist and the therapy and by showing complete acceptance of those thoughts and feelings, the therapist is already contradicting what Judy anticipated would happen in the therapeutic dialogue, which is likely to increase her interest in what it might consist of.

THERAPIST: Thanks for that, Judy. I'm glad that I got it right! Of course if I'm just going to tell you what to do and not get it, this would be a waste of time. Sure it would! If your parents don't listen and I don't listen because I'm working for them, there is no way that this meeting is going to help you at all. No way! If no one here listens to what is important to you . . . how you see things.

JUDY: No one ever did!

THERAPIST: Ah! So it seems to you that your parents never listen to what you want . . . to what you think . . . and you're sure I won't either. If that's right, if your parents never listen, what is that about? Why don't they?

JUDY: Because they just want to protect their shiny reputation! That's more important to them than I am!

THERAPIST: Oh my! No wonder you don't want to be here! It seems to you that you're not very important to your parents—less than their reputation. So if they brought you here, it must be to fix you so that their reputation is left shiny, not because it would be good for you or for both you and them.

JUDY: Don't you listen? I just told you! It's not about me and them. It's only about them!

THERAPIST: If that's how it is—if that's how it seems to be—no wonder you're annoyed about being here. It's like it seems to you that you're not important to your parents at all. Except maybe if you are able to help them with their reputation!

JUDY: That's about it!

THERAPIST: So you don't feel part of the family at all then, if that's what it seems to you. You're all alone, living with people who don't know you and maybe even don't care about knowing you.

Comment: The therapist has established Judy's perception that her parents care about their reputation more than about her. However, this only gives her reason to continue her anger and resistance to engagement in treatment. If the therapist is to move the dialogue along so that it will become therapeutic, he needs to help her to go more deeply into the consequences of her perception, that is, that she experiences herself as all alone in her home. If she can acknowledge that, she is likely to become a bit vulnerable and may be more receptive to a way out of her isolation.

JUDY: They don't!

THERAPIST: How hard that would make it! In some ways living alone, even if you're living with them. Not feeling in their minds or hearts at all.

JUDY: I'm not!

THERAPIST: How do you handle that?

JUDY: I don't think about it!

THERAPIST: Ah, another reason to not want to be here! I'm asking about it.

JUDY: Yeah, it's a waste of time.

THERAPIST: I think I get it now, Judy. I think I get it. Why talk with me and your parents if it seems that no one here wants to hear you, wants to understand you? It's hard not to be understood and even harder if the other person doesn't want to understand.

JUDY: You're right again, shrink.

THERAPIST: Thanks, again, Judy. I'm glad that I get something about you. Now, if you're okay about it, I want to talk with your parents—while you listen to me—and see if I can tell them what I understand about you now, and see if I think that they understand at all, and more importantly see if I think that they want to understand you at all. And after that, I'll let you know what I think and you let me know what you think about their understanding what you said, what I said, and also what you think about whether you agree with me or not. Okay?

JUDY: Go for it. Yeah.

THERAPIST: Thanks, again, Judy.

Comment: Here the therapist chose to not lead Judy into even greater vulnerability as she is not likely to go further unless she has a bit of confidence that her parents would respond differently than her perception of them would have her believe. Instead, she only has to listen to the therapist and her parents engaging in a similar dialogue. If the therapist is able to help them to become vulnerable as well (possibly acknowledging sadness over her isolation and their not being close to her, or a sense of failure as parents because she does not trust them very much, or their sense of hopelessness that they do not know how to engage their daughter), then she is more likely to go with the dialogue herself. Of course if he is not able to elicit such vulnerability from them, then she is probably not safe to continue to become more vulnerable herself and the therapist might decide to see the parents alone to see if he can help them to move under their defensive stance.

IV. A Final Example

The following example focuses on the therapist's role to encourage the safe expression of experience within the family, where the expression of the experience of one person does not have to hurt the other person. If it does hurt the other, the important experience of hurting and being hurt within the sharing of experience then becomes explored. The core assumption is that the personal truths of the family members, when accepted and understood by each other, will generate a greater reduction of hurting and being hurt within the family than is likely to have been the case before the family entered treatment. In fact, the personal truths, when expressed and responded to intersubjectively, often deepen and include—in positive ways—the importance of the relationships with the other members of the family. In the healthy parent-infant intersubjective dance, the infant's deepest interests and joys are embedded in the relationship and the joyful dialogues that were occurring between him and his parent. At the deepest level, the infant's "selfishness," creating his greatest pleasure, was being engaged intersubjectively with his parent. The therapist's task now is to help the family members to rediscover the reality that when each one is truly focused on his or her own best interests, a joyful and meaningful relationship with the parent or child is a central feature of that self-interest.

SAM [15-year-old]: Why don't you just leave me alone? You really don't care about me anyway! You just care about your wonderful reputation in the church and in the neighborhood!

MOM: That's not true!

THERAPIST: Wait a second, Gail. I hear Sam telling us his experience that you don't care about him—or at least less than you care about what others think of you.

MOM: But that's not true!

THERAPIST: Stay with me for a moment. We're talking about his experience, not whether or not he is accurate about your thoughts or values. I need to help you and me to understand his experience before responding to it. I know that it is hard for you to hear, but it is important that we understand what this means to Sam before we respond.

GAIL: Okay.

Comment: Here Sam is expressing his wish for his mother to be less engaged in an aspect of his life, and his reason for this wish—he does not believe that she cares for him more than for her reputation in the community. The therapist's goal now is to understand his wish more fully as well as his belief that his mother's motives are more about her reputation than about him. In doing so, the therapist will try to understand what Sam's belief about his mother's motives implies about the nature of his relationship with her, why he thinks that she would care more about other people's perceptions than about him, and related issues.

Gail finds it difficult to accept Sam's wish that she be less engaged with him as well as the importance of really understanding Sam's experience. While this most likely was explored with Gail before the joint sessions with Sam were begun, it nevertheless is often hard to accept and work to understand a family member's experience of us when it is negative.

THERAPIST: Sam, could you tell me more about that? It seems to you that your mom doesn't care as much about you or your thoughts or wishes as she cares about neighbors.

SAM: Yeah, she always worries about what others think but she never worries about what I think.

THERAPIST: If that's right, Sam, that your mom doesn't care much what you think and want, what does that mean?

SAM: It means that I'm not that important to her.

THERAPIST: And if that's right, Sam, that you're not that important to your mom, what does that mean?

SAM: I know that she loves me. I just don't feel it very much anymore.

THERAPIST: That must be hard, Sam.

SAM: It's just the way it is.

THERAPIST: Then I'd guess that you don't feel very close in the family now, Sam. That you feel all alone in the family.

SAM: Yeah, you're right. I don't.

Comment: Now the therapist attempts to help Sam go deeper into his experience of his mother not caring for him. He is able to say that it makes him think that he is not important to her. The therapist suggests that belief would be hard for Sam and leave him feeling alone. Sam agrees and adds that he does not feel his mom's love much anymore. The therapist throughout accepts where the dialogue is taking him and wonders if there are related experiences (feeling alone). There is never any effort to suggest that his experience is right or wrong. However, when the therapist asks Sam about his experience of his mother's motives, she is clear that he may or may not be right about his mother's motives. His experience of her motives could be different than her experience of her motives. Here the therapist implies that Sam is guessing his mother's motives when she asks, "If that's right, Sam, what does that mean?"

Once the therapist is able to assist Sam in becoming aware of his experiences more deeply and to communicate them, she asks him to talk with his mother. Such direct communication, rather than simply asking Gail to respond to what she heard Sam tell the therapist, will deepen the intersubjective communication between the two of them.

THERAPIST: Would you be willing to tell your mom that, Sam?

SAM: What?

THERAPIST: Would you be willing to say, "Mom, often lately it seems to me that I'm not really important to you. Like others are more important. And then I don't feel very close to you or the rest of the family."

SAM: Okay. Mom, she's right, that is what I often feel. Like you and I are worlds apart. I don't feel close like we used to be. It seems to me that you don't know me anymore, you don't even want to. I know you love me, Mom, but I just don't feel it anymore.

GAIL: But I do love you, Sam, of course I do.

THERAPIST: Would you start with Sam's experience, Gail, and hold yours till later?

GAIL: What do you mean?

THERAPIST: Would you tell him—if it's true—that you are sorry that he doesn't feel your love anymore? That you did not realize that he thinks that you care more for others than for him. That you are sad that he feels alone in the family now . . . all alone.

GAIL: I am sorry, Sam, if you can't feel my love. I really am. And I'm sorry that you think that I am more concerned about what others think than what you think. I can understand why you would feel so alone now at home if that is what you are feeling.

SAM: I am, Mom. I really am.

GAIL: I am so sorry, Sam. I really am. I want to be close to you. I love you so much and I'm sorry that you haven't felt it lately. And maybe that I haven't been showing you my love very well lately.

THERAPIST: Would you say that again, Gail? I thought that it took courage for you to say that last sentence.

GAIL: Maybe I haven't been showing my love for you very well, Sam. I'm sorry. I love you.

Comment: In this intersubjective dialogue, the goal was simply to assist Sam in going deeper and deeper into his statement that he wants his mother to leave him alone. If the therapist had stayed on the surface of that wish, he could have been left exploring why his mother was evaluating or trying to direct some of his behaviors and whether or not her efforts were justified by the nature of his behaviors or his age or related issues. A more fruitful exploration involves Sam's deeper perception of their relationship, and how that is affecting him. If the intersubjective experiences of both can be elaborated and then communicated, often the dialogue leads to a deeper reciprocal understanding and expressed desire to repair any breaks experienced in the relationship. The crucial therapeutic stance requires that the therapist does not evaluate Sam's experience and works to ensure that his mother does not evaluate it either. If the therapist and mother are able to hear his experience with acceptance, curiosity, and empathy, he is likely to more fully communicate his experience and acknowledge any vulnerabilities that lie within them. Then he will experience their experience of his experience and his original experience is likely to change somewhat—it will be influenced by their experience. This will occur naturally without power or consequences or lectures. This process will also greatly facilitate relationship repair.

EXERCISES

Intersubjectivity

1. Within a parent-infant intersubjective relationship:
   A. The parent and infant are having a reciprocal impact upon each other.
   B. The parent is impacting the infant's organization of self but this impact is not reciprocal.
   C. The parent is selecting behaviors that the infant can imitate.
   D. The infant, until 12 months of age, is not capable of an intersubjective relationship.

2. Conflicts are often based upon:
   A. Confusing facts with experiences of the facts.
   B. Having different experiences.
   C. Not taking the time to accept and understand the other's experience.
   D. A and C.

3. Attunement is:
   A. Another word for intersubjectivity.
   B. Defined by Stern as the intersubjective sharing of affect.
   C. Defined as the process of taking turns.
   D. Imitating the actions of the other.

4. Intersubjectivity can refer to a relationship between:
   A. A parent and child.
   B. Partners.
   C. A teacher and student.
   D. All of the above.

5. Intersubjectivity involves a form of learning that is an example of:
   A. Reinforcement theory.
   B. Association theory.
   C. Rote practice.
   D. None of the above.

6. To facilitate joint awareness within the therapeutic relationship with a child:
   A. The child gets to go first.
   B. The child's experience is evaluated calmly.
   C. The therapist presents an agenda for the session.
   D. All of the above.

7. Therapists who clearly express their experience of their clients are demonstrating:
   A. A neutral therapeutic stance.
   B. An unethical behavior.
   C. An intersubjective therapeutic stance.
   D. Their sensitivity to their clients.

8. Which of the following intentions held by the therapist is the child most likely to accept?
   A. I want to help you to change.
   B. I want you to like me.
   C. I want to tell you stories.
   D. I want to get to know you.

9. An intersubjective relationship is characterized by:
   A. Reciprocity.
   B. Contingency.
   C. One person being dominant.
   D. A and B.

10. When the therapist communicates his experience of the client, the following is likely to occur:
    A. The client will become dependent upon the therapist's view of her.
    B. The client will learn to change the behaviors that the therapist does not like.
    C. The client will feel safe to explore aspects of self within the therapist's unconditional positive regard.
    D. The client will become the therapist's friend in a truly reciprocal relationship.

Case Examples

1. Which of the following would not be considered an intersubjective therapeutic response to this client statement: "She never lets me do what I want!"
   A. If that is so, why do you think she doesn't let you do what you want?
   B. How hard that must be for you if your own mother never lets you do what you want.
   C. What is that like for you, if your mother does not let you do anything that you want?
   D. I think that you know that she must sometimes let you do what you want.

2. If a teenager shouts at the therapist, "You don't have a clue about what I think," which of the following would most likely be an intersubjective response?
   A. The therapist replies calmly, "That must be hard for you."

B. The therapist matches the intensity and rhythm of the teen's voice and replies, "Then help me to know! Help me to know what you think!"

C. The therapist replies with sadness, "I can't know what you think if you don't tell me."

D. The therapist suggests, "I do know what you think. You don't want to believe that."

3. Which of the following is likely to be an intersubjective response to the parent saying: "He never does what I tell him! He always wants his own way!"

A. That would be so hard if you think that your son never does what you ask of him!

B. If that is so, what might that mean about your relationship?

C. When you think that, do you worry that you are not as important to him as you were in the past?

D. All of the above.

4. If a child says to her father, "You care more about your job than about me," which of the following would be an intersubjective response from the father?

A. Of course I care about you! How could you think that?

B. If I did not work you could not have the things that are important to you.

C. That really hurts me to hear you say that!

D. If that's your experience, I am very sorry for not showing better what I feel about you.

5. A client says to his therapist: "This is just a job to you!" What would be an intersubjective response?

A. Yes, this is my job.

B. That's true but I still care for you and worry about you and your family.

C. Why should that matter if my ideas are helpful to you and your family?

D. None of the above.

Experiential Exercises

1. Think of friends and relatives that you know who have a baby at home. Ask if you could come over and observe the parent and baby engaged in the intersubjective dance. Note their reciprocal interactions and the presence of the three components of intersubjective interactions.

Now ask if you could interact with the infant yourself and try to be aware of your own experiences that are being elicited by the interaction itself. Notice your impact on the baby and the baby's impact on you.

Reflect, too, on what aspects of the experience might be similar to the intersubjective experience in therapy. Note any differences.

2. In this exercise, observe the intersubjective dance between a parent and toddler. Interact with the toddler yourself and be aware of the intersubjective features of the interaction for both you and the toddler. Note any similarities and differences between your intersubjective experiences with the infant and the toddler. Reflect on the experiences with a toddler and those in therapy.

3. Reflect upon a time when someone with whom you have a very close relationship (partner, parent, child, sibling, best friend) told you something that he or she thought (felt, wished for) that did not make any sense to you. What was your response?

_____

_____

Would you consider your response to have been intersubjective?

_____

If it was not intersubjective, why do you think it was not? _____

_____

4. Reflect upon a time when someone with whom you have a very close relationship told you something about yourself that he or she thought (felt, wished for) that did not make any sense to you. What was your response?

_____

_____

Would you consider your response to have been intersubjective?

_____

_____

If it was not intersubjective, why do you think it was not?

_____

_____

ANSWERS AND SUGGESTED RESPONSES

Intersubjectivity

1. A.
2. D.
3. B. Attunement is only one of three components of intersubjectivity. It relates to joining the other's affective experience, not imitating their behavior.
4. D. An intersubjective relationship can occur in any relationship where the two individuals are interacting in a way that helps them to understand and be responsive to the experience of the other.
5. D. The closest of the three theories is reinforcement theory because of the notion of contingency that is central to both theories. However, a major difference is that intersubjectivity requires that it be a reciprocal relationship where each member of the dyad is responsive to the other and able to influence the other. This is not a requirement of reinforcement theory. Also

in their practical applications, reinforcement theory implies that the purpose of the behavior (reinforcement) is to increase the likelihood that the person will do that behavior again. The purpose of intersubjectivity lies within the present moment—simply to join each other in joint affect, attention, and intentions.

6. A.
7. C.
8. D.
9. D.
10. C. The client is unlikely to become dependent upon the therapist's view because the therapist is most pleased when the client is increasingly able to develop his own autonomous sense of self and what is best for him, and that is not to depend on the therapist. The therapeutic relationship is not a friendship in which there is equal space for the narratives of each member of the friendship. Here, the client's narrative and its coherence are the central focus of the intersubjective time together.

Case Examples

1. D. Here the therapist is trying to point out "proof" that the client's experience is invalid.
2. B. In the first response the therapist is not matching the affect. In the third response the therapist is implying that it is the teenager's fault that the therapist does not understand him. In the fourth response the therapist states that the teenager does not believe his own experience, that he is lying to himself and/or the therapist.
3. D.
4. D.
5. D. The second response is the closest to being intersubjective. It does not attempt to understand the child's experience but rather makes an assumption about it and then tries to reassure the child about that assumption. There also does not appear to be matched affect for the child's experience.

3 | Affective-Reflective Dialogue

Therapy of any form—individual, couples, family—and involving any theoretical orientation consists of communication. As Allan Schore stated, "Therapy is not a 'talking cure' but rather a 'communication cure.'" (2001). Through the art of communication the therapist is able to influence clients in a manner that addresses their reasons for initiating therapy and facilitates changes in the intrapersonal and interpersonal patterns that are of concern.

How does therapeutic communication influence clients in such a manner that they begin to change? Problem-solving communications that analyze maladaptive patterns and recommend alternative patterns often bring short-term or limited results. Lectures given in the name of change are likely to be even less successful. Telling a person what he should be doing rather than what he is doing is likely to elicit frustration and possibly shame, but little change.

For centuries, interpersonal influences that have evoked change in many cultures, among many communities, involve communication through storytelling. Elders have told stories involving the wisdom of the "ancients" that have been passed down over the generations and that offer guides for living that may become embedded in the emerging stories of the younger members of the clan or community. The content of the story contains the collective knowledge that was embedded in the experiences of those who came before. However, just as important, and possibly even more so, is the manner in which the shaman, guru, witch doctor, priest, or rabbi tells the story. As Schore (1994) suggested, it is the nonverbal expressions of the storytellers that carry the story into the minds and hearts of those listening.

This nonverbal, attuned dance among those who are communicating is where the affective component of the dialogue lies. It generates safety, deep interest in the story, and a momentum within the dialogue that calls for increased coherence within the story being created. It invites new events into the storytelling process in a way that makes them much less likely to be avoided or defensively engaged. Once this safety and momentum for completion are generated, there is an openness to making sense of the story that is evolving. This process leads naturally into a greater readiness to reflect on the events that have affected a person, to understand their impact and to invite them into the story.

Affective-reflective (A-R) dialogue is the heart of attachment-focused family therapy. It is an integrative activity, involving both the emotional meaning of an event and its affective expression as well as the cognitive understanding of the event and its place within reflective awareness. Without the affective component, the dialogue tends toward intellectualization and without the reflective component, the dialogue tends to be an exercise in catharsis. A-R dialogue is the primary means whereby the intersubjective presence of the therapist within the family can generate, deepen, and expand the intersubjective presence of the family members for each other. From that safe, open, and creative presence, the family becomes empowered to fulfill its mission of interweaving autonomy and secure attachments within the narratives of all the members of the family.

Much focus in this chapter is on the process—not the content—of A-R dialogue. When the process becomes established as the primary way in which the family members communicate with one another both in therapy and at home, then the relevant content is able to be shared, understood, and safely integrated within the narratives of those engaged in the dialogue. Communicating about important content before the process is established is likely to make it very difficult to successfully address and, when necessary, resolve it.

IN THIS CHAPTER

I. The Process of A-R Dialogue

  A. Initiate and Maintain the Momentum of the Dialogue

    1. The therapist's affective experience of the family members and the present dialogue itself are very clear in his nonverbal expressions.

    2. The therapist moves from light to stressful, and from well-integrated events to those that are poorly integrated.

    3. The therapist assists with the transition from one event to another, making it as natural as possible by being alert to possible associations between the two events and by maintaining the same nonverbal expressions, especially relating to voice prosody and facial expressions.

    4. The therapist ensures the reciprocal nature of the dialogue by adopting a follow-lead-follow orientation to the dialogue.

    5. The therapist ensures that the natural ebb and flow in the dialogue is accepted when it occurs.

    6. The therapist's nonverbal communications about the story are congruent with his verbal expressions.

  B. Addressing the Challenges to A-R Dialogue

    1. When a family member shows a lack of congruence between the verbal and nonverbal, the therapist brings this to awareness by addressing it.

    2. When a family member is engaged in the story with little or no evident affective

expression for the events of the story, the therapist accepts this and then may be curious about the lack of affect.

3. When the family member conveys little or no affect, the therapist may also lead the client into a deeper affective experience through expressing, with very clear nonverbal expressions of voice prosody, facial expressions, and gestures, his own affective experience of that event.

4. The therapist takes the lead early in the session in modeling A-R dialogue with one or more members of the family in order to interrupt the prevalent, nonproductive family patterns of communication.

C. Facilitating A-R Dialogue

1. The meaning of the A-R dialogue is likely to deepen if the parent and child are able to engage in direct conversation with each other in a manner that conveys acceptance, curiosity, and empathy for each other's story.

2. Speaking for a child, or even a parent, can be such an effective way of leading a client into a deep and productive exploration of her inner life that she then can often directly communicate to her parent (or child).

3. When the child (or parent) shows distress in response to her engagement in the story, the therapist speaks about the person to others in the family in a manner that removes all felt demand to remain engaged in the story and assists her in downregulating her emotional state.

II. The Content of the A-R Dialogue

A. Ten Important Factors

III. Obstacles to A-R Dialogue

A. Monologues—Including Venting

B. Giving a Lecture About What a Client Should Do

1. Alternatives to Lectures

C. Problem Solving

1. Intersubjective Alternatives to Problem Solving

IV. Transcript of Affective-Reflective Dialogue

I. THE PROCESS OF A-R DIALOGUE

The primary therapeutic activity in AFFT is cocreating the individual narratives of the members of the family as well as the family narrative itself. The therapist and clients are engaged in storytelling and the characteristics of storytelling are present throughout the session. A-R dialogue is literally the process of the narrative or narratives being cocreated in the session by the therapist and clients. Because our focus is on the process, no particular content is more important than the storytelling—narrative creation—itself.

A-R dialogue is an intersubjective process. For that reason the therapist strives to initiate and maintain matched affect, joint awareness or attention, and a complementary intention throughout the dialogue. This is harder to maintain in family treatment than in individual treatment because while the therapist may be intersubjectively present with one member of the family, one or more of the others present may not be.

The movement of the story creates a momentum that carries the dialogue forward, with a natural ebb and flow, varying in intensity but with an organizing plot and subplots. The story being created has an inherent coherence, organized in a consistent manner that genuinely feels like it makes sense.

The therapist is responsible to ensure that the momentum of the story is present, with a goal of making the narrative coherent. The therapist keeps his "third ear" on the act of the storytelling itself to ensure that it continues to engage the members of the family and is being cocreated by all. The therapist is ensuring that lectures and problem solving do not become the central components of the dialogue—and are likely to not be present at all.

His goal is to assist in developing a plot—or theme—that can be interwoven in the narrative of the individual or family. When the therapist loses the plot, the story is likely to begin to drift and its coherence is likely to be lost.

For the narrative to be intersubjectively experienced and cocreated, all members need to be engaged. It needs to be a reciprocal process and not a monologue by any member present. Even if most of the verbal communication is being carried by one person, it remains reciprocal if the listeners are responding nonverbally and the speaker is aware of and receptive to those nonverbal responses. The therapist is ensuring that when a monologue begins, he inserts himself into the other's verbal expressions, often through matching the affect of the nonverbal expressions, moving these expressions into a dialogue.

There are affective and reflective components to the story. The affect is communicated mostly by the nonverbal communications, animated curiosity, and empathy, but also by the emotional content of the story. It represents the impact that both the content of the story and the act of sharing the story have on the members of the family and the therapist. The affective component provides the ongoing momentum of the story, with its inherent ebbs and flows. The reflective component is conveyed by the verbal content but also by the interest and curiosity being openly conveyed. The reflective component deepens when there is no judgment about what is being conveyed. The reflective focus is on the family members' experience of the events in the story, more than on the events themselves (e.g., "What is it like, listening to your mom tell how that affected her?"). How the events impact the thoughts, emotions, wishes, intentions, perceptions, beliefs, and memories of those involved in the story and its telling is the key. These features of the inner lives of those involved are explored, deepened, elaborated, and—hopefully—made more coherent by the A-R dialogue.

Most moments in the dialogue contain both the affective and reflective components, with one tending to be primary and the other secondary. In most sessions the affective component is likely to be primary early in the session. It moves the participants into the narrative, building its energy and deepening the experience. As the events are being explored, the emotional content is experienced and coregulated in order for the client to be able to remain fully present in the story. As the story about the event begins to unfold, it begins to make sense. The A-R dialogue enables the client to experience the story in a more coherent and comprehensive manner. As it makes sense, the therapist begins to reflect on its emerging meaning. The affect recedes and the reflective component of the dialogue tends to be primary toward the end of the session. The big picture is now experienced in a safe and meaningful manner.

Often the client does not remain engaged in the story and the therapist needs to reestablish this joint engagement before continuing with the content. The emotional content of the story may be stressful to the client and/or he may have failed to make sense of the event from the past that is being explored. Often, simply exploring the story lightly, with minimal detail and then taking a break from the story for a while is sufficient for achieving some integration of the event into the narrative. Certain clients do not generally have a reflective storytelling habit. They tend not to be sufficiently aware of what they think, feel, or wish about an event. Or if they have such an awareness, they do not have the ability to communicate it to another. It may be especially hard to remember the event itself, their experience of the event, and then to communicate it to another all at the same time. Other clients may be able to do all three in general, but cannot around specific events. These events tend to be associated with thoughts, emotions, or wishes that the client does not consider to be acceptable to the self or they may be traumatic (i.e., they generated an extreme emotional reaction that could not be integrated into the narrative). These clients are discussed further in Chapter 8.

A. Initiate and Maintain the Momentum of the Dialogue

It is the therapist's responsibility to ensure that the process of the dialogue is occurring throughout the session. He sees to it that there is a momentum—rather than a drift—to the dialogue. If the family is able to achieve this focused, intersubjective movement in the dialogue, the therapist participates but does not have to lead the dialogue. But if no family member is able to ensure that such a movement is occurring—and this is often the case with families who are not accustomed to A-R dialogue—then the therapist takes the lead. The following features of the therapist's interventions are often present.

1. The therapist's affective experience of the family members and the present dialogue itself are very clear in his nonverbal expressions. The therapist's nonverbal expressions—which often may seem quite dramatic—tend to hold the clients in the present moment in a way that facilitates affect regulation as well as a heightened interest in understanding more deeply the themes being explored. The therapist's clear nonverbal expressions support the ongoing intersubjective nature of the dialogue with its sharing of affect, joint attention and awareness, and complementary intentions.

In the following example, the momentum for the flow of the dialogue was the therapist's experience of the experiences of both father and son, enabling each to deepen their experiences of what was occurring in the events between them.

EXAMPLE

JOHN [age 10]: I don't know why we have to go to the dumb lake anyway! There's nothing to do there!

STAN [DAD]: It's not always what you want, John! What the rest of the family enjoys doing is important too!

THERAPIST [with some urgency]: Wait a second! I hear you, Dad. You need to think of the whole family, not just one member. Can we understand more about what John is saying first before responding? I need to know what he's experiencing about the lake more.

STAN: That's fine.

Comment: The therapist immediately interrupts a lecture and makes it clear by her sense of urgency that the therapeutic process primarily involves helping each other to understand and communicate each one's experience. The therapist is implicitly communicating the nature of A-R dialogue and her commitment to maintaining its process throughout the session.

THERAPIST: Thanks! Thanks. I really want to know, John, I really want to know. . . . What makes it hard for you to think of spending a week at the lake? What makes that so hard?

JOHN: It's so boring! We never do anything!

THERAPIST: Ah, okay, John. So are you saying that for you it's boring? That there is nothing that you enjoy doing there? Nothing?

JOHN: All we ever do is read. Or I could go for a walk—big deal!

THERAPIST: Ah . . . okay. . . . If that's it—reading or walking—I can see where you could get kinda bored! I can see! . . . Wait a second! I remember talking a few weeks ago about how you wished that your dad did not work such long hours . . . that he would be home more so that you could do more things together. . . . I remember your saying how important that was for you. . . . So now you and your dad are together all week! He's not at work. And it is boring? What makes it boring if you are with your dad all week?

Comment: Remembering a prior dialogue that involved John's dad working long hours and not being available to him, the therapist seems perplexed that John is anticipating that he will be bored when he will be with his dad all week. However, he does not jump into giving advice now regarding the two of them doing things together during that week. He simply struggles with what he remembers and explores it with PACE.

JOHN: He never wants to do anything with me! All he does is read!

THERAPIST: Ah! Ah! Now it is making more sense. You want time with your dad, and when you have time with him at the lake, nothing happens that you enjoy with him. That would be hard!

JOHN: He never wants to do anything with me! He says "later" and then he says "when I'm done with this book." And then he does something with mom.

THERAPIST: So you ask your dad and still you two don't do much. What's that about, John? Why do you think you don't do much then?

JOHN: He doesn't want to spend time with me. He doesn't enjoy being with me!

THERAPIST: Ah . . . John . . . how hard that would be if you think that your dad does not want to spend time with you. That he doesn't enjoy being with you! How hard! . . . Would you tell your dad that, John? Would you say to him, "Dad, it seems to me that you just don't want to do anything with me."

Comment: The therapist is touched by John's experience of his dad not doing things with him and she wonders with John what he thinks his father's motives are. Then, when John guesses that his father's actions suggest that he does not want to spend time with John, the therapist shows how she imagines that belief must impact John and then asks him to convey that to his father. She first enables John to experience and communicate his vulnerability about his father's behavior—through experiencing the vulnerability herself. This will make it more likely that the resultant direct communication between the two will have deeper meaning to them both.

JOHN: Dad, you don't want to do things with me! You always say no or "later."

STAN: It's not that, son. I just like to relax when I'm at the lake. I work so hard the rest of the year.

THERAPIST: So when you relax, Stan, you tend to read. To just want to be alone.

STAN: Yeah, to have no demands.

THERAPIST: Ah! No demands! So when your son wants to do something with you, it's more like a demand. . . . It's hard to feel relaxed while doing things with your son.

Comment: Stan's initial response sidesteps John's concern by giving a reason—relaxing and being alone with no demands—that can be viewed as not reflecting anything about the father-son relationship. The therapist's curiosity makes the connection between Stan's behavior and his relationship with his son more explicit.

STAN: I guess . . . though I don't like saying that. I just don't know what to do with John that we would enjoy together.

THERAPIST: Ah! That's sad, Stan. You would like to be able to relax with your son, but you don't know how to do it! What makes it hard to know how to do it?

STAN: My father never did anything with me. I guess I never learned how a father and son could have fun together.

THERAPIST: Ah! So when you were little it was the same for you as it now is for John! That is sad. You wanted to be closer to your dad, just like John wants to be closer to you.

STAN: I want to be able to relax with John. I love him. I just don't know how, I guess.

THERAPIST: Ah, Stan . . . that is wonderful what you just told me! That took courage to say. Would you tell your son that?

Comment: The therapist has enabled Stan to go deeply into his uncertainties regarding how to relate to John, how these uncertainties connect to his relationship with his own father, and how he wishes that he had a deeper relationship with his son but does not know how to create it. This becomes an opportunity for the therapist to facilitate direct father-son communication that is devoid of defensiveness and problem solving.

STAN: I do love you, John. I do want to have more fun doing things with you. I want to be the dad for you that I wanted from my dad. I'm sorry, son. I just don't know how.

THERAPIST: Wait, Stan! Wait. If it is true . . . would you tell your son that you would like to learn how to be a dad? To enjoy being with his son and to enjoy relaxing with his son?

STAN: I do, John, I do want to be that kind of dad! I don't know how very well.

THERAPIST: Do you want that too, John? Do you?

JOHN: Yeah.

THERAPIST: I knew it! Stan, ask your son if he will be patient with you while you learn how. Ask him.

STAN: Will you be patient with me, John, while I learn how to be the dad that you want me to be . . . that I want to be?

JOHN: Yeah, Dad. I'll be patient.

THERAPIST: Great! Great! You both want this. You both love each other and want to show it more in the things that you do together. And we have the lake coming up in a couple of weeks. So many possibilities there!

STAN: But I'm not an Eagle Scout!

THERAPIST: Ah . . . Stan, I think that John knows that. . . . He knows that. He doesn't want to spend a week with an Eagle Scout. He wants to spend a week with his dad! You can learn about the lake and woods and frogs, and water skiing, and secret places, and building dams, and building campfires, and telling ghost stories and cooking hot dogs and burning marshmallows together! Fathers and sons together can learn most anything . . . if you are patient with each other. Will you be?

STAN: I will!

JOHN: Me too!

Comment: The dialogue moved quickly from the conflict around a vacation at the lake to the sad and vulnerable feelings that both father and son have about their relationship. The therapist kept the focus on the father's and son's experiences of the event, gradually enabling each to experience the other more fully, more openly, and with less judgment and defensiveness.

2. The therapist moves from light to stressful, and from well-integrated events to those that are poorly integrated.

EXAMPLE

THERAPIST: Hey, you seem to have a bit more energy this week than last. Something up? I remember you mentioned that you were going on a school trip this week. Is that it?

CHILD: Yeah, it was great!

THERAPIST: Great! All right! Tell me about it.

CHILD: Just regular stuff.

THERAPIST: Regular stuff! That is great! Give me an example of that regular stuff.

CHILD: Well, the teacher said that we could have pizza delivered to our rooms and . . .

However, if a stressful theme is present at the onset, do not avoid it in order to begin with something lighter.

EXAMPLE

[The 10-year-old appears to be frustrated and discouraged as he sits down, not like his usual more engaging beginning of the session.]

THERAPIST: Hey, you seem to be having a hard time. What is it?

CHILD: Nothing much.

THERAPIST: My guess is, it is more than "nothing much." Something come up today?

CHILD: Just seems to me that I never get to do what I want! It's always poor little Janet that needs to be kept happy.

THERAPIST: Ah, so you are having a hard time. Sometimes it seems that what she wants is more important to your parents than what you want. That would be hard!

CHILD: Yeah, but that's no surprise. It's always been that way and always will be.

THERAPIST: You are really discouraged. Seems to you that she is more important and that it's always going to be that way. Wow! That would be hard if it seemed that way.

Comment: The therapist stays with this experience and leads it toward deeper meanings, being ready to follow any sign that the child is withdrawing from the dialogue, possibly because the child does not want to begin the session with such difficult content.

3. The therapist assists with the transition from one event to another, making it as natural as possible by being alert to possible associations between the two events and by maintaining the same nonverbal expressions, especially relating to voice prosody and facial

expressions. A stressful event is placed in the context of the dialogue, which is simply serving the purpose of getting to know the family members better. The less that the client believes that a certain theme is the problem as it is being explored, the more likely that the exploration will deepen the experiences for all and elicit some resolution. The therapist's voice tone, rhythm, and flowing, storytelling quality in the discussion remains stable. He does not move into a serious, problem-solving tone even if the content becomes more stressful for the client.

EXAMPLE 1

THERAPIST: Let me get this right. You lost your ring—the one that your friend bought for you—and your mom found it in the salad bowl?

SARAH: Yeah, it was kind of slimy. Thousand Island dressing all over it.

THERAPIST: Wow! How did you guess that it would be there?

MOM: Sarah was helping with dinner and I had asked her to make the salad, and I thought that it might have fallen off then.

THERAPIST: That's neat! So do you guys often get dinner ready together?

MOM: Maybe a few times a week.

THERAPIST: That's great. 'Cause I know that you two haven't been feeling real close at times lately because of the arguments about school. Do you mind helping your mom with the meals, Sarah?

SARAH: No, it's okay.

THERAPIST: Sounds like it's a habit that you two have had for awhile. Almost a tradition.

SARAH: I guess.

THERAPIST: And maybe it brings some closeness to your relationship that helps to get you through the hard times. Do you think?

SARAH: I guess.

THERAPIST: Are you glad that you both have that?

SARAH: I guess.

THERAPIST: How about you, Mom?

MOM: Me too.

THERAPIST: I'm glad for you both. It can help to get you through the hard times. Sarah, do you remember if your mom had brought up school while you were preparing the salad?

SARAH: I don't know.

THERAPIST: I just wondered if you got a bit tense and your finger shrank a bit and your ring slipped off.

SARAH: That doesn't make any sense.

THERAPIST: I guess not. I try to understand too much, I guess, even why rings end up in salads. But anyway, what is it like for you when your mom brings up the school troubles?

SARAH: It's like, here we go again! I'm going to be told what I need to do one more time!

THERAPIST: Ah! That would be hard if it seems that way to you—and maybe your finger would shrink a bit. But do you wonder what makes your mom bring up that stuff?

SARAH: She doesn't have any confidence in me that I can handle it.

THERAPIST: Ah! Yes, that would really be hard! Have you told your mom that?

Comment: If the therapist had ended the lost ring incident, sat silently for a few seconds, and then seemed to start a new, unconnected conversation about the school troubles, Sarah most likely would not have become engaged in the conversation so openly.

EXAMPLE 2

THERAPIST: So you guys were able to work it out and get the reservation for the concert after all. Great!

MOM: Yeah, it was really important to Greg, so we made it happen.

THERAPIST: That's nice. Even nicer for you, I imagine, Greg.

GREG: Yeah.

THERAPIST: You'll have to let me know if the concert is as fabulous as they say. Oh, yeah, and I was also wondering how that argument turned out that you were having a few weeks ago. You know, Greg, when your mom would not let you visit your friend in Philadelphia and you were really upset about it. [The therapist's voice cadence, pitch, and flow were unchanged as was his interest in this event, relative to the concert. It is all part of the narrative, and all can be explored and integrated into the narrative equally.]

4. The therapist ensures the reciprocal nature of the dialogue by adopting a follow-lead-follow orientation. When the client is willing and able, she initiates the conversation and the therapist follows her expressed experience. The therapist will lead the conversation into related areas when this seems natural or he may introduce new themes that have not yet been explored. These themes may relate to particular problems that the therapist believes that the client is avoiding or which are difficult for her to discuss. In either case, the therapist immediately follows the client's response to the therapist's lead, rather than pushing forward in spite of the client's resistance to doing so. If the client's response suggests that she does not want to explore that theme, the therapist responds with PACE, sometimes being curious about the reasons for client's intentions in focusing on something else.

This orientation is neither directive nor nondirective. The therapist's natural curiosity about the client's narrative causes him to lead into new themes that have not yet been explored, especially if those themes seem to have had a significant—positive or negative—impact on the client's life. The therapist does not wait long periods of time for the client to introduce that theme if he believes that the client is likely to have much difficulty doing so.

5. The therapist ensures that the natural ebb and flow in the dialogue is accepted when it occurs. After exploring a stressful theme, it is often quite natural to take a break and move through a lighter theme before returning to another, more difficult, theme.

EXAMPLE

THERAPIST: Dad, would you tell Jack that you are sorry that this argument has gone on so long and that you are glad that he took such a big step toward making it easier to resolve today?

DAD: I am glad, son. And proud of you. That wasn't easy, what you told me. And I heard you . . . and I hope that I'll continue to listen better to what you have to tell me.

THERAPIST: I think this was an important step forward in your relationship with each other. It was so clear to me how important it is to both of you. So obvious and I'm glad about it.

JACK: Glad that we made you happy too.

THERAPIST: Yeah, Jack, I do appreciate all that you guys have done for me. In fact, I remember how your dad said that you do a good job of cutting the grass at home. I have a big lawn and wonder if you could make me even happier by coming over and cutting my grass this weekend.

JACK: Sure, for $50.

THERAPIST: You don't pay him that much, do you?

DAD: No, but I get the family discount and you're not part of the family.

6. The therapist's nonverbal communications about the story are congruent with his verbal expressions. They are clear and not understated since much of the social and emotional meaning of the story is conveyed nonverbally. When there is a lack of congruence, the dialogue tends to become more of a lecture or monologue.

EXAMPLE

THERAPIST: Wait! Wait! Did you hear what you just said? Did you hear yourself?

ALISON: What?

THERAPIST: When I said that when you reached your dad from the hospital and he cancelled the important meeting that he had just started in order to be with you in the emergency room when they were putting the cast on your leg . . . and I wondered why he did that and did not find some relative to go and get you there . . . you said . . .

ALISON: Because he's my dad.

THERAPIST: That's it! That's it. And the way you said it! Like any idiot would know why he would cancel the meeting and hurry over to be with you there. Like, why did I have to ask?

ALISON: Yeah. So . . .

THERAPIST: So . . . it means that you know in your guts, at that deepest level of who you are . . . how much your dad loves you and how important you are to him. You mean that much to him. . . . I think you might forget that when you two are arguing about stuff. You mean so much to him.

ALISON: Yeah, I know that.

THERAPIST: And sometimes you might forget.

ALISON: Yeah.

THERAPIST: Would you tell that to your dad? That you are glad that you mean so much to him? You're glad that he's your dad.

ALISON: I am glad, Dad. I'm glad that I mean that much to you and that you're my dad!

DAD: I am very glad that I'm your dad, too, Alison. And you do mean *so* much to me.

Comment: Here the therapist's excitement about a seemingly small verbal expression made by Alison when she said that her dad did something for her because he was her dad led Alison into a stronger realization of the depth of security and commitment that existed in her relationship with him.

B. Addressing the Challenges to A-R Dialogue

A central therapeutic goal is to establish and maintain A-R dialogue. When obstacles to the nature and flow of the dialogue arise, the therapist needs to pause to reflect on those obstacles, making them into new content for the dialogue, as in the first sentence in the example below. The therapist must remember that the overarching goal is to seek an intersubjective context and connection between the inner lives of the people in the room.

1. When a family member shows a lack of congruence between the verbal and nonverbal, the therapist brings this to awareness by addressing it. When the nonverbal is connected to matching words, a deeper, more open level of communication often results.

EXAMPLE

THERAPIST: Jane, when your husband said that he tries hard to support you, you agreed that he does but you said it with a tone that seemed to suggest that what he does is not very supportive.

JANE: Well, I know that he tries. I know that he does, but he really is not being very helpful when he tells me what I should do differently and then he goes and yells at our son, which just makes Nathan madder at me!

THERAPIST: Would you say that to your husband? Would you say, "Ron, I know that you want to help me, but when you just tell me and Nathan what to do differently it does not help."

JANE: I know that you try, Ron, but you are not being helpful when you tell us what to do.

RON: What do you want me to do? [With some frustration in his voice.]

THERAPIST: Would you tell Jane that you do want to help her and this time say that you are sad that you have not been that helpful to her and you want to learn how to help her better?

RON: He's right. I am sad that I can't help you better. I know that it's hard for you, doing most of the work raising Nathan. I know it's hard and I want to do what is helpful, not what makes it worse. [Ron has lost the initial defensiveness and now his voice shows some concern.]

JANE: Thank you, Ron. You just helped me more by what you said than you have in weeks.

RON: What did I say?

JANE: It's more how you said it, Ron. I felt your caring for me. . . . I felt that you really do care and sometimes when you've tried to help I sensed more that you were frustrated with me that I can't manage the problems with Nathan better. So, thank you.

RON [soft and open]: And thank you for working so hard and for being patient with me.

2. When a family member is engaged in the story with little or no evident affective expression for the events of the story, the therapist accepts this and then may be curious about the lack of affect.

EXAMPLE

THERAPIST: Darlene, when you mentioned that Sarah hardly talks with you anymore, you said that in a sort of detached way. It was hard for me to tell if you have any feelings about that.

DARLENE: I don't know if I do.

THERAPIST: Because . . .

DARLENE: It's been that way for months now. I used to feel, it used to bother me, but I think that I've just gotten used to it . . . or maybe worn out, like it's too hard to feel anymore.

THERAPIST: Ah! Too hard to feel . . . worn out . . . you sound exhausted . . . and discouraged.

DARLENE: I guess I still feel that. I am discouraged . . . so discouraged.

THERAPIST: Because . . .

DARLENE: Because she is my daughter. My daughter. And I wanted so much more. And I still do! I still do. And I'm terrified that I'll never be close to her. That we'll never be close.

THERAPIST: Discouragement, sadness, and now terror.

DARLENE: Yes, terror! And I don't want to feel that . . . so I try not to feel anything.

THERAPIST: She means so much to you. So much! [Darlene begins quietly crying.]

Comment: When the therapist simply notices a lack of emotion when the client is discussing a theme, often the emotion naturally emerges—with awareness the emotion steps forward. This must be done with acceptance. If the therapist conveys a sense that the client should have a feeling or must have a feeling that he is denying, the client is likely to respond with resistance to what might be experienced as an intrusion into his inner life.

3. When the family member conveys little or no affect, the therapist may also lead the client into a deeper affective experience through expressing, with very clear nonverbal expressions of voice prosody, facial expressions, and gestures, his own affective experience of that event. When this occurs, the client is first experiencing his experience vicariously through the therapist's experience of the event of his story.

EXAMPLE

ANNE: I miss my dad. [He was killed in a car accident a few years before. Anne seldom talks about him and is more distant from her mother than she was before he died.]

THERAPIST: What are some things that you miss? [Anne calmly describes some activities and trips that they did together, without any hint of sadness or grief.]

THERAPIST: Such a lovely memory! Just the two of you . . . on the path in the hills near the ocean. Sharing the beauty of it. And then the story that he shared with you. How beautiful and how sad that he had shared the same view with his dad. Ah! The same view with his dad. And I imagine that he had tears when he recalled that.

ANNE [With a look of surprise over her emerging emotion and her voice beginning to crack]: He did! And I did! And I squeezed his hand. [Anne's tears begin to flow.] And I told him that I love him and . . . that I always will!

THERAPIST: And you do . . . and you always will.

ANNE [with trouble speaking]: Yes, . . . I always . . . will.

Comment: Therapists might worry that such an intervention is telling a client what she should feel. I do not believe that clients are likely to experience it that way. When the therapist shares his experience of the client's story, the client's experience—if it is similar—tends to become activated and it deepens, often eliciting emerging affect. If it is not similar, or if the client is not yet ready to experience that affect, the client is likely to simply move the discussion on without affect.

4. The therapist takes the lead early in the session in modeling A-R dialogue with one or more members of the family in order to interrupt the prevalent, nonproductive family patterns of communication. The therapist demonstrates the qualities of A-R dialogue that convey an intersubjective stance and the qualities of PACE. He does this naturally, without a lecture, and he does it early, before a defensive stance begins to permeate the experience of the family members.

EXAMPLE

RUTH [mom]: I get mad at her because she just wants to spend all her time in the room and does not want to be a part of the family!

THERAPIST: Okay, I think I understand what you are saying. Is it that it bothers you that your daughter spends a lot of time in her room because you think that she is doing that because she does not want to spend time with the family?

RUTH: Yeah, she'd rather be alone than with us.

THERAPIST: So that's what you think is her reason for being in her room a lot. If you are right about that, what bothers you about it?

RUTH: She should want to be with the family more!

THERAPIST: Because . . .

RUTH: I don't know! She just should!

THERAPIST: Could you stay with me a bit on this? . . . I think that it is important. If your daughter does not want to do things with the family much—including being with you—that is hard for you. What makes that hard for you?

RUTH: I don't know. [Softer voice] . . . Sometimes I just worry that . . . we're growing apart . . . that I'm not that important to her anymore . . . that maybe I've done something wrong and she does not get much from being in our family anymore.

THERAPIST: Ah . . . I can see how that might be hard for you if you were not important to your daughter anymore, if your love for her did not mean that much to her anymore.

RUTH: I don't want to think that!

THERAPIST: Ah . . . so it would reassure you . . . that you are important to her, if she spent more time with you and the rest of the family, and less time in her room.

RUTH: I guess that's it. That's why I get angry with her about that.

THERAPIST: Yet, you seem a bit slow to show her your fear, and sadness, and sense of dread that you and she might not be that close in the years ahead. What stops you from showing that?

RUTH: Maybe I don't want to cry, like I'm beginning to do now.

THERAPIST: Because . . .

RUTH: I'd be afraid that she'd not believe me, that she means so much to me. Because we fight so much.

Comment: Dialogues such as this, which may emerge when the therapist leads the family into A-R dialogue with PACE, are often a better therapeutic alternative than asking the girl why she stays in her room and then negotiating a schedule around some balance of solitude and family time. Helping the members of the family to understand and express the meaning of each other's behaviors often leads to an attitude of PACE toward one another that generates natural solutions.

C. Facilitating A-R Dialogue

1. The meaning of the A-R dialogue is likely to deepen if the parent and child are able to engage in direct conversation with each other in a manner that conveys acceptance, curios-

ity, and empathy for each other's story. While the therapist facilitates the dialogue early in the session, his goal is to have the parent and child continue in the same A-R dialogue process throughout the session. The ultimate goal is for the parent and child to be able to engage in similar dialogues at home. The therapist, at the onset of the therapy, spends some time with the parents, presenting the model of A-R dialogue and PACE, and giving examples of ways to become engaged with their child when the child is telling them about his experience.

AN IDEALISTIC EXAMPLE

THERAPIST [to Kevin, age 8]: So, Kevin, let me get this right. Sometimes you get *really* mad at your dad when he says that you cannot go outside and ride your new bike. You want to ride it so badly and he says, "No, you can't!" [Kevin nods in agreement.]

THERAPIST: And you said that you think that your dad sometimes says no because he doesn't care about how unhappy that makes you. That what you want isn't important to your dad. That he doesn't even care that you are unhappy!

KEVIN: Yeah, sometimes I don't think he cares!

THERAPIST: Ah! So no wonder you get mad then—if your dad does not care whether or not you are happy! No wonder you get mad if that's what you think! Would you tell your dad that, Kevin? Would you say, "Dad, sometimes I don't think that you care about my being unhappy when you say no to me. Sometimes I don't think you care, dad!"

KEVIN: That's right, Dad. Sometimes I don't think you care that I get really unhappy when you say no!

DAD: Son, I didn't know that! Thanks for telling me. I'm so sorry if you think that I don't care about your being unhappy when I say no to you. I'm sorry, son, if you think that your happiness is not important to me. No wonder you get mad at me if that's what you think!

KEVIN: Then why do you say no, Dad?

DAD: Kevin, I say no for a lot of reasons. Sometimes it is getting too dark to ride your bike or the weather is not good or there is not enough time before dinner or before we're going somewhere. When I say no to you it's because I think it is best for you or the family if you do not do something right then. I don't believe that I ever said no because I wanted you to be unhappy.

KEVIN: But it feels that way to me, Dad.

DAD: I know that now, son. Thanks for telling me. I'm going to have to work harder to show you that I really do want you to be happy—and I'm sad when I know that you might be unhappy when I say no to you. Maybe I have to let you know what my reasons for saying no are. Maybe I have to give you a hug when I see that you are unhappy. Or accept your anger better. Sometimes you just do not like it at all when I say no! I need to understand that better and show you that I understand it.

KEVIN: Okay, Dad.

DAD: Thanks, Kevin, for helping me to understand better why you get so angry with me when I say no to you.

Comment: It is not realistic to assume that most parents would naturally speak with the child in such a manner when the child conveyed his anger and his belief that the parent did not care that he was unhappy. However, it is realistic to assume that most parents, when given information about PACE and A-R dialogue, while experiencing PACE themselves with the therapist, can begin to approach such dialogues with their children. If parents feel safe with the therapist, they are often willing to be coached by the therapist in front of the child. Such coaching does not diminish the child's trust in what the parent is saying. Rather, it tends to help the child to experience the parents' commitment to improving their relationship with their child.

2. Speaking for a child, or even a parent, can be such an effective way of leading a client into a deep and productive exploration of her inner life that she then can often directly communicate to her parent (or child). Many clients are not in the habit of reflecting on or communicating their inner life to others. Others are able to do it well but are anxious, discouraged, or ashamed about something and cannot find a way to get the dialogue started. In these situations, the therapist is often able to ensure the momentum of the A-R dialogue by speaking for the client.

When a child (or parent) has difficulty finding the words for an experience of an event, the therapist speaks for the client, serving as her spokesperson, leading her into a possible experience of that event. Speaking for a child, or even the parent, is often an effective way of leading them into a deep and productive exploration of their inner life. This often generates an increased experience of an event, with a more evident affective experience of the event as well as a greater ability to explore the event in meaningful detail. When the therapist talks for a client, he does so with the client's permission. He indicates clearly that he is guessing what the client might want to say, and that the client should interrupt or correct the therapist at any time that she experiences the therapist's words as not reflecting her inner life. The therapist needs to observe the client's nonverbal response to his speaking for her and if there is evidence of distress, indifference, or disagreement, the therapist should stop speaking for and explore the client's nonverbal response.

EXAMPLE

THERAPIST [to child, Emma]: Your mom and I have been exploring the problems you've been having with your friends for awhile now and I don't think that we're helping much. I wonder if I could speak for you right now about the frustration that you seem to be having over our discussion. Is that okay?

EMMA: Yeah, you can talk for me.

THERAPIST: Thanks. I wonder if you were thinking—while your mom and I were talking— "I know those things! I know what I am supposed to do about peer relationships! Don't you think I'd do it if it were that easy? I try! I just get so tired of trying. I know that I have a lot to offer but I can't feel it. I feel that I'm not as good as them. I really do! No matter what you guys say!" Is that close to what you might want to say to us now, Emma?

EMMA: Yeah, it is! Yeah . . . no matter what you say! I don't feel that I have much to offer!

MOM: But . . . you . . .

THERAPIST: Just hear her, Sally, just hear her. What she experiences about herself is what we need to hear right now. Not what you experience or I experience.

MOM: But she does . . .

THERAPIST: Sally, let me say it differently. Emma, can I speak for you to your mom, now? [Emma nods, and the therapist then speaks for her.] "Mom, I know that you think that. But I don't! And you don't understand. You think that I can just say those things to myself and it will all be fine. But it's not! It's not that easy, mom! And you don't believe me. So I don't tell you how hard it is. You won't understand. You'll just try to talk me out of what I feel!" [To Emma.] Is that what you might want to say to your mom, sometimes?

EMMA: Yeah, I don't tell her a lot. [Sad and discouraged.]

SALLY: I'm sorry, honey. [Putting her arms around her and pulling her close.] I'm sorry that it's so hard. But I'm especially sorry that I haven't helped you that much. I have not understood. I've wanted to fix it . . . and I guess I haven't wanted to really understand just how hard it is for you. I just wanted to try to make it easier for you by telling you what to do. And I made it harder by making you have to handle it by yourself. I'm sorry, honey. You won't be alone with these feelings again.

Comment: Speaking for a child, when done in the manner described, often generates a sense of relief within the child—now someone finally gets it. The relief is even greater at times in that when the child hears the therapist speak her story, she often understands it better herself. Hearing the therapist speak in the first person for her often enables her to begin to find the words and become more empowered in knowing and communicating her inner life.

3. When the child (or parent) shows distress in response to her engagement in the story, the therapist speaks about the person to others in the family in a manner that removes all felt demand to remain engaged in the story and assists her in downregulating her emotional state.

Speaking about a child (or parent) is both similar to and different from speaking for him or her. When the therapist speaks about the child to the parent, he is maintaining the flow of the dialogue when the child and parent are at a loss for words. He also is reflecting on what was just happening in the dialogue, integrating the discussion thus far so that the underlying themes are more clear and able to be explored in greater depth. When he talks about the child, he is not attempting to increase the child's affective experience or to increase her engagement in the dialogue. Rather, he is offering a chance to withdraw into the background of the storytelling experience. The child can now pause and reflect, with less affective intensity. In the background, the child is under no pressure to respond to what is being said.

As is the case when the therapist talks for the child, when he talks about her, the child can interrupt and correct at any time if she disagrees with what is being said. She can speak for herself if she chooses. It must be clear that when talking about the child, the therapist is always bringing out the child's strengths or vulnerabilities. He never says anything that could be interpreted as a negative evaluation of her. As he speaks about the child to the parents in such positive tones, he is enabling the parents to experience their child, intersubjectively, through the therapist's experience. This could prevent the parent from sliding into what might be a more common negative judgment of her child.

EXAMPLE

JIM: It just seems that he's always harder on me than he is on Jackie!

THERAPIST: I get it. . . . So it was more than your dad being angry over your not finishing your chore. . . . It seems to you that if Jackie doesn't finish her chore . . .

JIM: He just lets it slide. Or he might "suggest" that she get it done. But with me he yells!

THERAPIST: Ah, okay. If it seems that he treats Jackie better than he treats you . . . if that's so . . . what does that mean?

JIM: That she's more important to him than I am! She's his favorite!

THERAPIST: Ah, I get it. . . . If it seems to you that your dad treats Jackie better than you . . . and if he does, it's because she is more important to him! Wow, I get it . . . why you got so mad about your dad telling you that you had to get the job done. Why it was really hard for you. . . . Does that make sense? What do you think, Jim?

JIM: I don't think anything. I'm tired of talking about it.

Comment: Jim's last response indicates that the emotion and theme are becoming too stressful for him and he has begun to detach from the experience and from there he might become defensive or angry. If he had stayed fully engaged with the discussion, the therapist might have asked him to talk with his parents, or spoken to them for him. However, that would only intensify his affective state, already too high for him. Thus, the therapist would do well to speak about Jim to his parents, removing all expectations on Jim to remain engaged or respond, helping him regulate his affect, and helping the parents to accept his expressions.

THERAPIST [to parents]: I think Jim is saying that he needs a break from this discussion. I'm glad he noticed that and I'm glad that he told us. If we continue further along this discussion it might just undermine the gains that we've made. I believe that Jim has been very honest with us, even when he knew that you guys might not like what he had to say. So that took some courage. And I'm glad about that. Jim showed courage to work on this. It is important to him, just like it is to you two. And he's saying, "Enough for now! I need a break!" So I say we respect that and talk about other stuff now.

II. THE CONTENT OF THE A-R DIALOGUE

For a person's narrative to be coherent, all of the events of his or her daily life need to be fully experienced and accepted into the narrative. For that reason, all events are welcomed into the dialogue. All interests, strengths, vulnerabilities, and doubts are welcome. This includes events associated with pride and shame, courage and fear, joy and sadness, anger and excitement. A welcoming interest creates a normalizing context for all aspects of a person's life, and presenting problems no longer dominate the person's narrative, nor the nature of the family relationships.

The primary contents of the A-R dialogue tend to be associated with attachment-related themes. The therapist is continuously gazing beneath the behaviors, the problems, and the events themselves to see if they reflect themes involving a lack of attachment security. These can include:

- Unexpressed or unmet needs for safety within the family
- Fear of rejection for having certain experiences (thoughts, feelings, wishes)
- Fear of rejection for certain behaviors
- Fear of psychological or physical abandonment
- A nagging sense that love is conditional
- Difficulty relying on others for comfort, support, and guidance
- Difficulty reflecting on one's own inner life or the inner life of attachment figures
- Difficulty regulating emotional experiences, positive or negative
- Difficulty repairing attachment breaks due to conflicts, discipline, or avoidance

The purpose of A-R dialogue is to make the ongoing communication safe enough to explore any of the above themes or others that are interfering with the development of attachment security, emotional regulation, and the development of coherent narratives. The following points tend to reflect general ways in which various content are explored.

A. Ten Important Factors

1. Generally, the session begins with lighter and more positive themes. These tend to initiate the flow of the dialogue and establish its momentum. Within the natural flow of the dialogue, the therapist then guides the focus toward themes that are more important to members of the family and more likely to involve conflict, shame, fears, or problems that one or more members would like to resolve. Once the momentum of the dialogue has been established, family members are more open to exploring stressful content.

However, if the family begins the session expressing intense emotion around an event, the therapist does not avoid that theme in order to begin with light content. The intense emotion, when responded to with acceptance, curiosity, and empathy, tends to easily create the narrative flow that the therapist wishes to develop. The therapist's task then is to quickly join in the dialogue around that theme—often a living family conflict—and ensure that an A-R dialogue develops along with the attitude of PACE.

For example, a parent may begin, "This kid can't follow rules!" The therapist can accept that and answer with curiosity, "How do you know?" The parent describes the child's behavior, saying, "He stole from us again this week!" However, the therapist follows the parent's feeling (not the child's behavior) with acceptance and curiosity, while preparing to reflect with empathy on whatever comes next: "What's that like for you?"

2. When specific conflicts or symptoms emerge naturally or are invited into the dialogue by the therapist, the goal of the therapist is to understand their meanings. The focus is what lies under the symptoms—the thoughts, feelings, intentions, and other qualities of the person's inner life—that the behavioral events reflect. Here again, an attitude of PACE facilitates such exploration and deepening of experience. A problem-solving attitude is to be avoided as it tends to remain at the surface level of behavior and to quickly seek solutions that often do not enter the narrative, do not address emotions, and are not likely to last. If there is value in exploring any cognitive-behavioral strategies, such explorations tend to be toward the end of the session, after emotions have been explored and the meanings of the interactions have been clarified and communicated. This leaves family members feeling heard, understood, open, and motivated to apply specific interventions to facilitate change.

3. The therapist is alert to specific thoughts, emotions, wishes, memories, or other aspects of the family members' view of self, other, and family that are not welcome into the individual or family narratives. These are unwelcome because they deviate in some way from the unspoken norms, interests, beliefs, or values. Certain intense emotions such as expressions of anger, sadness, fear, pride, joy, or love may also not be welcome. The family may have secrets that are not to be discussed or even thought about.

4. The presence or absence of relationship repair in the family needs to be understood and facilitated if necessary. When relationship repair is missing, families often become locked in cycles of escalating conflicts or patterns of avoidance. Then the safety and joy of attachment security is not evident. Repair within adult-child relationships remains the responsibility of the adult, since the adult needs to communicate that the relationship is more important than any conflict.

5. When the content is becoming stressful for one or more family members, the therapist steps back from the content, focuses on the immediate process, and coregulates the emerging affect. Taking a break from that particular dialogue may be helpful until members are able to safely reengage in it.

6. The relationship between the parents is certain to have an impact—for better or worse—on the overall family functioning and the functioning of each member as individuals within the family. The nature of the attachment between the parents is observed, and then addressed whenever necessary to facilitate the functioning of the family as a whole. When parents resist such an exploration, the resistance is explored with PACE.

7. The nature of the parents' own attachment histories within their families of origin will also be explored for connections between the parent-child or partner relationship patterns that existed in the past and those manifested in the present. Again, resistance to such explorations is welcomed and explored with PACE.

8. The content of the A-R dialogue is more about the experience of events than about the events themselves. Throughout the dialogue the therapist is conveying the attitude that the individual members' experiences of an event are valid. Any differences are accepted and understood, rather than argued about and rejected. The implications embedded in these differences as to the unique qualities of each family member and the relationships within the family are then much more able to be explored.

9. As specific experiences of events are explored with PACE, new meanings of the events are likely to emerge from the dialogue. These new meanings tend to contain much less shame, anger, doubt, fear, isolation, avoidance, and hopelessness than did the old experiences. Symptoms that were embedded in the old experiences of self and relationship tend to dissipate. In their place is safety within the self and among family members as well as an openness to explore and understand the events that confront the family narratives. These new meanings—as they emerge within the context of attachment security—lead toward more coherent narratives for one or more of those present. ("My life makes sense after all.")

10. The content of the dialogue, as it generates new experiences of events and more coherent narratives, may suggest changes in interaction patterns within the family that would impact upon daily life. These changes may be acknowledged, with some confidence that the patterns are now likely to shift for the better, or they may suggest the need for specific recommendations for the family. This process is not so much problem solving as it is discovering and verbalizing ways to make the new understandings more relevant and stable within the family's daily life. Any recommendations made by the therapist need to be congruent with the attachment-focused model of parenting that is the central feature of this model of treatment (i.e., focus on the relationship, emotion, and meaning of behavior, rather than a focus on behavior).

III. OBSTACLES TO A-R DIALOGUE

A-R dialogue provides an alternative to typical communication patterns that are central to the family's inability to understand each other and resolve conflicts and differences.
Typical patterns are:

1. **Angry criticism and defensiveness.** Often family members communicate in a manner characterized by defensiveness, arguments, trying to establish proof about what happened, and proving that the self is right and the other is wrong.
2. **Alternating or competing monologues**. While there is much talking, there is little lis-

tening and communication. Each person is primarily interested in developing his own position, not in understanding the position of the other.

3. **Evaluations of the other's behavior and inner life.** This may be done without anger but with reason and is experienced by the other as shaming. The evaluator is taking a stance of judgment over the person without any sense of empathic understanding of the person's perspective.

4. **Emotional distancing.** When the family wants to avoid conflicts, they tend to distance themselves from the emotional component of the dialogue. The themes being explored elicit comments such as, "It doesn't matter" or "I don't care."

The therapist models A-R dialogue as a more productive manner of family communication and interrupts—with PACE—efforts of family members to engage in maladaptive patterns.

A. Monologues—Including Venting

Often parents begin the first session under intense stress, struggling with serious family distress about which they have felt helpless or enraged for a long time, possibly months or years. Some parents are able to express their distress, often with great emotion and in much detail, while still maintaining a reciprocal relationship with the therapist. They are able to respond to her empathy and to follow her curiosity. Though she has said little, they are in an A-R dialogue because they are allowing themselves to be impacted by her nonverbal responsiveness. Other parents essentially are engaging in a monologue in that the therapist's nonverbal responsiveness is not noticed, and such parents may vent for an hour if the therapist allows herself to become increasingly passive in response to the monologue.

The therapist needs to be aware whether the parents' intense expressiveness is reciprocal or if it is a monologue. The therapist's bodily response to the parent's venting is often a credible sign as to whether it is a dialogue or monologue. If the therapist experiences herself as being engaged, responsive, empathic, and deeply interested, then she can be confident that the venting is a dialogue, with the parent responding to the therapist's nonverbal responsiveness. If the therapist experiences herself as becoming tense, tired, possibly irritated, then it is more likely that the parent's venting is a monologue. Before having confidence in her bodily response to the venting, however, the therapist is wise to first reflect on whether or not the venting—content or process—is activating materials from the therapist's own attachment history.

When the therapist concludes that the parent's venting is a monologue, the therapist is wise not to become passive or the venting is likely to only continue without benefit. Rather, the therapist might interrupt the monologue by matching the nonverbal affect being expressed and then joining the parent's content with her own congruent verbal and nonverbal communication. Such interruptions may require relationship repair before continuing, but if the therapist persists, often the parent begins to vent in the manner of a dialogue. Essentially, the therapist is guiding the parent to learn how to vent in a manner that is therapeutic.

EXAMPLE

Martha, the [mother of a 12-year-old girl, Jenny, had just described briefly and rapidly a conflict that she had with her daughter, barely noticing the therapist.

MARTHA: And that wasn't all! The next day . . .

THERAPIST [interrupting]: Just a second, Martha. I want to understand that better . . .

MARTHA [interrupting]: It just doesn't stop. The next day . . .

THERAPIST [interrupting]: Wait, please, I need to understand what you said before we go on. So, you said that she laughed at you when you said that she needed to get off the phone and do her homework. And the laughter seemed to really bother you.

Comment: The therapist is interrupting to insist on a dialogue rather than to passively accept a monologue. If Martha had seemed responsive to his empathic facial expressions, gestures, and brief vocal responses, he would have listened to the next example. Then he would have had confidence that Martha wanted to understand his thoughts, questions, and possibly ideas. Though Martha was doing all the talking at that time, it is certainly possible that it was a dialogue, not a monologue. The therapist needs to be aware of which it is.

MARTHA: Of course it bothered me! She just doesn't listen to me at all and then she laughs too! Why it's like . . .

THERAPIST: Please, Martha, I am sorry if you thought that I was suggesting that her laughter shouldn't be bothering you. I wasn't suggesting that at all.

MARTHA: Then why did you say that? And why do you keep interrupting me?

Comment: If Martha had been receptive to the therapist's thoughts, she most likely would have accepted his interruption as representing his desire to understand her better. When a person is annoyed with an interruption, it tends to confirm that the person was engaged in a monologue. Still, the therapist first repairs the relationship before continuing, making his motive clear. He does so in part by becoming more animated when she becomes annoyed with him. He is matching her affect, without matching the emotion, to demonstrate how intense he is about wanting to be helpful to her.

THERAPIST: Oh, Martha, again I'm sorry if you think that I don't want to hear about your experiences with your daughter. I truly do! What I'm doing is trying to understand what you're telling me better so that I might be of help. This has been so hard for you that you seem to have so much to say. I'm trying to slow it down a bit so I can understand what you're going through. So I can help to make sense of it. So, does her laughter . . . does it seem like she's making fun of you?

MARTHA: Sure it does. How else would I take it?

THERAPIST: Again, I'm not suggesting that you should not have that response. I'm trying to understand exactly what it is. It sounds like it is really painful! Your own daughter seems to enjoy making fun of you.

MARTHA: She does! And after all that I've done for her.

THERAPIST: Yes, you've done so much for her. And now it seems like she is moving further and further away from you and your influence in her life. How do you manage that? It must be so hard!

MARTHA: I don't know. Some days it's all that I can do just to come home after work. Knowing that she'll be there. Like she's waiting for me . . . to make my life harder.

Comment: There is now a shift in the discussion, with Martha being engaged in the A-R dialogue with the therapist. She now is allowing him to go with her into the distress of her lack of closeness with her daughter. She experiences his empathy. She may drift back into the monologue, but if the therapist can catch her a number of times, she may gradually begin to more deeply experience the value of the dialogue over a monologue.

THERAPIST: Ah! How hard that must be. Not even wanting to go home after work. And your daughter's presence doesn't make it appealing at all, but just the opposite!

MARTHA: You can say that again.

THERAPIST: And my sense is that you want a close relationship with her. She's growing up. Becoming a teenager. And from what you told me a few weeks ago, you never were close with your mom and you so want to have a better relationship with your daughter.

MARTHA: And she doesn't seem to want it.

B. Giving a Lecture About What a Client Should Do

In a lecture, the parent is focused on controlling or influencing the child but is not receptive to being influenced by the child. This is very evident to the child, who is likely to become defensive and angry. Parents fear that if they have a reciprocal dialogue, the child will think that they are giving in to him and he will argue all the more. This may be the child's assumption the first time, but he usually understands that the parent is rather trying to understand his inner life better, and this may or may not influence the parent's decision about the child's behavior.

In the next example the therapist gives a lecture to a child regarding his inner life and in the second example the therapist begins to lecture the parent. After presenting these two examples of lectures, I present the same examples a second time, this time demonstrating A-R dialogue. The client's response to A-R dialogue tends to be much different than it is to the therapist's lectures.

EXAMPLE 1

CHILD: It doesn't bother me. I don't care.

THERAPIST: I hear you, Steve, but if you don't start to care about this and work at it, things are likely to just get worse for you.

CHILD: I said that I don't care.

THERAPIST: I can only do so much for you, Steve, if you don't cooperate. I want to help you with this, but if you don't work too, there is not much that I can do for you.

CHILD: Then don't bother.

THERAPIST: I want to bother because I care for you, Steve, I really do. I want what is best for you, which is why I want you to try harder to change some of your habits.

EXAMPLE 2

PARENT: I get so angry with him sometimes. He says that he'll do the job and then he just ignores it.

THERAPIST: I know that it is hard to be patient with him when he promises something but does not do what he says. I can understand your frustration. It's hard, but you just have to hold onto your patience and not yell at him.

PARENT: Easy for you to say. After it happens so many times, you'd have to be a saint not to get upset about it.

THERAPIST: Yeah, of course it is harder when it happens again and again. It is important to remember that he had some hard times at school recently and he is likely to let it out at home.

PARENT: So he can take it out on me?

THERAPIST: I didn't say that. I just said that he needs more patience or he'll never start doing what you want him to do.

PARENT: I know, I've got to work harder.

THERAPIST: Yes you do.

Comment: In this example the therapist begins the dialogue with an effort to convey empathy but does not go more deeply into the parent's experience to truly understand it. It is as if he does not have confidence that an intersubjective dialogue will be enough to help the parent to reduce the anger directed toward his child. Later he might not have confidence that the lecture would help at all, but at the time, it may have helped the therapist reduce his own sense of failure and uncertainty about how to be of help.

1. Alternatives to Lectures

EXAMPLE 1

CHILD: It doesn't bother me. I don't care.

THERAPIST: Wow! You don't care anymore. You found a way to stop caring.

CHILD: I never did.

THERAPIST: Since it made your life so difficult, I wonder if you cared a long time ago. But it is hard to care and be always disappointed! I can see where you would find a way to just stop caring, and even forget that you once did.

CHILD: I guess.

THERAPIST: Yeah! Hard to care—and care alone—about something that was important. Makes sense to find a way to make it less important. And my sense is that you found a way to do that with most things in your life—make them not important. So there wasn't much left that meant much to you.

CHILD: Yeah, that's about it.

THERAPIST: I'm sorry, Ted, how alone you've been with this for so long! And I'm sorry that things that were once special to you became not special. And you still have to face all that too, and still seem all alone.

EXAMPLE 2

PARENT: I get so angry with him sometimes. He says that he'll do the job and then he just ignores it.

THERAPIST: You count on him to do what he said what he would do. And he doesn't! It gets so upsetting when it happens over and over.

PARENT: Yeah, after it happens so many times, you'd have to be a saint not to get upset about it.

THERAPIST: One time, yes! We all make mistakes. But over and over. How do you handle your anger? How do you keep trying to work it out with him?

PARENT: Sometimes not very well. I try to remember that he's having some hard times at school lately. He's got a lot happening to him too.

THERAPIST: So your empathy for him keeps your patience alive—though just barely at times, from what you're saying.

PARENT: Yeah, you've got that right! But I'll never lose it with him. He's a good kid. He's my kid, and I love him! We'll get through this together. We always do and we always will.

THERAPIST: Yes you do. Your love and commitment are big! They'll keep finding patience for you when no amount of advice will.

C. Problem Solving

Problem solving is similar to a lecture without the "should" so clearly implied. It offers a solution to a problem in a clear and direct manner. While this seems straightforward, it often is not helpful when it has been tried many times before, or when the behavior is simply the tip of the iceberg. Often it is necessary to understand and resolve the meaning of the behavior before its function as a problem is eliminated. **The following two examples are presented twice to first demonstrate a therapist's problem-solving followed by the therapist establishing A-R dialogue.**

EXAMPLE 1

CHILD: My little brother just drives me crazy! He keeps getting into my stuff and when I take it back and tell him not to, he just cries and follows me around until I give him something to play with to shut him up. I wish he'd just leave me alone!

THERAPIST: Have you thought of giving him something of yours to play with before you start playing yourself? If you initiate something with him, he is likely to get bored after a bit and then he'll probably leave you alone.

CHILD: What if he doesn't?

THERAPIST: Then maybe schedule a time to play with him every day. Tell him how long it is and keep to the schedule. Once he gets used to it he will probably accept the schedule.

EXAMPLE 2

PARENT: Sometimes I just don't know what to do. I tell him what he needs to do over and over again, but he just does whatever he wants. It gets so tiring.

THERAPIST: Just tell him once. Then if he does not do it, have a consequence ready, tell him what it is, and don't argue with him.

PARENT: I wish it were that easy. He'll just get more worked up and then I'll have a battle over enforcing the consequence. I start feeling that it is just not worth it!

THERAPIST: I know that it is hard to break these patterns. If you are consistent and firm without getting all worked up, he will eventually respond.

Comment: When the therapist focuses on problem solving as an alternative to establishing an intersubjective relationship, the client often does not sense that he is being understood as a unique person with unique problems. Rather, the client is likely to experience himself as being a case and the therapist as being an expert who believes that he knows best for him. It is hard then for the client to experience empathy from the therapist for his struggles. Also, because it is not intersubjective, the therapist is not likely to fully experience the client's experience and the problem solving is less likely to be on target. After establishing an intersubjective dialogue the client is likely to have more confidence in the therapist's ideas, and the therapist's ideas are more likely to best fit the client's unique situation. Problem solving, if it seems like it is still needed, is more likely to be beneficial toward the end of the session after the meanings have been explored and all are motivated to reduce the conflict and deepen their relationship.

1. Intersubjective Alternatives to Problem Solving

EXAMPLE 1

CHILD: My little brother just drives me crazy! He keeps getting into my stuff and when I take it back and tell him not to, he just cries and follows me around until I give him something to play with to shut him up. I wish he'd just leave me alone!

THERAPIST: How hard that must be for you! Sometimes you just want to play by yourself, with your own stuff, and he messes it up for you. Being a big brother isn't so great sometimes.

CHILD: I mean, he's a good kid and I love him, but why can't he just leave me and my stuff alone sometimes?

THERAPIST: That makes it so complicated! You love him and that is probably one of the reasons that he follows you around. You know that he loves you too and wants to be with you and be like you, including playing with the stuff that you play with.

CHILD: Yeah, maybe I should just turn into a mean big brother! [Laughs.]

THERAPIST: I get it! Be a meanie and he won't want to hang around with you.

CHILD: Yeah, but I'd never do that. He's just being a little kid.

EXAMPLE 2

PARENT: Sometimes I just don't know what to do. I tell him what he needs to do over and over again, but he just does whatever he wants. It gets so tiring.

THERAPIST: You just wish he'd listen to what you tell him and take care of it. At least sometimes!

PARENT: Yeah, is that asking too much?

THERAPIST: My guess is that you don't think it is—that you try to be reasonable about what you ask.

PARENT: It is reasonable!

THERAPIST: Oh, I hope that you did not think that I thought that you were being unreasonable! I'm sorry if I communicated that poorly.

PARENT: No, it's okay. It's just that it seems that someone is always telling me something to do but no one gets that I've tried most of that already. Everyone always has some advice for me.

THERAPIST: Like they want to help you and don't know what else to do but try to find a way to fix it for you.

PARENT: I wish they could. I wish you could. Maybe I am doing something wrong.

THERAPIST: Like we all do sometimes. Any sense about why you tell him to do it over and over?

PARENT: Because what I ask is reasonable and I think that if he could just see that it's reasonable, he'd do it.

THERAPIST: Ah, and maybe he doesn't want to do it—and doesn't—even though it is reasonable—and he knows it is.

PARENT: You mean he might not want to do it even though it's reasonable?

THERAPIST: Maybe.

PARENT: That means that I'd have to tell him to do it—even if he doesn't want to—simply because I said to do it. Just like my mother used to say to me and I always said I wouldn't do that. I'd show my kid the reasons and then he'd do it!

THERAPIST: And he won't cooperate! You got an unreasonable kid.

PARENT: Imagine that! [Laughs.] Maybe my mother was right—at least this time!

IV. TRANSCRIPT OF AFFECTIVE-REFLECTIVE DIALOGUE

This dialogue represents an abbreviated version of a typical treatment session between a parent and adolescent child. In this session, the key event that is brought into the dialogue involves a recent conflict between the mother, Andrea, and her 16-year-old son, Peter. As is often the case, as they entered the therapist's office, the conflict had not been resolved and the relationship had not been repaired, leading to some distancing and avoidance.

After speaking with Andrea about her current experiences and the events within the family since the last session, the therapist invites Peter to come into the office and sit on the couch with his mother.

THERAPIST: Peter! Good to see you again. It has been much too long.
PETER: Yeah, right.
THERAPIST: I don't quite hear your usual enthusiasm.
PETER: I don't think you ever heard it. It's your fantasy.
THERAPIST: I think you're right, now that you mention it. How come?
PETER: Yeah, like my favorite activity to do in my day is to talk with a psychologist.
THERAPIST: It's not? Is this because I don't listen to the music that you like?
PETER: No, it's because you're old. I like to talk with people my own age.

Comment: The therapist begins with an animated greeting of the child or teen so that he has the experience that the therapist is truly glad to see him, and he is more than a client but is also an individual whom the therapist enjoys and hopes to get to know better. In this situation, he is not matching the teen's somewhat bored and distant stance but rather leading them both into a more animated joint experience. Playfulness is often helpful at these moments, keeping the discussion light at the beginning. If the teen thinks that the playfulness is in any way making fun of him, then the therapist responds with empathy, and possibly a brief relationship repair.

THERAPIST: What makes you think I'm old?
PETER: You're not only old, you're nuts.
THERAPIST: Is that what this is about? You got stuck with a nutty psychologist?
PETER: I don't like any psychologist.
THERAPIST: That's not fair! You're judging me because I'm a psychologist, not for who I am.
PETER: You're all the same!
THERAPIST: See, that's my point! Would you like it if an adult said all 16-year-olds are the same? I'm not the typical psychologist who wants to fix you. I just want to get to know you.
PETER: Right, you want me to stop giving my parents a hard time—to earn your money.

THERAPIST: Not fair! I have not once said something with the goal of making you into a good boy. Not once!

PETER: Yeah.

THERAPIST: Think of one! Go ahead and tell me one time that I did.

PETER: I don't remember what you say!

THERAPIST: So you made that up then! I'm right and you know it. I work to make sense of things for your family and you know that. I have not once said to you that you need to be good for your parents. Not once!

PETER: Okay! Let it go!

Comment: While being playful, the therapist is alert to moving the dialogue to a deeper, possibly more open and vulnerable level. Here, when the teen says that the therapist is just like other psychologists, the therapist has an opportunity to lightly complain, "That's not fair!" which is likely to elicit a response that is more engaged and open. Since teens often stress fairness and not being stereotyped, this gives the therapist an opportunity to move the teen toward a more open conversation. At the same time, it is more than a playful dialogue. The therapist conveys an urgency regarding his wish to get to know Peter better, not to change him in order to collect his parent's money. This urgency conveys to Peter that their relationship matters to the therapist and that Peter's perception of the therapist matters too.

THERAPIST: I'm happy to do that. Let me prove it. What was that about anyway, the yelling that went on between you and your mom on Wednesday night?

PETER: See? I was right! You want me to be good.

THERAPIST: You are not right. I want to make sense of how angry you two got with each other.

Comment: When the therapist moved into the discussion about the conflict between Peter and his mother, he did so without changing his voice tone, rhythm, or overall storytelling tone. He was careful not to adopt a serious, problem-focused tone. This fosters the teen's likelihood of remaining engaged in the discussion as it moves into a stressful theme.

PETER: Ask her! She's the one who started yelling when I got home!

ANDREA: And why did I start yelling, as you call it?

THERAPIST: Wait, you guys! I don't need an example of your yelling now. I believe you when you say that you did. I just want the facts. What was it about?

Comment: The therapist takes the lead quickly when he senses that the mother and son are likely to simply reexperience their earlier conflict, reenacting the same defensive and aggressive stances that they had assumed before. The therapist wants to ensure that this dialogue is experienced differently, and so he quickly breaks up the old defensive patterns.

ANDREA: Peter came home 45 minutes late and he hadn't been where he said he would be.

PETER: And she reacted like it was the end of the world. Her son was a delinquent who just embarrassed her in front of the neighbors!

ANDREA: That's not fair, Peter. I never said any of that!

PETER: Well, it sounded like that's what you were thinking!

THERAPIST: Now we're getting somewhere. Thanks for telling me what you were thinking, Peter. It seemed to you that your mom was angry with you because she thought that you were causing trouble in the community—even doing something illegal—and that she was embarrassed by you.

PETER: That's what it sounded like!

THERAPIST: Thanks for helping me to make sense of it, Peter. If that's what you thought about your mom's anger, I could understand where you would become angry too, if she thought that you were a delinquent and that she was embarrassed by you. If your own mom were embarrassed by her son, that could be hard for the son. Could we hold those guesses about your mom's motives for getting mad, Peter? I'd like to hear your mom's memory about what she was thinking and feeling at the time.

Comment: After Andrea stated what event caused the conflict, Peter quickly stated his assumption about why she was angry with him (i.e., he was doing something wrong that would be an embarrassment to her). The therapist made it clear that he now understood Peter's anger if he thought that was his mother's motive. At this point the therapist can choose whether to deepen Peter's experience that was based on his assumption about his mother's motives or turn to Andrea and help her clarify her motives, and communicate them more clearly to Peter. Such acts of deepening experience followed by communicating the emerging experience to the other family member create a sense of vulnerability in the person who is uncovering his own experience. For this reason, especially early in the treatment, the therapist often engages in this process with the parent first.

PETER: Go ahead.

THERAPIST: Thanks, Peter. [To Andrea] So, I think now I know what led to that big argument between the two of you. Help me understand, Mom, why you were so angry with Peter when you knew that he wasn't where he said that he would be and then came home late.

ANDREA: Are you saying that I shouldn't be mad about that?

THERAPIST: Oh, Andrea, I'm sorry if I said that in a way that seemed like I was judging you and criticizing your anger. I did not mean to be critical. I just want to understand what is under your anger.

Comment: Without any judgment, the therapist has elicited a summary of the events that led to the conflict. Now he begins the process of exploring each person's experiences of the events. This moves the dialogue into the intersubjective context that is needed for therapeutic engagement. However, when questioned by the therapist, Andrea responds defensively, assuming that his curiosity implies that he is critical of her anger. Such assumptions are common, since often in dialogues individuals will question each other's motives. The therapist quickly repairs the breach in the relationship caused by her assumption about his curiosity.

ANDREA: What do you mean, "under my anger"?

THERAPIST: Oh, I know what Peter did, but what do you think led you to be angry about it? In the context of your relationship with your son, just you two, not society or other families, just you two . . . what do you think led you to experience anger right then?

Comment: The therapist is facilitating a reflective attitude within Theresa toward her own inner life. He wants her to look inside and wonder more about her thoughts, emotions, and wishes associated with her son and her relationship with him.

ANDREA: I just need to know where he is and when he'll be home. And to keep his word about it.

THERAPIST: Because . . .

ANDREA: Because . . . if I can't trust that he is where he says he will be and will be home when he says he will be . . . I won't be able to stop worrying about him.

THERAPIST: And what would be behind your worry? Do you think that he is not responsible?

ANDREA: It's not that! He's probably more responsible than most teenagers. . . . It's just that . . . he is a teenager . . . and I'm his mother.

THERAPIST: And that means . . .

ANDREA: That I worry if I don't know where he is!

THERAPIST: Because . . .

ANDREA: He's my son. And I love him. And I want him to be safe! And he's just not as safe in town or with other people as he would be at home.

Comment: With the therapist's gentle focus on her experience, Andrea is able to explore how her anger connects to her need to trust Peter's word so that she will worry less when he is away from home. And under her worry is her love for him and her desire for his safety. By asking whether she believes that her son is irresponsible, the therapist wants to know if she believes that his behavior away from home gives her additional reasons to worry.

THERAPIST: So, maybe he can stay home whenever he's not at school.

ANDREA: You can't mean that! He needs to be independent. He needs to learn about life and the world in ways that he cannot learn while near me at home. I know that, but it's hard and knowing where he is and when he'll be back makes it . . . makes me let go more easily.

THERAPIST: So . . . you got angry with him for not being where he said he would be and not being home when he said he would be . . . because you worry . . . because you love him . . . because you know that he needs his independence from you and from home . . . and because if you know that he will do what he agreed to do . . . you are less likely to go crazy with fear or be tempted to try to keep him near you all the time.

ANDREA: I guess that's about it . . . but I'd never try to make him dependent on me.

Comment: The therapist somewhat playfully suggests that Andrea keep her son home all of the time in order to help her clarify her motive: She does not want to make him dependent; she simply wants to worry less when he is exploring his independence.

THERAPIST: I have a better sense now about your anger at Peter the other night. And I think that he might too. Would you tell him what we just explored as if he had not heard us?

ANDREA: Peter, I am sorry for how I yelled at you. You mean so much to me. . . . I love you so much. . . . That's why I worry. . . . I get so scared. My life would be destroyed, broken to bits if I were to ever lose you. So, I guess that I try to control everything, like I could when you were two, so that I can keep you safe from everything. I know I cannot keep you in a bubble. . . . You need your independence. I know that. And when you are older and living on your own, there might be days when I don't know where you are and who you are with and what you're doing. But, now, knowing those things helps me to let go. Helps me to deal with the worries that I have when I'm not nearby. Knowing those things helps me to keep going on with my own life and trusting that you are safe.

PETER: I didn't know how much . . . how important it is to you, Mom. To know where I am and when I'll be home. I don't want to hurt you, Mom. I'm sorry. I think sometimes that you just think you need to make all my choices for me. I need to remember that you might have confidence in me, and still worry. And I can help your worries if I do what we agreed I would do when I go out. I will, Mom, I will.

ANDREA: Thanks, son.

Comment: The therapist asks Andrea to speak directly to her son about her reasons for becoming angry with him when he does not keep his agreement with her about his time away from home. This will facilitate his intersubjective experience of her experience and enable him to be less defensive about her anger and more receptive to her motives. This, in turn, is likely to reduce her use of anger to disguise her worry . . . and her love for him.

While Peter's response might seem a bit unrealistic, such responses do occur after the parent shows her vulnerability and motives for her behavior.

THERAPIST: And, Peter, you're willing to do that for your mom, because . . .

PETER: Because I didn't know that she worried so much. And I thought it was because she did not think that I could handle things . . . that I was irresponsible.

THERAPIST: And now you know . . .

PETER: That she just worries about me.

THERAPIST: Because . . .

PETER: She loves me.

THERAPIST: So you're doing this for her because she loves you . . . and . . .

PETER: I don't want her to worry so much.

THERAPIST: Because . . .

PETER: I love her too.

THERAPIST: Ah. . . . Would you tell her that?

PETER: I love you too, Mom. I really do.

ANDREA: Thanks, Peter. It feels wonderful hearing you say it.

Comment: After Andrea took the lead in expressing her inner life to her son, and thus being in a vulnerable position herself, the therapist asked the son to do the same, thus deepening the overall intersubjective experience for both mother and son.

EXERCISES

Questions

1. A-R dialogue stands for:
   A. Acknowledgment and remorse, which is crucial for conflict resolution.
   B. Two components that facilitate problem solving.
   C. Two components that facilitate cocreating a narrative.
   D. Anxiety reduction and trauma resolution.

2. Ensuring that the dialogue is maintained is the responsibility of the client because:
   A. The client is ultimately responsible for deciding the treatment goals.
   B. If the therapist takes the lead, the client is made dependent.
   C. If the therapist takes the lead, the client will lose control and become anxious.
   D. The therapist is responsible for ensuring that the dialogue is maintained.

3. When the content of the dialogue moves from light to serious, the therapist:
   A. Maintains the same nonverbal affect expression as he enters the new theme.
   B. Adopts a serious tone that is congruent with the serious content.
   C. Alerts the clients that he intends to move into a serious theme.
   D. Tells the client what he wants to explore and elicits the client's consent.

4. In general, as the session progresses from start to ending:
   A. The reflective aspect of the dialogue predominates early in the session.
   B. The affective aspect of the dialogue predominates early in the session.
   C. The reflective aspect is at the beginning and end and the affective part in the middle.
   D. There is no general pattern; it varies greatly from individual to individual.

5. Within A-R dialogues, monologues have an important role early in treatment because:
   A. They allow clients the opportunity to vent and hence feel understood.
   B. They allow clients the chance to set a slower pace and hence feel safe.
   C. They encourage the development of listening skills for all family members.
   D. Monologues are never given an important role in A-R dialogues.

6. When the client is telling important themes of her story with an absence of affect:
   A. The therapist notes the absence of affect and is curious about it.
   B. The therapist notes the absence of affect and expresses empathy for the need to make it disappear.
   C. The therapist expresses his affective experience of that theme.
   D. All of the above may be appropriate interventions.

7. When the client is exploring a difficult theme and begins to distract from it:
   A. The therapist needs to challenge the distraction and focus on the theme.
   B. The therapist needs to avoid that theme because it must be too stressful.
   C. The therapist needs to ignore the distraction and continue with the theme.
   D. The therapist needs to accept the distraction, see its value, be curious about it, and then follow the lead of the client regarding whether to take the theme further.

8. Talking for a child serves to:
   A. Assist him in discovering and giving expression to his inner life.
   B. Reduce his affect arousal.
   C. Teach him what he is thinking and feeling.
   D. Teach him new problem-solving skills.

9. Talking about a child serves to:
   A. Give him a break from a difficult discussion.
   B. Reduce his affect arousal.
   C. Assist the child's parents to see aspects of the child that they may have overlooked.
   D. All of the above.

10. When one member of the family is not engaged in the dialogue, the therapist:
    A. Confronts that member about needing to participate fully in the treatment.
    B. Accepts the lack of engagement and expresses curiosity about its presence.
    C. Interprets the lack of engagement as a sign of a break in the relationship.
    D. None of the above.

Case Examples

In the following cases, first choose what you think is the best type of response for the situation to facilitate A-R dialogue. Then create a response that you believe would facilitate such a dialogue.

1. Early in the session, the mother begins what is likely to become a long, critical story about her son's functioning since the last session. She states: "I just don't know why I bother coming here! I thought last week that he wanted to improve things between us, but this week he is worse than he has ever been! I am doing all the work and he's not doing anything!"

   THE THERAPIST:
   A. Waits until she finishes and then gives the son a chance to talk.

B. Tells her that she is not engaging in A-R dialogue and reminds her of the expectations.

C. Waits until she finishes and then initiates A-R dialogue.

D. Breaks into her venting to initiate a dialogue about the possible meanings of the behaviors to her and to her son.

The best type of response and the reason for your choice:

_____

_____

_____

_____

Write here what your response might be:

_____

_____

_____

_____

2. A boy enters the treatment room expressing anger about having to come for therapy. "This is such a waste of time. I don't know why I have to come here! I'm not crazy! They always blame me because they won't admit their mistakes. My parents are never wrong! And you're just like them! You'll just believe them and blame me!"

THE THERAPIST:

A. Explains why the boy has to come.

B. Ignores his anger and tries to engage him around a lighter theme.

C. Ignores him and relates to his parents.

D. Has empathy for his distress and expresses curiosity about its origins.

The best type of response and the reason for your choice:

_____

_____

_____

_____

Write here what your response might be:

_____

_____

_____

_____

3. A teenager says that it does not bother him that his dad seldom has time for him. "I don't care! He has never made time for me and it doesn't bother me. If that's what he

wants, it's his choice and I don't need him in my life. I have other people who like being with me."

THE THERAPIST notes the lack of affect and responds in the following manner:

A. He tells the boy that he does not believe that it does not bother him.

B. He explores with the boy the experience of no longer feeling close to his dad.

C. He suggests that the boy would be wise to not give up on having a relationship with his dad.

D. He changes the focus of the discussion since the boy's defense is very strong.

The best type of response and the reason for your choice:

_____

_____

_____

_____

Write here what your response would be:

_____

_____

_____

_____

4. An older child became upset as he explored his difficulties with his parents. He cried, then accepted comfort from them, and then became somewhat uncomfortable.
   THE THERAPIST:

A. Sat in silence, waiting for the child to express himself.

B. Asked the child why he was uncomfortable.

C. Reflected on the experience with the parents while mentioning their son's strength and openness.

D. Reassured the child that he was not too old to be comforted by his parents.

The best type of response and the reason for your choice:

_____

_____

_____

_____

Write here what your response would be:

_____

_____

_____

_____

5. As the dialogue moved naturally from a deeper experience to a lighter one, the mother impatiently brought the discussion back to the deeper one and the child did not become engaged with it.

THE THERAPIST:

A. Encouraged the child to discuss the theme awhile longer.

B. Encouraged the mother to wait awhile before continuing with the theme.

C. Ignored the mother's statement and continued with the light theme.

D. Spoke for the child to the mother about reasons for his disengagement.

The best type of response and the reason for your choice:

_____

_____

_____

_____

Write here what your response would be:

_____

_____

_____

_____

Speaking for and Speaking About

1. Speaking for:

A. The therapist is exploring with a 9-year-old child a fight that he had with his 7-year-old sister. The boy becomes agitated and looks away. The therapist could guess what he is thinking:

_____

_____

B. The therapist is able to help a 12-year-old girl realize that her anger at her mother for refusing to allow her to do something was related to her belief that her mother did not care that what she wanted to do was important to her. She would not tell her mother that, but allowed the therapist to speak for her:

_____

_____

C. A teenager said that he did not need to be in therapy. The therapist asked a few questions about the teenager's reasons for his belief, but the teenager would not respond. The therapist tentatively spoke for the teenager about what he might say if he chose to do so:

_____

_____

2. Speaking about:

A. An 8-year-old boy became angry about the dialogue and shouted "Shut up!" to the therapist. The therapist turned to the parents and spoke about the boy:

_____

_____

B. A 15-year-old girl became irritated with the therapist not agreeing with her about her parents' limits. The therapist glanced out the window and spoke out loud (to herself) about the girl:

_____

_____

C. After a stressful session in which two parents and a teenager were able to express the reasons for their anger at each other and attain some understanding—without judgment—of the other's perspective, the therapist:

Spoke about the teenager to the parents:

_____

_____

Spoke about the parents to the teenager:

_____

_____

Experiential Exercise: Impaired Dialogue

Researchers in attachment theory and early childhood development have developed the "still face" paradigm, in which the parent, while interacting with his or her infant, is told to "freeze" and make no facial expressions while sitting in front of the infant. Researchers then study the impact on the infant when the parent—though present—is completely unengaged, neither initiating actions nor responding to the infant's initiatives. This has a disorganizing effect on the infant's physiological, emotional, cognitive, and behavioral functioning.

In the exercise, the reader is asked to find a partner. One person is the talker and the other is the listener. The talker thinks of an interesting or humorous story to tell the listener, taken from the talker's life. The entire story needs to last about 4 minutes. The talker should not choose a stressful theme. For the first 1 minute and 15 seconds the listener is actively engaged in the story with appropriate verbal and nonverbal responses. Then, for the next 1 minute and 15 seconds the listener puts his head down to avoid all eye contact and tries not to respond to the story either verbally or nonverbally. Then for the final 1 minute and 15 seconds the listener becomes actively engaged again. The talker is asked to make an effort to continue the story during the middle section of time. However, if it is too hard to do so, the talker should wait until the third section to continue or should just discontinue the exercise at any time.

This exercise is an excellent way to experience the power of nonverbal communication in maintaining any dialogue and in contributing to the meaning of the story. It also demonstrates that the distinction between talker and listener is not that clear: the listener's continuous, contingent responses to the telling of the story actually contribute to the development of the story.

Following the exercise, the talker is asked to process the experience with the listener. He might reflect on any cognitive, emotional, motivational, or physical impact that the still face of the listener had on him while telling the story. The listener might then comment on the impact that his disengagement had on him as well. An additional discussion might follow regarding the possible implications of this exercise for being a therapist. It is customary for the talker and listener to then switch roles and do the exercise again.

SUGGESTED ANSWERS AND RESPONSES

Questions

1. C. The two components, affective and reflective, create a dialogue that tends to facilitate a coherent autobiographical narrative.
2. D. Many clients do not have the skills or habits needed to engage in this reciprocal, therapeutic dialogue. It is the therapist's responsibility to ensure that such a dialogue is present in the session.
3. A. By maintaining the same nonverbal voice prosody, the therapist is conveying that any theme is able to be safely explored in the dialogue and she has no assumptions about the client's experience of a theme prior to the client expressing his experience.
4. B. As events are explored, the more affective components of the experience are expressed first generally and the lived meaning is then felt. This enables the person to go more deeply into the experience of the event. The more reflective awareness follows, enabling the affective aspects to be integrated more fully into the narrative.
5. D. Monologues are not seen as likely to be therapeutic since they negate the intersubjective experience—the person engaged in the monologue is not receptive to the other's experience of his story. One person can do all of the talking in a dialogue, when that person is being receptive to and influenced by the nonverbal responses of the other person. In that case it is a reciprocal dialogue, though one person says nothing.
6. D. All of the above are appropriate responses, depending upon the unique context of the dialogue at that moment.
7. D. Distractions have many meanings, so before the therapist decides on how to respond to the distraction, it would be wise to be curious about its particular meaning, accept it, and then respond. It is best then to follow the client's response to the therapist's response.
8. A. When talking for a child, the therapist needs to remember that she is guessing about an aspect of the child's inner life; she does not decide what that life is. When her guess is accurate, it often becomes associated with an increase in the child's affective experience at the time.

9. D. All of the above.
10. B. The therapist first needs to understand the meaning of the disengagement before responding to it. As a result, as in most cases, the first response is based on PACE.

Case Examples: Suggested Responses to Facilitate A-R Dialogue

1. The mother begins the session by stating: "I just don't know why I bother coming here! I thought last week that he wanted to improve things between us, but this week he is worse than he has ever been! I am doing all the work and he's not doing anything!"

D is likely to be the most successful response. If the therapist is able to break into the monologue and then join the content being presented by the mother, while moving to the meanings under the events that she is describing, or by raising other, more positive motives, he is likely to guide the mother into a more open exploration of the situation that facilitates a more empathic and hopeful stance. If the therapist waits till she finishes (A or C), the communications expressed by her extended, negative, judgmental tone are likely to make it very difficult to engage the child or the mother in an A-R dialogue. This passive therapeutic stance also implies that such venting is of value, and it suggests that the therapist is resigned to the negative stance of the parent and may even agree with it. B is not chosen since it suggests that the therapist may give a lecture when the parent is not following the rules and that such a lecture is of greater value than facilitating an intersubjective dialogue. It is more likely to facilitate a defensive response from the parent and lead to little A-R dialogue.

In choosing D, the therapist might choose to say the following, starting the dialogue by matching the intensity and rhythm of the parent's voice (this will minimize the experience of the parent of being interrupted and rather seem that the parent's distress naturally elicited a matched response in the therapist).

How discouraged you are! If you want so much to improve how things are going at home, and you are afraid that things might not improve. That this therapy might not be helpful! And a big part of your worry seems to be your fear that your son may not want to improve things as much as you do. And you fear that unless you're both working at this, nothing we do is likely to be helpful. If that's what you've been thinking, no wonder you've become more discouraged!

2. A boy enters the treatment room expressing anger about having to come for therapy. "This is such a waste of time. I don't know what I have to come here for! I'm not crazy! They always blame me because they won't admit their mistakes. My parents are never wrong! And you're just like them! You'll just believe them and blame me!"

D is likely to be the most successful means of facilitating an A-R dialogue with the boy. By conveying empathy for the boy's distress, the therapist is accepting his reluctance to be present and is experiencing empathic understanding for how difficult the situation must be for him. By then being curious about the nature of his distress, she is conveying a desire not to avoid his distress, dismiss it, or argue with him about it, but rather to simply understand it better. If the therapist responds with A, a lecture is likely to begin, which is only likely to foster even greater emotional withdrawal from the session within the boy, or an abrupt departure from the room. B is likely to be experienced as devaluing his experience of therapy—suggesting that it is irrelevant to the therapist. C is likely to be experienced as an even more comprehensive devaluing of the boy himself, while confirming his assumption that only the parents are important to the therapist.

In choosing D, the therapist would match the affective expression of the boy with his own voice conveying a similar level of intensity and speaking in a similar rhythm. He would reply:

Of course you would not want to come here if you expect to be blamed. Of course you would see it as a waste of time! And why would you trust me? I'm older than your parents! They're paying my fee. Does it always seem this way to you—when the family is struggling over something—that you are being blamed, that no one else has made a mistake? Does it always seem that way?

3. A teenager says that it does not bother him that his dad seldom has time for him. "I don't care! He has never made time for me and it doesn't bother me. If that's what he wants, it's his choice and I don't need him in my life. I have other people who like being with me."

B is most likely to facilitate A-R dialogue. The therapist accepts the boy's statement about his experience and then tries to understand central qualities about it, hoping to convey empathy for how he stopped caring and hoping to facilitate the teen reflecting more on his relationship with his father. A would invalidate the boy's experience. Even if the therapist thinks that the boy might be denying his caring for his father to protect himself from the pain of caring, the therapist needs to respect the boy's statement about his inner life. The therapist must not suggest that he knows his client's inner life better than does the client. C is likely to generate a lecture and disengagement by the teenager. D assumes that the teen's defense is strong without first exploring the defense. Addressing the defense, without challenging it or judging it, is often preferable to avoiding it.

The therapist might reply in the following way:

Ah! You don't care anymore about your sense that you and your dad just don't have a meaningful relationship. It seems to you that he doesn't care—that he hasn't made time for you and maybe it seems that you're not that important to him—so why would he be important to you? If that's been your experience, I can see where you would stop caring. Did it use to be hard when you did care? Do you remember when you first noticed that you were not caring much anymore? When did it start to get easier for you that you did not seem to have much of a relationship with your dad? When you didn't think that you didn't mean much to him?

4. An older child became upset as he explored his difficulties with his parents. He cried, then accepted comfort from them, and then became somewhat uncomfortable.

C is likely to be the most effective response for enabling A-R dialogue to continue. The child's discomfort suggests that the emotional experience was becoming too intense for him and he might be starting to feel trapped. To keep the focus on him is likely to only intensify his distress. Talking about him with his parents allows him to withdraw psychologically into the background while the therapist and parents remain engaged with each other. A is likely to be the most stressful for the child as he is likely to experience the silence as if everyone is looking at him and waiting for him to say something. Both B and D tend to highlight his discomfort, which is only likely to increase it, rather than decrease it.

The therapist might talk about the child in the following way:

Your son showed great courage there to face some very stressful things and then rely on you guys for some support. Being a teenager can be hard at times and it's nice that he is able to acknowledge it, make sense of it, and turn to the two of you who know him better than anyone else in the world does. And he trusts you two that you're going to be with him in these things that he's facing, while not feeling that you have to rescue him from them. Yeah, he's quite a guy.

5. As the dialogue moved naturally from a deeper experience to a lighter one, the mother brought the discussion back to the deeper one and the child did not become engaged with it.

Either B or D is likely to be the most effective in facilitating further A-R dialogue. Both responses acknowledge that the child does not want to continue with the deeper theme and both responses validate the child's wish to stay with the lighter theme. D has the value of giving words to the child's nonverbal resistance to the mother's wishes, while making it clear that his resistance is understandable and accepted. B might be preferable earlier in the therapy if the child was not yet ready to be open about his differences with his mom.

A gives priority to the mother's wishes over the child' wishes, while C disavows the mother's wishes, indicating that they do not even merit an acknowledgment.

The therapist might say:

My sense, Bill, is that if you were to talk with your mom about what you are feeling now, you might say, "Ah, Mom, I just don't want to talk about that anymore! I've done enough talking about it for now. Can't we take a break? Can't we just talk about the trip to the zoo last weekend? Give me a break, Mom!

Speaking for and Speaking About

1. Speaking for
   A. The therapist is exploring with a 9-year-old child a fight that he had with his 7-year-old sister. The boy becomes agitated and looks away. The therapist could guess what he is thinking: "I think that you might want to say to me now: 'Okay, maybe I do get mad at her a lot and maybe sometimes I don't like her that much! But I'm tired of talking about it! I think that you're just trying to make me feel bad.' Is that close to what you were experiencing now?"

   B. The therapist is able to help a 12-year-old girl realize that her anger at her mother for refusing to allow her to do something was based on her belief that her mother did not believe that what the girl wanted to do was important to her. She would not tell her mother that, but allowed the therapist to speak for her: "Mom, sometimes when you say no to me it seems that you just don't care about what is important to me! Maybe even that I'm not important to you! And that's why I get mad at you, Mom, that's why."

   C. A teenager said that he did not need to be in therapy. The therapist asked a few questions about the teenager's reasons for his belief, but the teenager would not respond. The therapist tentatively spoke for the teenager about what he might say if he chose to do so: "I wonder if you might say, 'You just want to get me talking and trick me into thinking that you really understand! And that you really care. It's just a game and I'm not going to play!' Is that close to what you are thinking now?"

2. Speaking about
   D. An 8-year-old boy became angry about the dialogue and shouted "Shut up!" to the therapist. The therapist turned to the parents and spoke about the boy: "I think that your son is letting us know that this is getting hard for him and he needs a break. I could see him becoming a bit tense and I'm sorry that I did not suggest that we take a break. Glad he was able to tell us so we didn't go faster than he is able to handle it.

   E. A 15-year-old girl became irritated with the therapist not agreeing with her about her parents' limits. The therapist glanced out the window and spoke out loud (to himself) about the girl: "I wonder if Jane is thinking that I'm just like all adults. I just don't get it. Or maybe that I'm on her parents' side. I'm not sure how to help her to believe me that I'm looking for a way to help her with this. Maybe I just need to listen to her now. She's feeling all alone with this and that must really be hard."

F. After a stressful session in which two parents and a teenager were able to express the reasons for their anger at each other and attain some understanding—without judgment—of the other's perspective, the therapist did the following.

Spoke about the teenager to the parents: "I really admire your son! He really feels strongly about this but he was willing to try to understand your point of view, to work something out that you'll all be okay with. You two are important to him and while you might disagree, he still loves you and is trying to find something that will work for you all."

Spoke about the parents to the teenager: "I think that your parents are really working at this! It is so nice to see that they don't just pull out power to get what they want. They respect you and your perspective and want to find something that makes sense to you all. It's nice that I can see their love under their anger, and I am especially glad that you can see it too."

4 PACE

Maintaining the attitude of PACE to facilitate affect regulation and the cocreation of a coherent individual and family narrative is the central therapeutic intention held throughout AFFT. The four attributes of playfulness, acceptance, curiosity, and empathy are central in the development of attachment security and intersubjectivity in the parent-infant relationship and they are also central in the development of these realities in this model of therapy.

The attributes of PACE are quite evident when you observe the interaction between a parent and infant. Imagine interacting with a baby who wants to be engaged with you without being playful. It is so evident in the parent's eyes, voice, face, gestures, and touch. During these interactions the parent is likely to be very accepting of whatever expression is shown by the baby. It does not matter what the baby does; the parent accepts it and becomes engaged with that expression. And during the activity the parent is continuously curious about what the baby is doing, what it might mean, and what the baby is going to do next. The parent is open to the baby communicating her inner life and the parent is actively engaged in gentle, flexible efforts to make sense—with the baby—of what the expressions might represent. And then when the baby shows any distress, the parent is quick to communicate empathy for the distress, to show that he or she is joining the baby in the distress, assisting her with it in a practical way if possible but assisting her with it just by being there if nothing practical is possible.

These features in our frequent interactions with babies and very young children are central in developing and maintaining our intersubjective stance when with them. We are not working to change them. We are simply active in being with them, getting to know them, and sharing our experiences with them, which will help them to deepen and organize their own experiences.

enjoyment that can get the family members and the family and therapist through the difficult work of relationship development and repair.

    C. Playfulness facilitates developing the positive in the relationship. Reducing the negative is not sufficient if the family is to be able to maintain a vibrant and enjoyable emotional atmosphere for all.

    D. Examples of playfulness.

II. Acceptance

    A. The therapist models the important role of acceptance in attachment security.

    B. The therapist makes clear the difference between experience, which is always accepted, and behavior, which may well be evaluated.

    C. Even when the therapist experiences major concerns about what she sees as the implications of an aspect of the inner life of the client, she still responds with complete acceptance while exploring it in greater depth.

    D. Examples of acceptance.

    E. Shame and Guilt

III. Curiosity

    A. The therapist is not judgmental in efforts to understand the family members.

    B. The therapist may have to take the lead in helping the client to be curious about possible thoughts, feelings, and wishes about an event.

    C. Examples of curiosity.

IV. Empathy

    A. The empathic intention of the therapist is simply to be actively present and responsive to the client's emerging experience, either of a memory or of the current interactions in the session.

    B. The intention of the therapist's expression of empathy is simply to assist the client to remain safely within an experience—if he chooses to do so.

    C. Empathy is not a technique that one gives to the client to achieve a therapeutic goal.

    D. Examples of empathy.

V. Obstacles to PACE

    A. Obstacles to Playfulness

    B. Obstacles to Acceptance

    C. Obstacles to Curiosity

    D. Obstacles to Empathy

We must consider each attribute separately though they are invariably interwoven. In AFFT, acceptance of the experience of every member of the family is always present as is curiosity and empathy for those experiences. Playfulness is not always so evident, though it is likely still to be in the background, conveying a sense of hopeful movement into the future, while emerging to the forefront periodically between stressful themes.

I. PLAYFULNESS

Playfulness—so often dominant in the intersubjective activities between a parent and infant— reflects the joyfulness and fascination with each other that is inherent in their meeting and time spent together. It reflects the positive, unconditional, deep interest in each other and in the act of being together. The therapist holds the same underlying attitude toward his clients and their presence in treatment. It represents a positive, optimistic presence and movement of the mind and heart of the therapist into the experiences of the individual and family. Playfulness searches for, and finds, the strengths that lie within each family member and the family itself. As the therapeutic relationship forms between the family members and the therapist, the family begins to develop a joyful fascination in the therapist as well, not so much in his own personal narrative as in his intersubjective experience of the family. The family members are having an impact on the therapist also, and they come to greatly enjoy this impact and look forward to its continuing development.

A. In adopting a playful presence, the therapist is conveying optimism and expressing a positive response to the strengths of each family member. There is a lightness about playfulness that communicates hope that no matter how difficult the conflicts and problems are, there is reason to believe that they will be successfully managed.

EXAMPLE

THERAPIST: Let me get this right. You two [the parents] canceled the vacation and held what you called a "retreat" in your own home, with no one going anywhere for 5 days, because you sensed that you guys were not doing well together and you wanted to build the relationships again.

MOM: Well, I wouldn't have described it quite that positively but I guess that is about right.

DAD: Let's say there was more grumbling than that and even a few comments about it being "jail."

THERAPIST: I know that—of course there would be mixed emotions about what you were missing and what you might be doing at home that was less fun. But still, the bottom line for me is that you guys—all of you—noticed that the family was struggling, and at some level you all wanted to get it working again—the right way!

DENNIS [teen]: As they said, "want" might be too strong a term.

THERAPIST: Good point, Dennis, so let me bring in some hindsight. Now that you see the results, is at least part of you glad that you guys did this?

DENNIS: I guess.

THERAPIST: And you, Sue?

SUE [10 years old]: Yeah.

THERAPIST: Mom and Dad?

MOM: Yes!

DAD: Definitely!

Comment: The therapist works—in a light manner—to establish consensus that they all saw value in what they had done. From there he is able to lead them toward deepening the experience.

THERAPIST: Because?

MOM: It seems to have worked.

DAD: I am hopeful that it has brought us together again.

THERAPIST: And you want that?

DAD: Definitely!

THERAPIST: So you are glad?

DAD: I am. Totally.

THERAPIST: That's my point! You guys made it happen. You were struggling so you took a big step to shake things up. You said, "This family is too important to us to let it get broken like it seems to be heading toward. This will cause some anger and disappointment for all of us, but we have to do it. We love each other and we want to do what ever it takes to get it done. And you did! Right?

FAMILY: [Various words of agreement.]

THERAPIST: So, you can do it once a month!

DENNIS: No way!

SUE: Oh, no!

THERAPIST: And I'll call you the Brady Bunch.

DAD: Don't get carried away with this now!

THERAPIST: And I'll get credit for developing a new treatment intervention.

DENNIS: It wasn't your idea!

THERAPIST: Good point again, Dennis. It must have been yours.

DENNIS: I don't think so!

THERAPIST: Yeah, you must have said something like, "Mom, Dad, let's forget the beach and just hang out at home so we can sit around and tell stories and have popcorn and turn off the cell phones and iPods."

DENNIS: You're nuts! Like I'd say that!

Comment: The therapist keeps the conversation light, while still bringing out the positive meaning of the event. With all engaged now in focusing on the event, he can choose to continue to explore the experience more deeply or use that to move easily in other directions.

B. The therapist engages in playfulness to build a sense of camaraderie and reciprocal enjoyment that can get the family members and the family and therapist through the difficult work of relationship development and repair. When individuals can smile, look at each other, and laugh a bit, they often are aware of the reasons that they are together and are committed to each other. When affection is still a bit down the road, playfulness can generate experiences of closeness that can be sustaining during the hard times.

EXAMPLE

THERAPIST: [After a long exploration of an ongoing conflict between Tim and his mother] So, Tim, I missed that. What did you say to your mom in the heat of the moment?

TIM: I called her an old witch.

THERAPIST: And she was not pleased?

TIM: You can say that again!

MOM: You can say that again!

THERAPIST: And you called her that because?

TIM: I was mad at her!

THERAPIST: I know that, Tim. But why do you think you were being so honest with her about what you were experiencing at that moment?

TIM: Because I didn't care if she got mad.

THERAPIST: And you didn't care because you are safe to express your anger with her. You are safe, knowing that no matter what—she'll still love you. You were able to call her an old witch because she is such a great mom.

TIM: I guess so.

THERAPIST: You guess so! Of course I'm right! Now thank your mom, Tim. Thank her for not turning you into a toad or knocking your lights out for calling her a witch.

TIM [laughs]: Thanks, Mom!

THERAPIST: And thank her for loving you so much that her love is still there after you call her an old witch.

TIM: Thanks, Mom.

THERAPIST: Now thank her for being your mom.

TIM: Thanks, Mom.

MOM [to therapist]: Should I thank you for this? I'm not real sure.

THERAPIST: Only if you want to.

MOM: Thanks.

Comment: That sequence would not have been appropriate early in exploring their experiences of the conflict, as it would most likely represent an effort to minimize it or rescue or distract them from the negative experiences. Once the experience was fully explored and relationship repair attained, then such a playful interchange would assist them with moving on and seeing the conflict in the context of their very special relationship.

C. Playfulness facilitates developing the positive in the relationship. Reducing the negative is not sufficient if the family is to be able to maintain a vibrant and enjoyable emotional atmosphere for all. Any progress is more likely to last if there is actual reciprocal enjoyment and shared activities and conversation that is emerging within the family and extending into the future.

EXAMPLE

CARL [age 13]: So I guess that means that you are going to let me do whatever I want.

MOM: Nice try. I guess it means that when I say no, I'll do it with more understanding about how hard it is for you when you can't do what you want.

CARL: Then make it easier by only saying, "Yes, my darling son."

THERAPIST: "Darling son"! Wow! Carl knows how to turn it on!

MOM: Yes, he does and that's one of the reasons he is my darling son.

THERAPIST: It's nice seeing you two this way after all that you've been through.

MOM: Yes it is. I can't remember when we laughed and joked with each other like this.

THERAPIST: How about when Carl was a cute little toddler?

MOM: Oh, yes, then, all the time! He was so, so darling then! And his dimples!

CARL: Okay, Mom, don't go freaky on me.

MOM: And he still has them. This one cute little 12-year-old, Millie, thinks that he is *so* handsome!

CARL: Mom!

MOM: Yes, my darling son?

Comment: Whereas therapy, almost by definition, focuses a great deal on difficult experiences, the act of moving through them and attaining some resolution and relationship repair is often a great opportunity to activate some relaxed closeness. This does not diminish the importance of the focus on the family conflict and stress. Rather it helps to help the family members to experience the distress in the context of the whole relationship, extending back to the beginning. Often, the most positive experiences that the family have had in months or years occur during such moments in therapy that follow the hard work.

D. Examples of playfulness.

1. NINE-YEAR-OLD BOY: I don't want to say. You're just going to agree with my dad.

   THERAPIST:

   - Agree with your dad? But look at his shoes! I'd never agree with someone who wears shoes like that.
   - I'm not a judge! All I know how to do is to help dads and sons figure out how to agree about stuff like this.
   - If I agree with your dad, I'll buy you a candy bar. If I agree with you, you buy me a candy bar.

- How smart you are! You figured that out before I opened my mouth. How did you do that? What if you're wrong?

2. DAD: Easy for you to say! How many teenage parties are you planning at your home this month?

   THERAPIST:

   - My home is a teen-free zone.
   - I'd love to help you out. I can't—this professional boundaries thing.
   - I can suggest some creative ways so that it would have to be canceled!

II. ACCEPTANCE

Acceptance—radical acceptance—where the experience of each member of the family is completely accepted by every other member of the family creates a level of psychological safety and intersubjective discovery within the family that is unsurpassed. Acceptance refers to the unconditional, nonjudgmental attitude that one family member has for the inner life of another. The thoughts, feelings, wishes, intentions, perceptions, beliefs, values, and memories of each member of the family are not evaluated by the others as being right or wrong.

Acceptance is central to the open communication of one's inner life. When a family member knows that his inner life will not be evaluated by others in the family, and when he is certain that the mind of the other is active in simply trying to understand—and assist his own efforts to understand—his inner life, then he is likely to trust the family with his thoughts, emotions, wishes, and memories. When a family member knows that his inner life will be evaluated by the others, he is very likely to keep his inner life to himself and not share it. He is also likely to spend less time reflecting on his inner life and understanding himself. This is the case with many adolescents who are very reluctant to express themselves to their parents. If they trusted that their inner lives would not be evaluated, they would be much more willing to do so.

Behavior is not always accepted. Parents often try to modify their child's behavior through guidance, direction, consequences, or direct means to prohibit it. A toddler who is about to hit the sleeping family dog with a rock will be stopped from doing that by the observant parent. Similarly, if the toddler attempts to walk into a busy street the parent will prevent him from that action. With good guidance and the development of the child's internal inhibitions, there is less reason for parents to limit the child's behaviors as his childhood proceeds. However, it is always necessary for the parents to have that option. They are ultimately responsible for the best interests of their child. Children are more willing to accept parents' limits and consequences for their behaviors when parents make it clear that while they are limiting the behavior, they remain accepting of the experiences (thoughts, emotions, wishes, etc.) that generated the behavior. "Misbehaviors" often represent experiences that are confusing or stressful for a child and about which he is reluctant to—or does not know how to—communicate to his parent. Often, once the experience has been communicated and met with PACE by the parent, the child's "misbehavior" fades away with no need for a consequence.

Acceptance is conveyed at least as much by one's voice prosody (nonverbal features) as it is by the words themselves. Acceptance is conveyed with voice features that are relaxed and casual, not diminishing the importance of what is being said, but rather simply showing an interest in them, a focus on understanding with no evidence of evaluating what is being said. The tone is light and the conversation almost has a meandering, flowing character, unless the client is expressing something very intensely and the therapist is matching the affective expression. This flowing character makes it clear that nothing will move the therapist into a critical, evaluative stance. Nothing will elicit shock or rejection.

Within a family atmosphere characterized by acceptance, differences are more often addressed rather than confronted. When a parent addresses her child's behavior, her first motivation is to understand it, and so she focuses on accepting, being curious about, and possibly having empathy for the inner-life factors that led to the behavior. When a parent confronts a behavior, she often does so without fully understanding the personal factors that led to the behavior. This often leads to a defensive response by the person who has been confronted, and greater unwillingness to accept discipline that might follow. When a child senses that his parent has an understanding about the factors that led to the behavior, but still evaluates the behavior as wrong, the child is more likely to accept any following discipline. (Of course, certain behaviors might best be confronted on the spot without any need to first understand the precipitating factors. For example, nothing would justify kicking a younger sibling. However, even in such situations, understanding the factors that generated the behavior is often important, after the behavior has been stopped.)

Acceptance also conveys a sense of confidence that whatever is being explored can be experienced, observed, understood, and addressed if necessary. Nothing is too big to handle or too frightening to discuss.

Finally, acceptance clearly demonstrates the need to differentiate a person's behavior from his inner life. Any evaluation is directed toward the behavior alone. This same differentiation between the inner life (i.e., the sense of self) and behavior is central in the differentiation of shame and guilt. For that reason, shame and guilt are discussed, along with their implications for treatment, at the end of this section on acceptance.

A. The therapist models the important role of acceptance in attachment security. When one member of the family does not accept the experience of another, the therapist interrupts the dialogue and points out that the person was expressing an experience that needs to be accepted and understood rather than criticized and judged as wrong. He may also have to repair the relationship with the person whom he interrupted, but the issue is so important that he cannot avoid the conflict that might follow the interruption.

EXAMPLE

ED [to his father]: Seems to me that you never have any confidence in me!

FRANK [father, annoyed]: That's just wrong, Ed!

THERAPIST: Frank, your son just mentioned his experience of whether or not you have confidence in him.

FRANK: And I'm telling him that I do have confidence in him!

THERAPIST: I hear that, Frank, and I can tell how much you want to convince him that you do. I think that he might be open to your experience more if you first really understand his.

FRANK: Okay, I'll listen.

Comment: The therapist prevents the start of what would likely be an angry, defensive exchange between Frank and his son. If Ed's experience is accepted, he is likely to be willing and able to communicate it more fully and thus be better understood. As it is explored—as experience, not fact—it is less likely to elicit a defensive response.

THERAPIST: Ed, could you tell us what it is like for you if you think that your dad does not have confidence in you?

ED: It sucks! Seems like he just thinks that I'm clueless about everything! Or that I'm the most selfish person in the world. He always seems to be evaluating me and most of the time he doesn't like what he sees.

THERAPIST: So it seems to you that your dad thinks that you're either incompetent or selfish much of the time and does not have confidence that you are able to—or will choose to—make the best choice.

ED: That's right! I'm never quite good enough for him.

THERAPIST: Would you tell your dad that, Ed? Would you be willing to say, "Dad, sometimes it seems to me that you often think that I'm either clueless or selfish—you don't have confidence in me."

ED: That's right, Dad. I often think that you think that I'm either clueless or selfish.

FRANK: I don't, son.

ED: That's how it seems to me, Dad.

THERAPIST: Would you let your son know that if he thinks and feels that about your thoughts about him, it would be very hard for him? Just that, Frank, just empathy for your son, now.

FRANK: It would be hard, son. If that's what you think, I'm sorry because it must be hard for you. I need to do a better job showing you what I really think about you.

THERAPIST: What do you really think about your son, Frank?

FRANK: I think that he's a great young man! I think that he's competent in so many things—and I never think of him as being selfish!

THERAPIST: What's your guess about why he would not know that and would think the opposite about how you see him?

FRANK: I guess I don't talk about the positive. I guess I just look for what I disagree with and focus on that.

THERAPIST: Would you tell your son that now, Frank?

FRANK: Ed, I do think that you're a great and caring young man and I have so much confidence in your abilities. And I'm sorry for not telling you that very often. I'm sorry, son, that you did not know what I think about you. I hope that you believe me.

ED: I think so, Dad. It just seems so strange hearing you say that.

FRANK: I can see why, son, I can see why. It won't be strange in the future. I'm going to let you know loud and clear what I think about you all the time.

ED [laughs]: Thanks, Dad, but don't overdo it.

Comment: The question might be why Frank's experience of annoyance at his son's experience of him was not given equal acceptance by the therapist, when he asked Frank to wait and understand his son's experience more before responding with his own. When he did wait and his son described it in more detail, Frank's annoyance vanished and he was able to experience empathy for his son and then repair the relationship by describing his positive experiences of his son to him. This is often the case—one's defensive response to another's experience tends to greatly decrease when the other is given the freedom to express his experience in more detail. If, after fully hearing his son, Frank's annoyance remained, then the therapist would have communicated that he fully accepted Frank's experience of annoyance and responded to it with curiosity and empathy. Even then, the therapist would have separated Frank's experience—which he fully accepted—from Frank's behavior that consisted of criticizing his son's experience.

B. The therapist makes clear the difference between experience, which is always accepted, and behavior, which may well be evaluated. If discipline or criticism is restricted to behavior alone (and not the underlying experience that led to the behavior), often the other individual, whether it be child, parent, or partner, will be much more ready to hear the criticism and respond to it without defensiveness.

EXAMPLE

GRANT [teen, to his mother]: Yeah, right, you fat cow!

THERAPIST: Grant, slow down. Words like that don't work in here.

GRANT: So you're taking her side! You said that I could say whatever I wanted!

THERAPIST: I said that you are free to tell us any experience that you have and that it will be accepted. But not to use any words that you choose. Swearing and name calling can be experienced as assaults, similar to actually hitting a person, so I don't accept all words. I think you chose those words to let me and your mom know that you are angry with her. So tell us about your anger without swearing and name calling.

Comment: It is wise for a therapist to clearly differentiate words that are likely to be experienced as verbal assaults, and thus defined as behaviors, from words that are seen as communicating the inner life of the person. I would evaluate swearing at a person and calling names as behavioral assaults, while telling a parent that she is "mean" or "selfish" or that she "doesn't care" or "doesn't love me" would be expressions of a client's inner life. Parents may well disagree with that differentiation and it is wise for the therapist and parent to work out some agreement regarding what words are acceptable means of conveying experience in therapy and what words are not. Similarly, some parents may object to their child's tone of voice when expressing anger, seeing it as disrespectful. It is wise for the therapist to help the parent to see value in the child being able to use his voice tone honestly in a manner that is congruent with his words. To say "I am angry with you" in a rational and calm manner minimizes the child's actual experience, and the resultant dialogue is not likely to be as meaningful.

GRANT: She is just so mean all the time! She never lets me do anything! Like she lives to make me unhappy!

THERAPIST: Now I get it better. So it seems to you that your mom never lets you do anything that you want and it seems to you that she doesn't let you because she wants you to be unhappy.

GRANT: Yeah! Like she enjoys it! Like she had a son so that she'd have someone to make unhappy.

THERAPIST: I get it. Would you tell your mom that? Would you say, "Mom, sometimes it seems to me that you like saying no to me. Like you want to make me unhappy! And that's why I get mad at you, Mom."

GRANT: That's right! Sometimes it *does* seem like you want me to be unhappy. Like that's the *only* reason that you say no to me.

THERAPIST: Judy, try to get into your son's experience and if you feel it, express empathy for him.

JUDY: Grant, I am truly sorry if you've felt that I say no because I want you to be unhappy. I really am. I can't imagine what it would be like to think that your mom takes pleasure in your distress. I am doing a poor job of showing you that I feel badly when you are unhappy over something that I say you can't do. I want your happiness, I really do!

GRANT: Well, sometimes it just doesn't feel like it.

JUDY: I get that, son, I do. I will work harder to explain why I am saying no and also to be more sensitive to how much something means to you before I make a decision about it.

GRANT: Okay, Mom. And I'm sorry that I called you an old cow! I didn't mean that.

JUDY: Thanks, Grant. It feels good hearing you say that.

Comment: If the therapist had accepted the "old cow" phrase from Grant, it is very unlikely that the dialogue would have led to such a good repair. It would have been unrealistic for Judy to experience empathy for her son when she was verbally attacked with those words.

It also would have been unfair to Grant to imply that his name calling of his mother was an appropriate way to express his experience of anger.

C. Even when the therapist experiences major concerns about what she sees as the implications of an aspect of the inner life of the client, she still responds with complete acceptance while exploring it in greater depth. She is open to the real possibility that if she understands the person's experience (thoughts, feelings, intentions, etc.) better, she may well come to the conclusion that her client's experience makes sense for him given his narrative. If she remains concerned after she understands that aspect of the client's inner life, she can express this concern about a possible behavioral implication of the client's experience, wondering if the client had considered that. The therapist might be quite cautious about evaluating and disagreeing with a client's intention itself. The intention to do harm to self or other would be a clear exception to this suggestion.

EXAMPLE

SUSAN [a star basketball player who is likely to get a university scholarship if she continues playing]: I'm not planning to play basketball my senior year. Mom and Dad have been yelling at me about it since I told them last week.

WENDY: "Yelling" is a bit strong. But we have been telling her that she is turning her back on a great opportunity and she should rethink that decision.

SUSAN: More than that, Mom. You said that you won't help me with college expenses if I don't play.

THERAPIST: Slow down a bit, folks, please. I need to understand something before we continue. Susan, it seems like you made a big decision that your parents disagree with. Would you tell me about it?

Comment: As is often the case, early in many sessions, and especially early in the course of therapy, the therapist slows down the dialogue when it quickly goes into conflicts, distancing, and defensiveness. She needs to understand the experience before she knows what to do with it, and she must begin by simply accepting it.

SUSAN: Yeah, I've been thinking about it a long time. I just don't enjoy it that much anymore. Yeah, it's fun to win and to have everyone get excited and pat me on the back and say how great I am. And it's nice to think that I could get a scholarship and save me and my parents a lot of money when I go to college. But . . . this may sound selfish . . .

THERAPIST: Hard to say it?

SUSAN: Yeah, I think that they [my parents] will think that I'm being selfish.

THERAPIST: So what you think you want may be selfish? A desire in itself may be selfish?

SUSAN: If I do what I think that I want to do.

THERAPIST: I can see your deciding that an action might be selfish, and that might affect your action. Where I struggle is understanding why you think that just having a desire—a wish—is selfish in itself.

SUSAN: Okay, maybe not the wish. Okay, here goes. I want my college years to be special and I don't think that they will be if I have to practice all the time throughout the season. It is most of the academic year. I want to be able to wander around, make friends, play sports when I feel like it, maybe go overseas for a semester or a whole year. I want to explore, to experiment, to see who I am away from home, and away from being a basketball star.

WENDY: You can still do those things! Take a year after you get your degree. It would just save so much money! It's just not very practical to give that all up!

Comment: The therapist might have interrupted Wendy here because her first comment was to argue with her daughter about her wish. She would have if Susan were to begin to withdraw or become defensive. Since Susan seemed to remain engaged in expressing her wish in greater detail, the therapist remained quiet and did not interrupt the dialogue that appeared to be productive.

SUSAN: I know that it's not practical! But I don't want to be practical at this stage of my life. I want to just—it sounds corny—follow my dreams.

WENDY: I thought that playing basketball was your dream.

SUSAN: Not anymore, Mom. I want to find out what it is! If I have to take out loans and go to a less expensive school, I'm willing to do that. I'll do it on my own if you and Dad can't help.

WENDY: It's not about the money, Susan. We can find a way to manage that.

SUSAN: Then what is it, Mom?

WENDY: I just thought that you'd regret your decision. And I still fear that you will. Basketball has meant so much to you!

SUSAN: It has, Mom, it has! But I don't think that it will in the future. I want to start exploring who I am and what's out there in the big world so that I can find something that will bring me joy and excitement just like basketball has done. I want to have something like basketball for myself all my life.

WENDY [tears]: You're growing up! I'm scared at what you might be leaving behind. And I'm proud at your willingness to do it, if you need to. It's not corny! I want you to have dreams and I want you to follow them. I do not want to get in the way of that. I want to help you with that if I can.

SUSAN [tears]: You just did, Mom, you just did.

Comment: When we are able to allow room—within the attitude of acceptance—for an experience to be fully expressed, it often deepens in such a way that it becomes fully understood. Such understanding often removes the original sense of threat that it created in others and if differences remain, they are often much more easily resolved.

D. Examples of acceptance. Acceptance is often embedded in curiosity or empathy, enabling both of them to be experienced by the client more deeply.

1. 13-YEAR-OLD GIRL: Sometimes I just wish that I'd go to sleep and never wake up!
   THERAPIST:
   - It sounds like you feel overwhelmed at times! Like there is nothing left to do.
   - How hard those days must be for you! Like you run out of energy to keep trying.
   - Ah! You feel that hopeless . . . to never wake up. . . . Is it that hard often?
   - You sometimes wish to never wake up. What do you think keeps you going? Keeps you trying?

Comment: With this comment the therapist might have a question about the possibility of suicidal intent. Regardless of that question, the therapist's first response is one that demonstrates acceptance of what the client wishes. As he explores the wish more deeply, the intensity of the wish will become apparent, as well as the likelihood that it will lead to action. If there is the possibility of a suicidal behavior, then the therapist needs to do a more formal risk assessment. However, such an assessment will be more productive if it is grounded in complete acceptance of the client's wish to never wake up.

2. MOM: Sometimes it gets so bad I hate her [daughter]!
   THERAPIST:
   - You become aware of hating Jen. How hard that must be for you!
   - You have such honesty to say that . . . to tell me that . . . and such courage.
   - You find yourself hating your daughter at times now. . . . Did you ever imagine being in this place when she was an infant?
   - You get so exhausted sometimes that you hate her . . . and maybe hate your life too.

Comment: As in the previous example, the therapist might have some concern that the parent's hatred of her daughter could lead to verbal, emotional, or physical abuse. This question is best addressed once the therapist has supported the client in giving full expression to the feeling of hatred toward her daughter. Such full expression is best facilitated by communicating acceptance—not evaluation—of that feeling.

E. Shame and Guilt. The differentiation of the inner life of the person from his behavior, which acceptance facilitates, is at the core of the difference between shame and guilt.

Shame and guilt are radically different emotions. Both involve evaluation. With shame, we evaluate the self and find it to be bad, either temporarily or permanently. With guilt, we evaluate our behavior as being bad or wrong. When we feel shame, we do not accept ourselves but rather devalue the self and evaluate it as worthless. When we feel guilt, we are able to continue to accept the self, while evaluating our behavior as being wrong. As a result, shame is much more painful, and it leads to denial of our behavior, hiding it from self and others. With shame, we want to hide and if this does not work, we respond with rage toward the perceived source of the shame.

Guilt focuses not on the self, but rather on the effects of our behavior on others. With guilt, we are more likely to face our behavior, experience empathy for the other who we wronged, and then be motivated to express remorse and repair the relationship.

This brief discussion of shame and guilt demonstrates the importance of acceptance in family relationships and family therapy. Within an atmosphere where the inner lives of the members of the family are habitually accepted, the members are able to acknowledge when they have caused distress to other members of the family, experience empathy for them, and be motivated to repair the relationships. Without acceptance of the self of a family member, that individual is much more likely to attempt to avoid responsibility for his behavior, to respond with intense anger or rage when it is addressed, and then refuse to accept appropriate consequences or work toward changing his behavior. When AFFT has been successful, there is often a significant reduction in the experience of shame among most, if not all, of the family members, while realistic guilt—which correlates with empathy—is likely to be more available to facilitate relationship repair. (Much of the research that summarizes these differences can be found in Tangney & Dearing, 2002.)

III. CURIOSITY

Once acceptance of the inner life of the client is clearly communicated, then the therapist can demonstrate his deep curiosity about the client's inner life, with some confidence that the client will begin to feel safe enough to explore it with the therapist and communicate it to him. Curiosity involves an active, nonjudgmental openness to—and interest in—the experience of the other. It represents a deep desire to know the other's experience, a fascination about the narrative that the other has developed to make sense of the events of her life. In simply joining the other in this narrative—through this active, not-knowing stance—the therapist is having an impact on the narrative that he is now experiencing with the client. By being with the other intersubjectively in her narrative, he is cocreating the narrative with the client. This is true with one client or with the joint narratives of all of the family members.

The intent of curiosity is not to gather information, although understanding the events that went into the development of the inner life of the other is important. Curiosity is focused on understanding how the person has developed and organized his experience of these events. The therapist does not assume that if he knows the events that a person encountered that he also knows how the person experienced those events. One "objective" act of physical abuse may be experienced by individuals in countless ways: with variations of anger, sadness, shame, fear, ambivalence, and disappointment, along with denial, preoccupation, repetition, seeking comfort, revenge, and restitution, as well as idealization, confusion, understanding, compassion, despair, and resilience. The abuse is not experienced objectively. There is no right or wrong way to experience it. The therapist truly does not know anything about how this unique individual experienced it. Actually, the individual may have hardly experienced the event at all, if he was overwhelmed by it, dissociated from it, and isolated the event in a corner of his mind that was not to be faced, explored, or understood. The initial task of the therapist then is to assist the client to begin to experience the event. Curiosity is the psychic state in which the therapist walks with the client within that aspect of his narrative.

Curiosity is not a solely rational activity, and possibly not even a predominantly rational activity. While it requires reflection and facilitates the development of reflection, it is embedded in affective states of interest, compassion, awe, fascination, and a deep desire to know. To simply understand, with no strings attached. Curiosity, when embedded in affect, easily conveys deep empathy and respect, while facilitating a sense that one is now safe to explore something that one cannot face alone.

A. The therapist is not judgmental in efforts to understand the family members. If at any time the client experiences her curiosity as being judgmental, the therapist perceives that as creating a break in the relationship with the client, and her primary intention then is to repair the break.

EXAMPLE

JANETTE: She just turns her back on me and walks away!

THERAPIST: And that seems to be very hard for you to experience.

JANETTE: Are you saying that I should be okay about it?

THERAPIST: Oh, my, I am so sorry if I communicated that in a way that made you think that I was saying that it should not bother you when she walks away. I apologize. No, no! I definitely understand why her turning away from you would be hard for you. I think that it would be hard for most mothers who love their daughters like you do.

Comment: Here the therapist tried to convey empathy for the mother's experience but her response was experienced by the mother as being a criticism. She immediately, with some urgency in her voice, expressed an apology for not communicating her intention well enough for it to be understood. That would not be a time to question why the mother experienced her comment as a criticism, as that would have minimized her experience as well as the stressful experience with her daughter that she was describing. If her perception of criticism in the therapist's comments appeared to be a recurring pattern, the therapist might well be curious about it at a later time, without implying that this pattern is wrong.

JANETTE: I try hard to be a good mom for her and it does not seem to be getting through.

THERAPIST: I know how hard you try, I do! What would you say is the hardest part for you when she walks away from you?

JANETTE: That I'm doing something wrong! That I'm letting her down somehow.

THERAPIST: Ah! I get it. You try hard to be a good mom, and it does not seem to be good enough. And you love her so much . . .

JANETTE: And it's not good enough!

THERAPIST: Yes, I get it! Having those doubts about whether she gets it—how much you love her and want to get it right—would be so hard to carry.

B. The therapist may have to take the lead in helping the client to be curious about possible thoughts, feelings, and wishes about an event. Many times clients do not have the habit of actively exploring their inner lives and for that reason they often do not know what they think, feel, or want about a certain event. In a similar way, they may have an incomplete memory about it. They may lack words to describe their inner life. In taking the lead in this exploration, the therapist raises possibilities and then waits to see if any of his guesses resonate with the client and generate recognition of something within his inner life about which he had not previously been aware.

EXAMPLE

THERAPIST [to Steve, age 10]: So what do you think, Steve, about what was happening? Why do you think that your dad said no when you asked him to help you work on your assignment?

STEVE: He said that he would later.

THERAPIST: But it really bothered you! So I'm guessing that there was something about his saying "not now" that was hard for you.

STEVE: I don't know.

THERAPIST: Ah, you don't know. But it bothered you a lot. I wonder what it was that upset you that much.

STEVE: I don't know.

THERAPIST: Okay if we try to figure it out?

STEVE: I guess.

Comment: When a child—or a parent—says that he does not know what he thinks or feels or what his motive is, it is important not to challenge that statement. Most often it is true and if it is not, the person most likely does not feel safe enough to reveal what he is thinking at that moment. The therapist might simply assume that the response is honest and the client might have some desire to understand his inner life better but not quite know how to begin. The therapist can take the lead with guesses. However, it is crucial that the therapist not assume that he is right and knows best what the client thinks, feels, or wants. The act of guessing always remains tentative until the client's nonverbal or verbal response validates it or not.

THERAPIST: Great! Okay, what might it be? . . . What might it be? . . . Maybe you thought that he didn't really want to. That maybe "later" was an excuse: he just didn't want to!

STEVE: I thought that he was a little annoyed when I asked.

THERAPIST: Okay, okay! So it was more like that! If that's what you thought, that he seemed a bit annoyed . . . why did your dad seem to be a bit annoyed? Why would he?

STEVE: I don't know.

THERAPIST: What might it be? . . . What might it be? Maybe you are worrying that he does not want to be with you that much lately. [Steve does not show any sign that he senses that the guess is right.] . . . Or maybe . . . it seemed that your dad thought that there were more important things to do then. [Steve remains quiet.] . . . Or maybe you thought that your dad thought that you should do it yourself.

STEVE [becoming suddenly alert as if remembering something]: He told me the other day that I should be working on the project because I did not have much time left to get it done!

THERAPIST: So maybe that's it! Maybe you thought that your dad was annoyed with you for not working on the project on your own. And that maybe he did not want to help you because he was mad at you for not working harder yourself.

STEVE: Yeah. I thought that he was mad at me for not getting it done before. And I didn't think that was fair! It was a long assignment.

Comment: When the guess touches on the child's experience, the child then often takes the lead in speaking about it in great detail.

THERAPIST: Would you tell your dad that, Steve?

STEVE: What?

THERAPIST: Well, if it seems to you to fit, would you say something like, "Dad, I got upset because it seemed that you didn't want to help me because you were annoyed that I hadn't finished it already on my own."

STEVE [to Dad]: I did think that, Dad. It seemed that you were annoyed with me. Like you didn't want to help me because I didn't work hard enough by myself.

DAD: I'm sorry, son. I should have been more clear, or talked with you about it when I saw that you were getting upset. I knew that it was a hard project and was planning to help you as soon as I finished the work that I was doing in the garage. I was actually annoyed with the job that I was working on, not with you. I'm sorry that I didn't tell you that.

STEVE: Sometimes, Dad, I don't feel that I'm working hard enough for you.

DAD: Oh, son, I am really sorry if I've given that impression. I am fine about how you get your schoolwork done. You're doing better than I did at your age. I know that you're 10 and have a lot of other stuff that you enjoy doing a lot. I'm proud of what you do regarding school . . . and everything else too.

STEVE: You are?

DAD: I am, Steve, I really am.

Comment: As a child develops his awareness of what he thinks and feels and wants, and when he is confident that he can tell his parents what is on his mind, often his communication skills greatly improve and conflicts are significantly reduced.

C. Examples of curiosity. Often an empathic statement precedes the curious one.

1. MOM: I've been so angry with my son for so long that I just don't care anymore, I just want to give up!

   THERAPIST:
   - Oh, how hard it's been . . . and still is! You find that it's hard to care anymore . . .
   - What's it like when you find yourself wanting to give up?
   - When did you first notice that you were beginning to not care?
   - When you are aware of these feelings, do you start blaming yourself?
   - Are there ever breaks from this? Ever times when you find some hope?
   - When you recall how close you were when he was an infant, how does that affect you now?
   - Do you find yourself doubting yourself as a mom when you are having this experience?
   - Any sense of what makes your anger that big for that long?
   - Does your anger ever affect you in other ways too?
   - What keeps you going?
   - Can you think of a time lately when you discovered yourself caring in spite of your anger?

Depending upon the context, some of those examples would not be appropriate. Also, the response to the first question would greatly influence where the next question would lead. Curiosity is not simply having a list of questions, no matter how insightful they might be. It involves walking together with the client, making sense of things along the way, constantly revising one's questions about the experience depending on the last response.

2. TEENAGER: You don't know anything! You're clueless!

   THERAPIST:
   - So it seems that I know nothing! How annoying that must be for you!
   - What is that like, being with someone who you think really does not know you?

- If I could convince you that I do want to know you better, would you be willing to help me?
- Are you aware of any adults who you think understand you pretty well? What is that like?
- If there were one thing that you would want me to understand about you, what would that be?
- Have you felt that way long? That no adult understands you at all?
- What is that like to feel that no one really knows you?
- Do you ever think that if someone understood you better, he wouldn't judge you so much?
- If I don't understand you very well, do you have any sense of what is getting in the way?
- If I understood you better, do you think that I might be able to be of help at all?

IV. EMPATHY

As the therapist accepts the client's experiences and is curious about them as they emerge and deepen, many of these experiences prove to be stressful, confusing, and potentially emotionally dysregulating. The emerging memories of events may be associated with shame, rage, despair, or terror and these emotions need to be regulated if the dialogue is to continue in a therapeutic manner. The therapist has an active role in assisting the client to remain regulated in the face of these emerging, troubling experiences. The therapist's primary task is to experience empathy for the client's distress and then to actively communicate—both verbally and nonverbally—his experience of empathy with the client. His experience of empathy, while he remains regulated himself, enables the client to experience his presence within his own experience and to sense that he is not alone in the experience. He senses that the therapist is regulated—the experience is not too much for him—and the therapist's confident, compassionate, intersubjective presence enables the client to remain in the experience and engage in the process of actively deepening the experience through accepting it and being curious about it together.

Sometimes therapists will experience empathy, communicate it, and then rush on to the "real work" involving giving recommendations to solve the problem. When the therapist does not have confidence in the psychological benefit of truly being with a person in great distress, the therapist is likely to understate the experience and devalue its importance. When the therapist does that, the client often does not experience its true healing and restorative features. The degree to which the therapist values empathy will be intersubjectively communicated to the client and the client's degree of benefit from the experience will be greatly influenced by the therapist's view.

Often when empathy is communicated, received, and experienced by the client, the deepest benefits of therapy occur. When, in family therapy, the therapist is able to communicate empathy and to facilitate the family members to experience empathy for each other, problems that had seemed unsolvable have easy, or doable, solutions. Relationships that were distant or conflict ridden are now on their way toward repair, healing, trust, and intimacy. When the intersubjective communications are embedded in empathy, these experiences dominate and behavioral strategies, when still necessary, are met with higher motivation and are easier to achieve.

Empathy, to be experienced by the therapist when present within the client's experience, requires that the therapist's own narrative remains coherent with regard to the type of event—and the client's experience of it—that is being explored. If the therapist's narrative is not coherent around this theme, his affective and reflective response in the present is likely to relate to unresolved aspects of his own narrative and not to the client.

A. The empathic intention of the therapist is simply to be actively present and responsive to the client's emerging experience, either of a memory or of the current interactions in the session. The empathic intention involves neither minimizing the experience, working to change it, or rescuing the client from the emotions that are emerging.

EXAMPLE

JESSICA [age 14]: They [parents] don't care about me at all! I told them that I don't want to move! I told them! I even cried—I never cry—and they still decided to move!

THERAPIST: Oh, my! How hard for you! You don't want to move. You so much want to stay where you now live. So much!

JESSICA: And we're still moving! They knew how much it would hurt me.

THERAPIST: So moving is hard enough. It's even harder because your parents decided to move even though you told them how much you did not want to. How much you don't want to!

JESSICA: It's all about what they want! It's not what I want at all.

THERAPIST: Oh! It seems to you that your parents only thought about themselves, and not about you at all! How hard that would be . . . if your parents did not think at all about what you wanted.

JESSICA: I used to think that they wanted me to be happy!

THERAPIST: Now you don't know!

JESSICA: They tell me how much they care about me!

THERAPIST: And now it seems that . . .

JESSICA: They don't care at all!

THERAPIST: How confusing that must be for you. How confusing! You always were so sure that your parents thought about you, cared for you, wanted you to be happy, and now you have doubts.

JESSICA: They don't!

THERAPIST: Would you tell them, Jessica, if that's what you think, would you tell them now that because they decided to move even though you so much don't want to, that you think that they don't care about you at all?

Comment: In this example the therapist makes no effort to talk Jessica out of her experience. He is also very slow to ask her to question her experience. Her intensity needs to be responded to with empathy and until it decreases, Jessica will not be receptive to another reason for her parents' behavior. The therapist would only ask Jessica to communicate to her parents her experience of their not caring if he was confident that they would also respond with empathy. He would have asked the parents in advance to respond with empathy, not becoming defensive nor rational, but simply being with Jessica in her pain. Afterward, they could gently explain their reasons for the move, not as an excuse, but to help her to see that their motives were not to hurt her.

B. The intention of the therapist's expression of empathy is simply to assist the client to remain safely within an experience—if he chooses to do so. The therapist then assists the client in cocreating new meaning of the event if he chooses to do so, but never exerts pressure on the client to do so. If the client chooses to leave the experience, the therapist accepts the choice, experiences empathy if the client found the experience to be stressful, and may express curiosity—without judgment—about the client's choice.

EXAMPLE

THERAPIST: Jim [age 9], you seem kind of unhappy today—what's happening?

JIM: Nothing!

THERAPIST: Usually you come in here and tell me about a half a dozen things that are happening. But today, it seems like you're not interested in much of anything.

JANET [MOM]: Jim's cat, Tinker, was hit by a car and killed over the weekend.

THERAPIST: Oh, Jim, I am so, so sorry! How hard that must be for you!

JANET: It has been hard for Jim.

THERAPIST: Of course! Of course. You've told me about Tinker and I know how important Tinker has been to you. How important!

JIM: I don't want to talk about it.

THERAPIST: There's no need to talk, Jim. Just sitting here close to your mom is the best thing you can do. Just letting yourself be sad with her, to let her help you with these big feelings.

JIM: I don't want you to talk about it either!

THERAPIST: Oh, I'm sorry, Jim. I won't if you don't want me to. [Turning to mom.] Jim is clear that here in therapy today he doesn't want me to talk about Tinker and the accident at all. I respect that. It's Jim's decision how he handles these really hard feelings. I hope that he decides to let you help him at home in any way that he thinks will be the most helpful. Whatever way.

JANET: I will.

THERAPIST: In the meantime, why don't I step outside for a bit and leave you two alone. I have a book here that you might read to Jim, if he wants you to. It's about a boy whose dog died. It might be helpful for Jim to hear that story. Or he might say "not now" and you can take it home with you. Call me when you want me to come back in, if Jim wants to talk with me at all about Tinker or about anything else. Whatever Jim decides is fine.

JIM: You don't have to go.

THERAPIST: Fine, Jim. I'll stay then.

JIM: I let Tinker outside! [Jim bursts into tears and is embraced by his mom.]

JANET: I let Tinker out when he starts howling to go out. I was busy and Jim did it.

THERAPIST: Oh, Jim, how hard that would be. You let him out! If there was some way of knowing! You wished you had known what was going to happen and you never would have. But how could you? How could you know? Nobody could know.

JIM: Why did Tinker have to die?

THERAPIST: I don't know, Jim. I don't know. I do know it hurts you that he did. Hurts you so much. I'm so sorry that he died . . . so sorry.

Comment: Often when a child's decision not to discuss something that is very painful is completely accepted, the child will then spontaneously begin to talk about it. This is especially true if he has had prior experience with A-R dialogue and PACE. The presence of empathy often gives the child the courage to go more deeply into the pain and then to stay with the experience while trying to make sense of it. Reason is not relevant in these experiences unless the child wants specific information. The adult's empathic presence is primary for safety and struggling with its meaning.

C. Empathy is not a technique that one gives to the client to achieve a therapeutic goal.
Empathy is an intersubjective experience that naturally emerges when fully present with the other's emotions and is resonating with the other's affective expressions.

EXAMPLE

SANDY [age 11]: She is such a little crybaby! Mom and Dad give her everything and never me! They always feel sorry for her and never care about what I feel about anything!

THERAPIST: You're really angry with her now. You think that she tricks your parents into feeling sorry for her and that makes you mad [said in a flat, rational tone].

SANDY: And then she laughs when they take her side! But she is sneaky and they don't see it.

THERAPIST: You also get angry with her for laughing about having your parents side with her. You might be angry at both her and them [again, matter-of-fact].

SANDY: Wouldn't you be mad if someone did that to you?

THERAPIST: Now you're wondering if I can understand why you are angry with her.

SANDY: You don't understand! Nobody does!

Comment: In this example the therapist did not talk her out of her experience, so in that sense he stayed with her in it. However, he did not engage her affectively in the experience. He was more of an observer of it and she was still experiencing it by herself. Empathy is not something that we give to people. It is an experience of being with another in his inner life, resonating with him as he expresses his emotion in his affective expressions.

D. Examples of empathy. Often empathy and curiosity become interwoven, with one creating an opening for the other.

1. BOY, 6 years of age, often angry with his 4-year-old sister: "She is so stupid! I don't like her! I wish she lived somewhere else!"
   THERAPIST:
   - Sometimes you *really* don't like your sister! Sometimes you just want to say, "Go away! I don't like you here!"
   - Sometimes you get *so* angry! Sometimes you don't like her at all!
   - Sometimes you just want to be your mom and dad's only kid! The only one!
   - Sometimes your anger toward your sister gets so big! I wonder why? Why do you think it gets that big?

2. MOM: Sometimes I think that I'm just not cut out to be a mother.
   THERAPIST:
   - Ah! You get really hard on yourself sometimes. Are you often that hard on yourself?
   - Oh my, you seem to be *so* discouraged. How do you take care of yourself when you get this down on yourself?
   - You have worked so hard . . . so hard . . . at being the mom you want to be . . . and now a part of you thinks that you'll never get there . . . you'll never be that mom.
   - And I know how much you've wanted to be the mom that you never had. To give your kids what you seldom got. And now these doubts . . . they must be so painful!

V. OBSTACLES TO PACE

A. Obstacles to Playfulness

A. A family member or therapist uses humor as a means to avoid or minimize conflict or distress.
   Probable causes and means to address them:
   1. a. Conflict or distress is perceived by the family as being wrong or too difficult to manage.
      b. The therapist is not comfortable with conflict or distress.

2. a. Efforts to avoid or minimize distress or conflict are met with PACE.

    b. The therapist reflects on his discomfort, including exploring his own attachment history.

B. Sarcasm is disguised as playfulness.

Probable causes and means to address them:

1. a. Anger in the family is expressed through sarcasm.

    b. Distress over sarcasm is minimized by saying, "You can't take a joke."

2. a. The therapist addresses sarcasm with PACE. Anger is acknowledged and expressed directly and then understood with PACE.

    b. The distress caused by sarcasm is noticed and responded to with PACE. Efforts to minimize this distress are addressed with PACE.

C. Playfulness is experienced as, "You're making fun of me."

Probable causes and means to address them:

1. a. The intent of the playful comment is ambiguous.

    b. The sense of humor of the family member is fragile.

2. a. The therapist repairs the relationship, clarifies his intent, and explores with the client the possibility of future playful dialogue.

    b. The therapist is more careful in expressing playfulness. The therapist also addresses the family member's discomfort with playfulness with PACE.

B. Obstacles to Acceptance

A. The parents have great difficulty separating the child's experience from his behavior.

Probable causes and means to address them:

1. a. The parents believe that the child's thoughts, emotions, and wishes should be evaluated as being right or wrong.

    b. The parents' reaction to the child's behavior is so intense that they have great difficulty separating the behavior from the experience that led to it.

2. a. The therapist takes a psychoeducational approach to the parents' objection. Then the therapist responds to the objection with PACE, including being curious about the possible origins of the parents' beliefs in their childhoods. The therapist commits to resolving this important difference of opinion.

    b. The therapist addresses the intensity of the parents' reaction with PACE, including the exploration of related aspects of the parents' attachment history.

B. The parents or child experience shame in response to any mistake or problem.

Probable causes and means to address them:

1. a. The parents' attachment history contained shaming or harsh discipline.

    b. The parents are raising their child as they were raised.

2. a. The therapist addresses the shame of their attachment history with PACE.

    b. The therapist helps the parents to consider new child-rearing ideas that will reduce their child's shame. The therapist helps the parents engage their child with A-R dialogue about the mistakes that they made and their regrets and commitment to change.

C. The therapist's negative evaluation of the parent-child behavior reduces his ability to accept the experience (thought, emotion, wish, intention) that led to it. Probable causes and means to address them:

1. a. The therapist has lost focus on the meaning of the behavior and has begun to address the behavior itself with problem solving.
   b. The therapist has joined the parents in focusing only on the child's behavior.
   c. The behavior of the family member is activating an aspect of the therapist's own attachment history.
2. a. The therapist returns to PACE and A-R dialogue as soon as possible.
   b. The therapist discusses with the parents the joint need for them to address the child's behaviors with PACE while also seeing other aspects of the child beyond the problem behaviors. The therapist responds to the parents' resistance with PACE and relationship repair.
   c. The therapist reflects on aspects of his own attachment history that are being activated by the behaviors, with PACE toward himself.

C. Obstacles to Curiosity

A. The parents believe that finding the reasons for behaviors are efforts to find excuses for them.
   Probable causes and means to address them:

1. a. The parents may have adopted a rigid behavior management philosophy that makes the meaning of behavior irrelevant.
   b. The parents' own attachment history lacked an emphasis on finding the meaning of the behavior.
2. a. The therapist addresses their concerns with PACE and psychoeducation.
   b. The therapist addresses their attachment histories with PACE.

B. The parents' curiosity is evaluative and critical without acceptance or empathy.
   Probable causes and means to address them:

1. a. The parents do not see the value of distinguishing between experience and behavior. They believe that the inner life of the child does need to be evaluated and criticized when necessary.
   b. The parents' own attachment history is activated by this theme.
2. a. The therapist addresses their concerns with PACE and psychoeducation.
   b. The therapist addresses their attachment history with PACE.

C. The parents—and possibly the therapist—view curiosity as not important in itself but simply as a means to beginning behavior management.
   Probable causes and means to address them:

1. The parents place less value on facilitating the development of their child's inner life and more on managing their child's behaviors.
2. The therapist addresses their concerns with PACE. If aspects of their own attachment histories are being activated, these are addressed with PACE.

D. Obstacles to Empathy

A. The parents believe that expressing empathy is suggesting to the child that the behavior is not serious and that the parent will be permissive about it.
   Probable causes and means to address them:
   1. a. The parents view relationship withdrawal as central to discipline.
      b. The parents do not distinguish between the child's wishes and behavior.
   2. a. The therapist addresses their concerns with PACE and presents how effective discipline does not create insecurity in the attachment relationship.
      b. The therapist explores again the importance of the difference between experience and behavior and explores any resistance with PACE. The therapist is sensitive to possible connections to the parents' attachment histories.
B. The parents believe that expressing empathy will cause the child to become dependent.
   Probable causes and means to address them:
   1. a. The parents view attachment and empathy as fostering dependency.
      b. The parents believe in the value of developing a stiff upper lip.
      c. The parents were raised without much experience of comfort and support.
   2. a. The therapist addresses their concerns with PACE and provides psychoeducation on the nature of attachment security.
      b. The therapist addresses their concerns with PACE and provides information regarding the value of comfort in fostering their child's development.
      c. The parents' own attachment histories are addressed with PACE.
C. The parents—and possibly the therapist—find it difficult to experience empathy for the child's distress because the distress activates an unresolved aspect of their own attachment histories.
   Probable causes and means to address them:
   1. a. The parents experienced so little comfort for their own distress when young that they have unresolved attachment experiences that are activated by the child's distress. Empathy only creates more discomfort for them.
      b. The therapist similarly has unresolved issues around stressful themes that are made more difficult when he experiences the child's distress more fully with empathy.
   2. a. The therapist addresses the unresolved themes from the parents' own attachment histories with PACE.
      b. The therapist reflects on his own attachment history with PACE. He seeks supervision or therapy for himself if needed.

EXERCISES

Questions

1. The purpose of playfulness is to:
   A. Give a client a break from difficult themes.
   B. Create a sense of hope and confidence.
   C. Facilitate enjoyment to provide a context to keep the difficulty in perspective.
   D. All of the above.

2. Playfulness:
   A. Distracts the client from his symptoms.
   B. Minimizes the symptoms so they can be addressed.
   C. Is inappropriate in treatment because it distracts from real problems.
   D. None of the above.

3. Acceptance is unconditional with regard to:
   A. All of the person's inner life.
   B. His thoughts and feelings, but not his intentions.
   C. His inner life and behavior.
   D. Certain experiences should not be accepted.

4. If the client intends to kill himself:
   A. The intention to kill himself is accepted while efforts are made to prevent any suicidal behavior.
   B. The intention to kill himself is evaluated as being not acceptable.
   C. The intention and any subsequent behavior are both accepted.
   D. None of the above.

5. If a teenager thinks that his father does not love him, and the father says that he does love his son, then:
   A. The teenager's experience is wrong.
   B. The father is not telling the truth.
   C. The teenager's guess about his father's inner life may be wrong, but his experience itself of his father's inner life is neither right nor wrong.
   D. The therapist's role is to convince the teenager that his father does love him, if the father says that he does.

6. Curiosity:
   A. Is inherently intrusive, so the therapist should restrict himself to no more than five questions.
   B. Has a place later in the session and the overall treatment.
   C. Can be effective, but only if the word *why* is avoided.

D. None of the above.

7. Curiosity:
    A. Comes from a strong not-knowing stance.
    B. Functions to move with the client deeper into his experience.
    C. At times, is needed to lead the client deeper into his experience.
    D. All of the above.

8. When the client interprets the therapist's question as suggesting that she should have acted in a certain way:
    A. The therapist is curious about the client's perception of the therapist's intention.
    B. The therapist repairs the relationship break caused by the client's perception of the therapist's intention, but is never curious about his perception.
    C. The therapist repairs the relationship break caused by the client's perception and only then is curious about the client's perception.
    D. The therapist overlooks the client's perception and continues with the dialogue.

9. Through the therapist's expression of empathy:
    A. The client experiences the therapist's presence within a stressful experience.
    B. The client is able to remember more information.
    C. The client experiences the event the way the therapist does.
    D. The client is able to realize that the event was not that bad.

10. In family therapy, empathy:
    A. Is difficult to maintain for all family members.
    B. Is not as important as teaching communication skills.
    C. Is a technique that can be applied to the family member in most distress.
    D. None of the above.

Exercises in Curiosity

Give three responses that reflect curiosity about the following statements made by a client.

1. Seven-year-old girl: She [mom] never lets me do what I want! Never!
    A. _____
    B. _____
    C. _____

2. Sixteen-year-old boy: Why should I bother? Nothing is ever going to change.
    A. _____
    B. _____
    C. _____

3. Mom: Sometimes I know that he says no just to make me mad! I can't stand that!

   A. _____

   B. _____

   C. _____

4. Dad: He has to realize that just because he wants something doesn't entitle him to get it!

   A. _____

   B. _____

   C. _____

General Exercises

In the following therapeutic scenarios, provide a few intersubjective, therapeutic responses that demonstrate PACE. Acceptance needs to be present in every response involving PACE. Try to provide an example of both curiosity and empathy for each scenario; try to include a playful response too, when appropriate.

1. Shortly after the therapist begins to explore with a child and his parents an incident in which he lied to them and became angry with them when they continued to confront him about it, the boy begins to focus on other recent events that are not stressful.

   A. _____

   B. _____

   C. _____

2. During a session, a 13-year-old says to the therapist, "They never let me do anything that I want! They always say no and refuse to discuss it!"

   A. _____

   B. _____

   C. _____

3. During a discussion with parents about their concerns about their child, the mother says to the father, "You don't seem to be that concerned about your daughter. Whenever there's a problem you disappear and expect me to handle it."

   A. _____

   B. _____

   C. _____

In each of the following examples, provide three or four therapeutic responses to the client's statement (playfulness would not always be appropriate).

1. ROBERT (age 16): "It seems to me that every time I walk into the house, mom has another chore for me to do!"

   Playfulness:

   _____

   Acceptance:

   _____

   Curiosity:

   _____

   Empathy:

   _____

2. THOMAS (dad): "If I keep doing this PACE stuff, the kids will think they got two moms!"

   Playfulness:

   _____

   Acceptance:

   _____

   Curiosity:

   _____

   Empathy:

   _____

3. SALLY (age 5): "Sometimes I'm so mad at Daddy I want to throw him in the river!"

   Playfulness:

   _____

   Acceptance:

   _____

   Curiosity:

   _____

   Empathy:

   _____

Experiential Exercises

1. Curiosity: Start anywhere.

    In this exercise, Person A shows an interest in the first thing that Person B says about anything such as a recent, small event ("I couldn't find my gloves so I wore my mittens," "I found this necklace in a yard sale," "I wasn't going for a hike yesterday but then that big rain came") or small talk in the here and now ("I hadn't noticed that small statue before," "This is a really comfortable chair," "Would you like a mint?"). See if you can express curiosity about the statement, with one question naturally following the last, reaching into aspects of the person's life in small steps so that they do not appear to be artificial or intrusive. See if whatever topic you start with can lead to more central aspects of the person's narrative. Try not to force the dialogue ("Don't push the river") but rather allow it to flow.

    Reflect upon the experience and then reverse roles.

2. Empathy: Matching affect or not.

    In this exercise, try to experience how matching the affect of the person is crucial in the expression of empathy for the other's experience. Person A makes a statement with the appropriate affect and Person B replies either with matched affect or in a matter-of-fact tone with little affect.

    A. PERSON A: I get so tired of having to correct him! It seems like it's all day. Every day!
       PERSON B:
       With matched affect: You sound exhausted! When will you get a break! When?
       With little affect: You sound exhausted. When will you get a break? When?

    B. PERSON A: I don't know if anyone can understand! I feel so alone with this!
       PERSON B:
       With matched affect: It seems like you're all alone with this! That no one understands!
       With little affect: It seems like you're all alone with this. That no one understands.

    C. PERSON A: You never listen to me! It's always what you want!
       PERSON B:
       With matched affect: You think that I never hear you! That I only consider what I want!
       With little affect: You think that I never hear you. That I only consider what I want.

    D. PERSON A: I really don't care anymore! I'm not going to change.
       PERSON B:
       With matched affect: You don't think that you'll ever change! So why bother trying?
       With little affect: You don't think that you'll ever change. So why bother trying?

3. Shame.
    A. Recall an incident in which you felt shame.

    How was shame experienced in your body?

    Why do you think you experienced shame rather than guilt (e.g., I just made a mistake)?

    When you are experiencing shame, how does it affect your communications and behavior?
    B. Recall a mistake that you made as a therapist.

    If you experienced shame, how were you likely to act next?

    If you experienced guilt, how were you likely to act next?
    C. Reflect on any incident where you felt shame and imagine what you might say or think if you were experiencing one of the following attitudes toward yourself.

    Playfulness:

    _____

    Acceptance:

    _____

    Curiosity:

    _____

    Empathy:

    _____

4. Reflect upon a habit that you have that you wish that you could change. While you reflect, maintain acceptance and empathy for yourself. Now adopt a not-knowing stance of curiosity about the habit, wondering:
    A. When it began.
    B. What factors are central to its continuing.
    C. What factors are central in your wanting it to change.
    D. How you feel about yourself when you think about having the habit.
    E. If the habit ends, imagine what your life might be like.

ANSWERS AND SUGGESTED THERAPEUTIC RESPONSES

Questions

1. D.
2. D.
3. A. Acceptance of all aspects of the person's inner life is crucial. Otherwise the client will experience the self as being evaluated, will feel less safe in relationships, and will be vulnerable to shame.

4. A. A clear separation between intention and behavior is necessary. Efforts to talk a person out of his intention to hurt himself tend to be met with resistance and to lead to secrecy. If the person's intention is accepted, he is more likely to communicate to another that experience and through sharing it, he is more likely to be open to changing it.

5. C. When the therapist begins to evaluate and judge if an experience is right or wrong, the client will not feel accepted and will be more likely to hide his experiences. When the experience is accepted and explored, it is open to the intersubjective experience created through communication, and the experience is more likely to change if it is not congruent with other experiences.

6. D. Curiosity, when conveyed with acceptance and empathy, is not likely to be experienced as intrusive. It facilitates therapeutic dialogue at every phase of treatment.

7. D. Curiosity involves having no assumptions about the client's experience of an event. It may follow and support the client in his initiatives to understand an event, and it can lead the client into further understanding.

8. C. Relationship repair precedes other interventions in that it supports the client's expression of his experience and works to reestablish the client's sense of safety in therapy.

9. A. Empathy has no other goal but to be with the client in his experience. Through empathy, other results may occur, but they are secondary and are not goals in themselves. Empathy cannot become a technique to achieve another purpose, or it has less or no impact.

10. D. Empathy has as important a function in family therapy as it does in individual therapy if the goals of providing safety for all as well as intersubjective exploration are to be achieved. The therapist can have empathy for all if he is able to approach the experiences of every family member with PACE, not evaluating one member's experience to be right or better than the experience of another.

Exercises in Curiosity

Give three responses that reflect curiosity about the following statements made by a client.

1. Seven-year-old girl: "She [mom] never lets me do what I want! Never!"
   A. How do you handle that if it seems that way to you?
   B. If she doesn't, what do you think is her reason? Why doesn't she?
   C. Does that make it hard to feel close to your mom? What's that like—not feeling close?

2. Sixteen-year-old boy: "Why should I bother? Nothing is ever going to change."
   A. What's that like? If it seems that nothing will ever change? Nothing?
   B. Has it seemed that way to you for a long time? How do you manage it?
   C. Are there ever times when you have a tiny bit of hope that things might change? What is that like?

3. Mom: "Sometimes I know that he says no just to make me mad! I can't stand that!"
   A. If he tries to make you mad on purpose, why do you think he'd do that?
   B. What makes it so hard for you that you get that mad?
   C. Are there times when he does something to make you mad and you don't get mad?

4. Dad: "He has to realize that just because he wants something doesn't entitle him to get it!"

A. What about his anger over not getting what he wants makes you think that he feels that he is entitled to what he wants?

B. Are there any other possible reasons why he gets that mad when you say no?

C. What is the hardest thing for you about his getting that upset when you say no?

General Exercises

In the following therapeutic scenarios, provide a few intersubjective, therapeutic responses that demonstrate PACE. Acceptance needs to be present in every response involving PACE. Try to provide an example of both curiosity and empathy for each scenario; try to include a playful response too, when appropriate.

1. Shortly after the therapist begins to explore with a child and his parents an incident in which he lied to them and became angry with them when they continued to confront him about it, the boy begins to focus on other recent events that are not stressful.

   A. (playful) I wonder if you would rather rake all the leaves in the neighborhood than talk about this.

   B. (curious) What would you say is the hardest for you now when we talk about that trouble you guys had? Do you wish that they would just forget it? What is the hardest about remembering it?

   C. (empathy) It is so hard sometimes to think about those big arguments with your parents. So hard! I wonder if you're thinking, "We finally were starting to get close again and now this guy brings that up! We'll just get mad again and I don't like it when we're mad!

2. During a session, a 13-year-old says to the therapist, "They never let me do anything that I want! They always say no and refuse to discuss it!"

   A. A playful response would easily be experienced as making fun of the child or calling the child a whiner, so the therapist would have to be very cautious if he were to attempt to be playful with this theme before it were fully explored and resolved.

   B. (Curiosity) What do you think that is about? If they never let you do what you want? What do you think is their reason?

   C. (Empathy) How hard that must be if it seems to you that they never let you do what you want. Your own parents we're talking about. How discouraging that would be!

3. During a discussion with parents about their concerns about their child, the mother says to the father, "You don't seem to be that concerned about your daughter. Whenever there's a problem you disappear and expect me to handle it."

   A. Again, playfulness early in this discussion would most likely be experienced as being patronizing or minimizing the experience.

   B. (Curiosity) What is that like if you think that your husband does not care for your daughter? If he withdraws that way, why else might he do it? How does that affect your relationship with him?

   C. (Empathy) How difficult that must be for you if you experience your husband as not caring for your daughter! And if he leaves you when you are struggling with her, I would guess that you would feel very discouraged then too. All alone with something that is very hard and also very important to you.

In each of the following examples, provide three or four therapeutic responses to the client's statement (playfulness would not always be appropriate).

1. ROBERT (age 16): "It seems to me that everytime I walk into the house, Mom has another chore for me to do!"

   Playfulness: Sort of like a toll booth between the front door and your bedroom.
   Acceptance: Sounds like you're thinking that your mom might be asking you to do too many chores.
   Curiosity: If that's what it seems like to you, have you wondered what that's about?
   Empathy: That would be kind of upsetting to you—if it seems that your mom is really loading you down with work.

2. THOMAS (dad): "If I keep doing this PACE stuff, the kids will think they got two moms!"

   Playfulness: And if your wife would start pushing the authority like you used to do, that would really confuse them!
   Acceptance: So using this PACE approach might be making all of you a bit unsure about what relationships are all about.
   Curiosity: And what's it like for you, relating to the kids in such a new way?
   Empathy: Ah! It has been a big change for you all. Hard for you to get used to also, I'd think.

3. SALLY (age 5): "Sometimes I'm so mad at Daddy I want to throw him in the river!"

   Playfulness: In the river! With the fish! Would you go fishing for him?
   Acceptance: So you get angry with your dad sometimes when he says no to you.
   Curiosity: He says no. Why do you think . . . why *does* he say no to you sometimes?
   Empathy: Wow! In the river! Sounds like you are really mad at your dad then. *Really* mad!

5 The Deepening Sequential Process of Attachment-Focused Family Therapy

As in any therapy—and in any relationship for that matter—typical sequences of interactions and themes develop over time. The first session is not the same as a middle session, which is not the same as an ending session. And yet, these sessions are the same with regard to many aspects of PACE, A-R dialogue, principles of attachment and intersubjectivity, and the need for ongoing relationship repair. This chapter briefly looks at the sequential process of AFFT, following threads of the elements of the treatment as they evolve over the course of treatment.

This movement into deeper levels of experience is evident in the ongoing interactions between parent and infant. Each time they are together, they read each other more quickly and easily. The parent comes to know what is unique about her baby through increasingly more subtle reciprocal communications. From day to day the infant feels both safer with this parent and more able to discover aspects of self, other, and the world through the intersubjective interactions. By the beginning of the second half of the first year of his life, the parent-infant communications are very intricate and facilitate the differentiated attachment that the infant has with the parent. Safety and intersubjective exploration are intimately interwoven.

A core assumption of AFFT is that within families intersubjective experiences with one another provide basic safety as well as the readiness and ability to explore self, other, and the broader social-emotional world. As we become openly aware of our experiences—including intersubjective experiences with our attachment figures—without terror or shame, we are able to develop a coherent autobiographical narrative upon which we develop the meanings that we give to our lives, including our attachment relationships and the larger world.

In this chapter I attempt to describe this process as it relates to eight separate, but interwoven, themes and interventions. An underlying factor permeates all eight of these areas of focus, consisting of the deepening of experience, both the intersubjective experience that exists between the therapist and family and the subjective experiences of all members of the treatment, including the therapist. I believe that this deepening of experience is the basic difference between the first session and the last. This chapter also briefly discusses the presence of unique sequential events as well as when AFFT might be terminated.

I. EIGHT FEATURES OF THIS SEQUENTIAL PROCESS

As new events, people, and objects enter our life, they become integrated into our narrative. For example, when we meet an individual and gradually develop a relationship with him or her, the relationship deepens over time. We know the person better, the emotional connections become stronger and more complex, and that person assumes a bigger and bigger place in our narrative. He or she has a bigger impact on our life, and vice versa. This deepening of experience becomes the core of our increasing knowledge of and affection for this person. As the experience deepens, we become aware of what is unique about that person as well as the unique contribution to our life.

The same occurs during the course of treatment in AFFT. With the cyclical repetitions of A-R dialogues, expressed within the attitude of PACE, the members of the interactions become more and more meaningful to one another. They are increasingly able to more deeply accept, discover what is unique, and experience a deeper sense of empathy for each other. This enables an increased ability to feel safe with each other, learn from each other, and experience a deeper commitment to the relationships and their repairs. AFFT facilitates this deepening of subjective and intersubjective experiences that the family was not able to successfully develop, but which are a central goal of family life. This deepening sequential process is a cyclical movement that exists from the first moment of the first session to the final moment of the final session. This process rests upon acceptance and the forward momentum of the A-R dialogue that is created by the alternating loops of curiosity and empathy.

Thus, in the background of the therapist's awareness, she is asking: Is the process of the A-R dialogue in place? Is the parent safe? Is the child safe? Is emerging affect being coregulated? When the answer is yes to those four features, then the natural movement of the therapy occurs from easier themes to more difficult ones, from experiential to reflective awareness of a given experience, and from coregulation and experiencing to autoregulation and experiencing. The first four features are likely to be easier to reestablish later in therapy, but they can never be taken for granted.

The first four features are continuously deepened throughout the course of treatment. They need to be in the background of the therapist's awareness to ensure that they are still present from moment to moment, session to session. It cannot be assumed that if they were present in the last session, they will be present in the present one. When the first four are deepening, then the progression of the final four is likely to occur.

A. The process of A-R dialogue precedes any focus on content in the dialogue. The therapist needs to ensure that the process of A-R dialogue is established before attending to any specific content. Many clients have had little successful experience engaging in A-R dialogue and the intersubjective experiences associated with it. Too often in families who seek treatment, dialogues are characterized by evaluations and criticism, angry assaults and defensive reactions, and alternating monologues, as well as emotional dysregulation or a lack of any emotional connection. The therapist needs to lead the family into A-R dialogue and model the nature of such dialogues.

As specific content is explored, the therapist always needs to remain aware of whether or not the process of A-R dialogue is still occurring. This process is constant regardless of the theme being explored. There is an openness to expressing one's own experiences and to understanding and being responsive to the experiences of the other. Differences regarding experiences are accepted as natural; right and wrong are not applicable to descriptions of these differences. Experiences just are; they are not right or wrong, good or bad. Within the dialogue, participants hold a nonjudgmental tone, a deep interest in knowing each other's experiences, and a readiness to experience empathy for any distress that the other experienced along with joy for the other's successes. As the process of the dialogue becomes more comfortable to the family members, stressful, conflict-ridden themes can be explored with a much greater sense of safety and opportunity for successful resolution.

B. Safety precedes exploration. The therapist needs to ensure that all members of the family are experiencing safety before beginning to explore difficult themes. Without safety, such explorations are not likely to be productive but rather elicit defensiveness, shame, anger, and fear. Without safety, the intersubjective nature of the explorations will be impaired, since one is less open to the experience of the other when one is not feeling safe.

When difficult explorations commence, the therapist is always alert to any disruptions to the sense of safety for all present. If there appears to be a lack of safety, the exploration is discontinued while the safety needs are addressed.

C. Coregulation of affect precedes cocreation of meaning. This feature naturally follows safety. The coregulaton of affect is often central to creating safety for family members as they explore stressful themes. When a family member experiences intense emotion that may become dysregulating, the therapist matches the affective expression of that emotion, which often enables the person to experience the therapist's empathic presence and to remain regulated. During the act of exploring stressful events, the therapist joins the family member in cocreating new meaning for that event. Intersubjective exploration is central for establishing new meanings of events that are experienced as shameful or frightening. As such events are explored, associated emotions tend to be elicited. These need to be coregulated as they emerge for the intersubjective exploration to continue.

D. Establishing safety for the parent precedes establishing safety for the child. If the parent does not feel safe, she will not be in a stable position to be aware of and responsive to the safety needs of her child. In fact, not being safe, she may be more likely to criticize her child so that the child is not safe either. Once the parent is safe with the therapist, the parent and therapist can work together to ensure that the child is safe within the session.

In order to first ensure the parent's safety, the therapist meets with the parent for one or more sessions before beginning joint sessions with the parent and child. Often at the beginning of the session the therapist meets with the parent alone before bringing the child into the office too. This enables the therapist to ensure that the parent is experiencing safety and is in a position to ensure safety for the child as well. If the parent comes to the session experiencing rage or despair about her child, the therapist is wise to first address these intense emotions before having the child enter. Parents might also be told to come alone if they believe that they are so angry that they would not be able to focus on their child's safety during the session. It is my experience that children accept and are not frightened or upset over the therapist meeting with the parents without them as long as it is explained to them. Often I have said something like, "Your mom and dad have been pretty angry lately about how things have been going on at home. We thought it best for me to meet with them alone to help them with their anger before we all meet together." When the therapist has been successful in helping parents with their anger, children are often relieved and appreciative that they did not have to participate in that session.

E. Lighter, positive, casual themes precede shameful, frightening themes. As engaging in the process of A-R dialogue becomes easier, the family is more able to move into more difficult themes. It is important for the therapist to communicate—nonverbally more than verbally—that the process of the dialogue is just as valid, and even more important with the stressful themes than with the easier themes. A-R dialogue ensures that the stressful themes can be addressed with the family members in a way that leads to resolution of the themes and a deepening of the relationship rather than toward escalation of conflict or emotional distancing. Through the successful use of A-R dialogue, areas of difference become opportunities for relationship development rather than being experienced as threats to the relationship.

F. Easier shameful, frightening themes precede more difficult ones. As in the previous step, with the increased ability to engage in the process of A-R dialogue comes an increased ability to explore more stressful themes. In the interests of safety and success, it appears reasonable for the therapist to direct the focus first on themes that appear to be less stressful to family members and from there introduce the more difficult themes. The exception to this guideline—and it occurs often—would be when it is important for the family to address a theme in that day's session rather than to wait.

Sometimes a parent may want to address a theme but the child does not. The parent may insist on it. It is important for the therapist to reduce the parent's sense of urgency and first explore with the child his reluctance to address that theme. If the parent's insistence is based on present anger over an incident, then it would be wise for the therapist to first address the parent's anger—most likely at the onset of the meeting with the child in the waiting room—before agreeing to explore it with the child. Often the parent's anger will prevent the child from experiencing safety. The child's fear or shame in response to the anger would make it very difficult for the child to engage in A-R dialogue. Similarly, the parent's anger would make it difficult for the parent to be truly receptive to engaging with PACE in the A-R dialogue.

G. Experience precedes reflection. Experience refers to the emotionally rich, fully present awareness of a here-and-now event or a past event that continues to impact one in the here and now. Reflection entails being aware of the event and the experience of the event as being something in the past that we are now observing and making sense of from a more detached stance. Reflection has a larger focus than does direct experience, seeing the specific event in light of aspects of the larger narrative.

Reflection has this more detached stance but it is never a lecture. Lectures tend to be rational efforts to influence another—to present reasons for doing something or behaviors to accomplish a goal. When the therapist or parent begins a lecture, that often means that they have failed to engage in an intersubjective experience and are attempting to influence the other through reason rather than through shared experiences. Reflection is simply a description of an experience, from a more distant stance where it can be observed rather than actually being in the experience. Reflection enables the more direct experience to be integrated better into the narrative. It also ensures that the experiential aspect of the session will be recalled more fully later and remain alive within the client's inner life.

H. Coregulation and meaning making precede autoregulation and meaning making. As the child develops, his social-emotional learning moves from being primarily based on his intersubjective experiences with his parents to learning both from his parents and from his own separate experiences and his reflective skills. As he matures, his sense of his own autonomy deepens while he is still able to maintain a deep, emotionally meaningful relationship with his parents. Autoregulation and meaning making do not signal an end of the intersubjective influence but rather the emergence of twin abilities for regulation and learning.

During the course of therapy these deepening autoregulation and reflective skills are apparent for the family members individually as well as for the family as a unit. There is a natural back-and-forth motion that integrates the family unit with the autonomy of the individual family members. Often when the family is able to balance the needs of the family and the needs of the individual member, there is no need for continuing therapy.

A background awareness of this sequential process needs to be continuously present in therapy. The therapist can never assume that since the parent is now safe she can focus on the child's safety. The parent may have been safe in the last session but is not safe in this session—even when it is the same theme. The therapist must experience the parent's safety now—moment-to-moment—while focusing on the child's safety. Similarly, the therapist may have seen all members of the family participate well in the process of A-R dialogue in the last several sessions, as well as the first 30 minutes of the current session. Suddenly one member of the family becomes angry or defensive and is not engaging intersubjectively. The therapist needs to actively explore the disengagement from A-R dialogue before proceeding with the theme that was being explored.

II. UNIQUE SEQUENTIAL EVENTS

A. Progress tends to generate some resistance to progress. Frequently when one member of the family—especially a child—has had a particularly meaningful session in which she experienced a deepening of her awareness of her narrative as well as her relationship with one or more other members of the family, the following session may show a return to more habitual patterns in her inner life and relationships. The progress in the prior session may have created anxiety or shame. She may experience difficulty becoming comfortable with the change and her uncertainty about trusting it. If the therapist—and parent—assume that the progress will continue to the present session, one or both may be discouraged or frustrated over this "regression" to a previous pattern of functioning. Worse still, the therapist or parent may begin to think that the previous session was not real, that is, that the child had faked it and said what she thought the adults wanted her to say. Given the nature of intersubjectivity, if that is how the therapist and parent come to perceive the meaning of the previous session, the child is likely to perceive it in a similar manner. In a fundamental way, then, the progress of the prior session did not last. It might be said that it did not even exist in the first place.

To ensure against this return to a prior pattern due to anxiety over adopting and believing in progress leading to a new pattern, it is wise for the therapist to acknowledge the possibility that the progress might bring along some anxiety and that there might be a return of some problems from the past. Parents and children are made aware of this possibility and encouraged to be patient with the process. The parent might be encouraged to keep the child close for a time after especially meaningful sessions and to have extra patience if the child's behavior takes a turn for the worse after such sessions. By presenting the possibility that the progress will create some difficulties, there are likely to be fewer difficulties. If they do emerge, they are likely to be more transient, with the progress being quick to return. They also will be less likely to undermine the meanings that were developing in the prior session.

B. Second-session withdrawal. Frequently, when the therapist has successfully prepared the parents for the first joint session, the session itself is a breath of fresh air for the family and their readiness and ability to explore important family-related themes. Safety permeates the here-and-now interactions and, with the therapist taking the lead in ensuring the momentum of the A-R dialogue, the child often shares her inner life more openly and fully than she may ever have done before. As a result, she is more exposed psychologically and is likely to experience some vulnerability. She also may experience more emotional closeness with her parents which, although it may elicit wonderful feelings, may also evoke anxiety. What was shared might be used against her and the closeness attained may be short-lived.

As a result of this vulnerability and anxiety that may be associated with the open and emotionally deep interactions that occurred in the first treatment session, the child—and possibly the parents as well—often withdraws from engaging in A-R dialogue and exploring similar themes in the second session. This sequence is so common that it has been called second-session withdrawal by two AFFT clinicians, Julie Hudson and Alison Keith.

The therapist might anticipate the possibility of a second-session withdrawal much the same way he integrated particularly meaningful sessions by verbalizing the possibility that there could be a return of some challenges to the progress after the session. He might tell the parents before the start of the second joint session that their child might be more reluctant to explore themes than she was in the first session. The therapist would assure the parents that this is not unexpected and is best met with PACE.

The therapist might also begin the second joint session by reflecting on the first session and acknowledging that although it seemed to generate greater sharing and closeness, it most likely also created some vulnerability and anxiety. By accepting the possibility that the child might be hesitant to engage in the session as she did the first time, the child's withdrawal is likely to be less intense. By reflecting on the first session the therapist is also beginning the second session with a more cognitive, and less experiential, stance. This is likely to help the child to feel safer as her vulnerable emotions are less likely to emerge.

C. Every session is unique. It is important to stress that each session is unique. While there are general sequences to anticipate, the therapist needs to maintain a background awareness that this specific family on this specific day may not follow the usual pattern.

The therapist can reduce the likelihood that she will assume how a family member will function at the beginning of a session based on one or two previous sessions. She does this by focusing on PACE—and especially acceptance and curiosity—before the session begins. When the therapist meets the family in the waiting room, she is wise to adopt a not-knowing stance where she is very open to experiencing each family member as he or she is at that moment rather than as she remembers them having been in the past few sessions. She also must accept where the therapy itself is at that moment, rather than becoming frustrated or disappointed that previous, seemingly resolved themes from the past have returned. By accepting the return of these themes, the therapist and family are more likely to be able to address them more quickly this time. When the therapist and family resist them, these themes are likely to return with greater intensity.

Thus, the therapist cannot assume that in a session 2 months after treatment began that the family members will engage easily in the process of A-R dialogue, that they will demonstrate PACE, and that they will repair their relationships whenever needed. If she begins every session with PACE, then she is likely to accept the family as they are, be curious about how they are, and experience empathy for them, as they are at that moment.

III. TERMINATION OF ATTACHMENT-FOCUSED FAMILY THERAPY

Families are most likely to seek treatment around a specific behavior (lying, anger, being noncommunicative and noncompliant) of their child that often can be seen as having a large relational component. The therapist in AFFT attempts to help the family to focus on the relational aspect of the areas of concern, believing that the solutions lie within the relationship itself. In bringing the focus to the relationship, the therapist can utilize attachment theory and research to serve as a guide as to how to strengthen the relationship so that it facilitates a resolution of the presenting problems.

Parent-child attachment facilitates safety for the child so that he actively becomes engaged in intersubjective exploration about self, other, and the world with his parents and secondary attachment figures. This therapy is embedded with interventions that are based on principles of attachment and intersubjectivity that facilitate the attachment relationship. These include A-R dialogue, PACE, and relationship repair and they facilitate the coregulation of affect and the cocreation of meaning along with enhanced reflective functioning. The therapist teaches these interventions to the parents, and then the child, primarily by having them experience them, with the therapist taking the lead with modeling and coaching and becoming engaged with them in the same way that he wants them to become engaged with each other. A psychoeducational component with the parents at the onset of treatment is also utilized, primarily to present the parents with a roadmap of the treatment and to increase their sense of safety with the therapist.

The therapist begins to think of termination not so much when there is a reduction in the problems that brought the family to treatment as when he observes that the parents are able to consistently utilize PACE to become engaged with their child in A-R dialogue. He also observes that the parents now consistently initiate relationship repair more quickly and openly than was the case in the past. When such relational patterns are evident, then the therapist can have some confidence not only that the presenting problems will be successfully addressed but also that future problems will be addressed as they emerge with the same attachment-influenced interventions. In essence, the therapist has not given the parents a fish, but rather has shown them how to fish.

If the parents and child have developed an intersubjective relationship with the therapist and consistently experience safety with him, they are very likely to contact the therapist in the future if family problems emerge. This prevents the response of shame that occurs with some families when they are again experiencing problems similar to the ones that they experienced before. Such shame would prevent them from seeking therapy. When the family does become reengaged in AFFT, often it is because they drifted away from the attachment-focused principles that they had developed during the prior course of treatment. Often they begin to utilize those skills again fairly quickly and the treatment tends to be short.

EXERCISES

Questions

1. The process of A-R dialogue:
   A. Enables intersubjective exploration.
   B. Needs to be developed within families when they begin treatment.
   C. Precedes the focus on the content of the dialogue.
   D. All of the above.

2. The coregulation of affect needs to precede the cocreation of meaning because:
   A. It ensures that the family is engaged in the discussion.
   B. It prevents the experience of anger.
   C. It prevents the experience of fear.
   D. It ensures safety is present when stressful themes are explored.

3. Safety is established:
   A. With the parents first and then for the child with the parents participating.
   B. With the child first.
   C. With both together.
   D. With the parents first and then the child separately.

4. Regarding the regulation of affect:
   A. Coregulation and self-regulation of affect are learned independently.
   B. Self-regulation of affect needs to precede coregulation.
   C. Coregulation of affect needs to precede self-regulation.
   D. Affect regulation is a neuropsychological process that develops alone.

5. Often in therapy, reflection about the session:
   A. Occurs consistently throughout the session.
   B. Must dominate over the affective experience of the session if it is to be therapeutic.
   C. Precedes the affective experience of the session.
   D. Is preceded by the affective experience of the session.

Experiential Exercises

1. For the next week, when you first see a member of your family or a good friend who you see daily, focus on the experience of not knowing how that person is at that moment in time. Try to maintain an awareness that he might be experiencing life differently than he was when you last saw him. Be open to the value of discovering his inner life as it exists right then. Try not to assume or anticipate how he is likely to be.

After your time together with your family member or friend, reflect on how it went. Did you notice anything that was different about him? Was it easier to become more fully engaged in a conversation with him than you might have otherwise been? Were you less likely to take him for granted? Did the conversation seem to be more enjoyable for him? For you? Did the conversation itself seem to contain more meaningful themes than usual?

2. The next time that you share an enjoyable activity with a family member or friend, find time later in the day to reflect on the experience with her. Comment on a few things that happened, how you experienced them, and then wonder how she also experienced them.

Later, reflect on the reflecting activity with her. Do you think that it changed the original experience in any way? Deepened it? Made it more likely that you would want to do it again? Do you recall more about it? Do you want to bring the activity into your joint history with her more fully?

ANSWERS

1. D
2. D
3. A
4. C
5. D

6 Repair of the Attachment Relationship

Relationship repairs are necessary to ensure that the attachment relationship creates and maintains safety for the child. When the child experiences his parent as being willing and able to do the difficult work of repair, he knows that the parent is committed to the relationship and that it will survive and even thrive. The relationship is more important than a particular conflict that they are experiencing. This chapter presents the core factors in initiating and maintaining successful relationship repair both from parent to child and from therapist to family members.

C. Address breaks as they occur between the therapist and one or more members of the family.

IV. Obstacles to Relationship Repair

A. When the therapist initiates relationship repair, he is taking a risk that the repair will be rejected.

B. When a parent initiates relationship repair, she is also taking a risk that her child will reject her initiative.

I. THE NEED FOR RELATIONSHIP REPAIR

As has been discussed throughout this work, the attachment relationship is a primary source of safety and interpersonal learning during childhood and throughout life. Intersubjectivity is a central means whereby both safety and social-emotional learning occur. When, within an attachment relationship, we have an attitude of PACE toward the experience of each other, we come to know each other below the surface and we come to trust that our knowledge of each other—as it deepens—generates safety and confidence in the ongoing nature of the relationship. Increasing intersubjective knowledge creates safety, and increasing safety creates an engaged reciprocity whereby intersubjective learning can flourish.

In every attachment relationship there will be misunderstandings, mistakes, and differing interests and purposes, as well as differing opinions about important matters. All of these factors can be the source of breaks in the attachment relationship and in the intersubjective experiences that are present. These breaks may last for seconds, minutes, hours, days, weeks, months, or years. Each break requires the act of repair to maintain the strength of the attachment relationship in the face of these common daily stresses on the relationship. Such repairs are necessarily active components of all secure attachments. Breaks vary from mild to severe.

1. Some breaks are self-correcting, barely noticed, accepted, and then lead to subtle changes in patterns of interaction that better meet the wishes and preferences of both members of the relationship.

2. Other breaks require a more elaborate repair in which the members of the relationship acknowledge them, explore them to understand them better, and then work together to develop new relationship patterns that better meet the interests of both.

3. Still other breaks require sufficient safety that one member of the dyad is able to become aware of and acknowledge that he or she has hurt the other. This person then expresses a sincere apology, is committed to try not to do that behavior again, and develops new behavior patterns to ensure that there is a true change. The other person accepts the apology and, seeing the remorse and changed behaviors, reestablishes a sense of trust in the other. Safety is ensured again.

In many families who seek treatment, these repair processes do not occur on a regular basis. Nor do they demonstrate the willingness to engage in them when necessary or the skill needed to generate successful relationship repair. In these families:

1. Differing experiences of events are not accepted.
2. Cycles of anger and defensiveness develop.
3. Avoidance of conflicts is thought to be central to the good of the family.
4. The family members believe they are no longer important to one or more of the others.

Without effective repair processes, the natural stresses that occur in the daily lives of autonomous individuals will lead the attachment relationship into maladaptive patterns in which either the relationship or the autonomy of the individual family members is compromised. One pattern may consist of repetitive, angry conflicts where the other is seen as an antagonist, the source of competition rather than cooperation. These conflicts follow one upon the next with few breaks in between and seldom a resolution to one before the next occurs. Another pattern may consist of increasing emotional distance where the attachment relationship becomes more of a practical bargain and a polite way of managing a life together that has sparse emotional intimacy. Physical safety may or may not exist, but psychological safety—confidence that the other will be there to comfort and support—is generally not present. In a third pattern within the attachment relationship between partners—or between parent and child—one may habitually initiate a conflict while the other habitually avoids the conflict.

Effective repair processes are characterized by the presence of intersubjective communications, in which the experience of each person is valued, of interest, understood, and accepted. Differences between experiences are noticed and, rather than being perceived as threats to the self and the relationship, are experienced as being normal factors in any family. This process—an inherently reciprocal one whereby the experience of one member of the family is influencing the experience of the other and vice versa—is not simply an exercise in building communication skills. Rather it involves deep, nonjudgmental fascination with the each other's experiential worlds. When mistakes and differences generate an intersubjective attitude characterized by acceptance, curiosity, and empathy rather than threats and defensiveness, repair occurs much more easily and the attachment remains secure. When there is sufficient safety within families to allow differences of experience, then repair becomes a natural part of the relationships and deeper experiences of safety are then created.

When families do not have a history of successful repair, establishing and maintaining the intersubjective process while engaging in repair is often difficult. In family therapy, a central goal for the therapist is to identify various breaks in the attachment relationship among the family members and then facilitate relationship repair. Breaks that occur in the present—in the therapy session itself—are excellent opportunities to teach and demonstrate relationship repair, with the goal that these repair experiences will be repeated at home. For that reason, the therapist takes the lead in ensuring that ongoing repair, and the underlying intersubjective stance that will facilitate it, is maintained during the dialogue. She does this through explaining the process but, more importantly, by becoming engaged in the intersubjective process herself. She does not adopt a neutral stance but rather maintains an intersubjective stance whereby her experience is influencing the experiences of the family members and vice versa. She is part of the intersubjective mix and is also actively engaged in relationship repair when needed.

When family members avoid conflict and try not to notice it, the therapist identifies it and creates a sufficient sense of safety so that the conflicts can be explored intersubjectively. When family members alternate between verbal attacks and defensiveness over differences, the therapist focuses on exploring the attack/defense patterns to determine their meaning in the context of the attachment relationships.

The intersubjective experience is a delicate process. Misunderstandings, themes involving shame or other threats to the self, differences in experience, conflicting intentions and cross-purposes, perceived expectations that are not welcome—all of these and more may generate a break in the intersubjective process. Such breaks need to be noticed, accepted, addressed, and repaired before A-R dialogue is able to continue. When the therapist is committed to the intersubjective process, he is willing to accept the breaks as much as he accepts the actual intersubjective experience itself.

II. RELATIONSHIP BREAKS

A. Identifying That There Is a Break

1. The first indication that a break is emerging in the intersubjective dialogue is often nonverbal. The person's voice may change. What was once animated, with a full range of expressiveness and a sense of aliveness, now is flat, one-dimensional, and plodding. Facial expressions also lose their vibrancy and become flat and ambiguous. Resonating, responsive gestures are now almost nonexistent. The person appears to be passive and disengaged. There is a lack of congruence between verbal and nonverbal communications.

EXAMPLE 1

MARY [age 12]: Dad, you just don't want me to grow up!

DAD: I know you think that when I say no about something you want.

MARY: Then stop treating me like a baby!

[Dad becomes tense and looks away, as if he wants to say, "Then stop acting like one!" but he inhibits himself.]

THERAPIST: I think that was hard for you to hear, Harry. What made it hard?

DAD: I try my best and it seems like unless I give Mary just what she wants, she thinks that I'm an insensitive tyrant!

THERAPIST: I know that it is hard for you when Mary tells you that she sometimes thinks that you're doing things wrong. Can I help you to take a deep breath and hear her now? That might show her clearly that she is not a baby to you.

Comment: Harry's avoidance of expressing his discomfort when Mary criticizes him is likely to reflect his strong desire to try to get along with her and possibly his lack of success in being able to resolve conflicts when they emerge. They may just escalate. The therapist sees the avoidance in his nonverbal expression and leads the dialogue to explore the conflict, hopefully guiding it toward a resolution this time.

DAD: Yeah, go ahead.

THERAPIST: Thanks, Harry. Mary, could you help us to understand more about what you mean that you experience your dad treating you like a baby?

MARY: He does!

THERAPIST: That would be hard for you if it seems that way to you. What makes you think that he treats you like you're a baby?

MARY: He's always telling me what to do! Like I can't figure anything out on my own!

THERAPIST: If he does that . . . why would he?

MARY: He doesn't think that I'm smart enough or old enough to handle things by myself!

THERAPIST: If he thinks that, it would be hard. Have you told him that? Have you ever said, "Dad, sometimes I think that you don't have confidence in me. You don't know that I'm growing up and can do things for myself now." Why not tell your dad that?

MARY: It's true, Dad. Sometimes it seems that you just think that I'm not able to make any decisions on my own. That you still think that I'm just a little kid.

DAD: I'm sorry that it seems that way, Mary, I really am. I know that you are bright and responsible and able to make many decisions on your own. I'm sorry that I haven't told you that enough.

MARY: Why won't you let me go out where I want to and come home when I'm ready?

DAD: Because I love you. I worry. I know that you can make many decisions quite well, but I also know that some of the things that you'll face out there are new to you. Some of the kids are older and come from families that have different beliefs. I want to help you get into the teenage world gradually, not all at once.

MARY: I'm worried that "gradually" means not until I'm 18.

DAD: I'm sorry if I've given you that impression. But you have to accept some of the reasons for my limits, Mary. You don't handle your basic responsibilities at home that well, so it makes me have a hard time giving you more freedom to be with your friends.

THERAPIST: Could you stay with Mary's fears, Dad? Could you let her know that you get it—how she fears that you won't see her maturing, but only focus on her mistakes?

DAD: I do know how well you handle some things, Mary. I really do. But I can't ignore your mistakes.

THERAPIST: I hear you saying how much you want to have Mary see you as being reasonable about the rules. You both have similar fears—she worries that you see her as being irresponsible and you worry that she sees you as being harsh.

DAD: I don't think she's irresponsible or that I'm harsh.

MARY: I know that I mess up, Dad! But I'm not irresponsible!

DAD: I know that you're not, Mary. I really do. I am sorry that I stress what you do wrong. Maybe the therapist is right—that I stress your mistakes so that you won't see me as harsh—so that I won't see myself as harsh.

MARY: You're not harsh, Dad.

DAD: Thanks, honey. I gotta stay positive more. I know I don't tell you enough how I think you are growing up so well. I really do have confidence in you.

MARY: I didn't know that.

DAD: And I'm sorry you didn't.

Comment: In this example the father was able to engage his daughter within an intersubjective dialogue with a few slips, but did not have the confidence to begin it. The therapist had coached him regarding the nature of PACE, and therapy provided the space where he could begin to use it. Repair is much more likely to occur when the parent is able to go beneath the angry outburst—"You're treating me like a baby"—and explore its meaning, as well as what makes it hard for him to hear the criticism.

EXAMPLE 2

STAN: You're right, Mom. I need to just do the chore and get it over with rather than spending so much time trying to get out of having to do it! I'm going to try to stop arguing so much.

MOM: Wow! It is wonderful hearing you say that!

STAN: Yeah, now to just be able to do it!

MOM [serious tone]: It is easy to make promises and much harder to keep them.

STAN [looks away and becomes tense as if he experienced his mother's serious "lecture" as evidence that she does not have confidence in him.]: I won't even bother trying then!

MOM: Now why did you say that?

STAN: It doesn't matter!

Comment: Janet appeared to not have confidence in her son's word (possibly because he had made similar promises in the past without results). It was not her words so much as the serious tone in which she said them. If she had said the same words with empathy, Stan might well have accepted them as a sign that she knew that it would be hard but she was glad that he was trying.

THERAPIST: Stan, when your mom said that it seemed to bother you. What was hard for you about what she said?

STAN: She doesn't believe that I mean it. I do plan to try but since she does not believe me I don't feel like trying!

THERAPIST: Could you tell your mom that? Could you say, "Mom, I don't think you believe me. And when you don't believe me, I don't feel like trying."

STAN: I don't, Mom. You don't believe that I'm going to try to just get the chores done without arguing about it. I meant that.

MOM: But you've said that before!

THERAPIST: Janet, are you saying that you don't believe your son when he says that he intends to try not to argue about his chores?

MOM: I know that he tries.

THERAPIST: Then can you stay with that? Can you say something like, "Son, I know that you try. I really do. And I know that doing chores is really hard for you. Is there anything that I can do to help you to argue less?"

MOM: I do know you try, son, and I'm glad that you do. I really am. I just worry that it will be too hard for you. Is there any way that I can help you with this?

STAN: Don't give me any chores! [Laughs.]

MOM: Nice try.

THERAPIST: I have some ideas if you two are interested.

Comment: When the therapist brought out the need to explore the reasons for the break, both participated easily. If Janet had been able to express her doubts about the probability of success with empathy and specific words that addressed it, rather than communicating her doubts with the serious tone and lecture, Stan most likely would have participated in exploring ways to address her doubts. The lecture led Stan to believe that his mom did not even believe that he was being truthful about his desire to address the problem.

2. The verbal content of the dialogue also quickly demonstrates that there is a break in the relationship. The person's words are distancing or angry. The content of the words and the apparent intent of the dialogue appears to be to control the other, to change the other's mind, rather than to relate intersubjectively with PACE. The response to this apparent effort to control tends to be defensive, resistant, and argumentative. The attack or distancing is happening without the parent or child being aware of what is happening.

EXAMPLE 1

KENDRA: Can't I just tell you why it is so important to me to go to New York with my friend and her family?

DAD (Ted): It does not matter why it is important to you. I've decided and nothing that you say will change it!

KENDRA: But you don't know anything about why I really want to go!

DAD: I said that it does not matter!

KENDRA: Nothing matters to you except what you want! You are so selfish!

DAD: Keep talking like that and there will be a lot more that you won't be doing!

Comment: In this example, Ted hides behind "because I say so" to avoid exploring the conflict that he has with his daughter. He may lack confidence in his position as to why she cannot go or possibly not even know why he opposes her wish and wants to avoid thinking about it. Or it may be a larger pattern where he defines parental authority in a rigid manner in which a parent's decision can never be questioned by the child. Either way, there is now a break in his relationship with his daughter that will make her be less communicative with him in the future and will cause their relationship to become more emotionally distant. Thus, the therapist addresses the break and attempts to understand Ted's reluctance to engage in a dialogue with his daughter about her wishes.

THERAPIST: Ted, help me to understand—if you don't know what your daughter's reasons are for wanting to go to New York, what makes you reluctant to listen to her?

DAD: She'll only get more angry about it when she realizes that after all the talking, she still can't go.

THERAPIST: What makes you sure that she will be more angry or even that you won't change your decision, if you don't know her reason for wanting to go and she doesn't know your reason for not wanting her to go?

DAD: Sometimes Kendra just has to accept my judgment when I say no without knowing the reason.

THERAPIST: And this is one of those times?

DAD: Yeah.

THERAPIST: Because . . .

DAD: You're as bad as her.

THERAPIST: I can sense that you are getting impatient with me for asking, Ted, but I'm exploring it because I think that it's important. If you two can resolve the conflict, that's great. But just as important, I think, even if your daughter remains upset because she can't go, is that she knows that you really understand why it is important to her and also that she sees that you will make the effort to explain your reasons to her, if only to make it easier for her to accept your decision. If she knows that you get it—why she wants to go so badly—it is likely to be easier for her to accept your reasons for saying no. If you guys don't explore this, I fear that your relationship will be a bit less close in the future— you'll be a bit less open to each other.

DAD: Okay, I know you're right. Kendra, I'll listen, I really will. . . . Why is it so important to you to go to New York with your friend and her family?

Comment: When conflicts are not able to be resolved, it is crucial that the different perspectives be understood and equally valid. When a respect for and openness to each other's thoughts and wishes are evident, the relationship can be repaired even when differences remain.

EXAMPLE 2

AARON: I really want that new video game, Mom. I really do!

MOM (Anne): I hear you son. I really do. But I have concerns about it.

AARON: No, I'm tired of your concerns! I want it and I don't want to talk about your concerns!

MOM: I know that it's important to you . . .

AARON: You don't know anything about me!

MOM: And whose fault is that?

Comment: In this example, Anne made an effort to understand and accept her son's wishes, but after he continued to verbally attack her, she became defensive and attacked him back.

THERAPIST: It seems like this conflict is causing you both to get angry and not feel close right now. Can I help? You really seem upset, Aaron. What's so hard for you now about your mom saying no about the game that you want?

AARON: She always says no! Always! She never lets me have anything!

THERAPIST: If that's right—that your mom never lets you have what you want—I can understand why you would get so angry. Why do you think that your mom does that? If you're right, why does she always say no?

AARON: Because what I want isn't important to her!

THERAPIST: And if you are right about that—what you want isn't important to her—that would be very hard. . . . Like you're not important to her!

AARON: I don't think I am!

THERAPIST: Ah! Tell her that. Say, "Mom, when you say no to me I sometimes think that I'm just not important to you."

AARON: I don't think that I am, Mom! I don't think I'm important to you.

MOM: I'm sorry, son, I really am. I'm sorry that I'm not better at explaining why I say no because you are important to me, really important, and I guess I'm not clear enough about that if you don't think that you are.

Comment: In this example, when the therapist sees that the conflict is beginning to move into reciprocal verbal attacks, he quickly interrupts and moves the dialogue into an intersubjective position rather than the angry/defensive pattern. He inserts himself into the conflict and relates to the child—who began the attack—in a manner that will lead to greater openness and vulnerability.

B. Identifying the Cause of the Break

1. The break may simply represent the natural rhythm of relationships. If a break is simply seen as a natural ebb and flow of connectedness, then it is not experienced as being wrong, avoidant, or resistant. Often the simple act of accepting the break in intersubjectivity reestablishes the intersubjective.

EXAMPLE

BRENT: We still got a lot of work to do on who's going to do what!

DAD: You got that right, son. You and I seem to have very different ways of looking at what needs to be done and who does it.

BRENT: Maybe we can talk about it again this weekend.

DAD: Great idea, Brent. We don't seem to be working much out now.

BRENT: I'll get you in a good mood before I bring it up again, Dad.

DAD: Thanks for that! I love it when you get me in a good mood.

Comment: In this example, Brent and his dad are clearly at ease with differences, can address and resolve them, and can delay resolving them when necessary and yet not be threatened by their differences. Such acceptance of differences promotes attachment security in that it is clear to both that the relationship is more important than the differences.

2. The emotional intensity of the communication may cause one member to withdraw a bit from the relationship (break) to regulate the emotion. The emotional theme being explored by one person may cause another person to interrupt the dialogue to regulate his own emotion.

EXAMPLE

HEATHER: I wanted so much to make the team!

MOM: I know, sweetie, I know.

HEATHER: I'll never be good enough! [Suddenly starts crying.]

MOM: Now, don't cry, honey, don't cry. It will work out!

HEATHER: No, it won't! Nothing ever goes the way I want it!

MOM: It will be okay. We'll find something else that you can do.

Comment: In this example, her daughter's distress caused the mother to pull back from the relationship because it was hard for the mother to experience it. Rather than experience empathy and comfort her daughter, she attempted to make her daughter's emotion go away and then distract her from it. This is often justified as giving reassurance and helping a child to cope with a hard time, when often it simply reflects a parent's discomfort with a child's difficult emotions.

THERAPIST: Betty, Heather is really struggling now with her distress over not making the team. Rather than trying to make her distress go away, would you just stay with her, express empathy, and give her a hug as she cries?

MOM: Yes, I could do that. Heather, I know how badly you wanted to make the team. I really do, honey. I can see why it is so hard for you now! So hard. [Moves over and hugs her.] We'll get through this together, honey. Yes, we will. I know it's hard. I really do.

Comment: At the onset of treatment, if the therapist explains the value of empathy and coregulating affect, many parents are able to become engaged with their child in that way. The reassurance and distraction simply reflect how they were raised and how they do not intuitively see the value of the other approach. With some parents, the explanation and coaching are not sufficient. Often those parents have unresolved aspects from their own childhood associated with a similar theme.

3. Often a break is caused by one person misperceiving the intention of the other. A child may think that her parent said no to her because the parent does not care what she wants. A mother may think that her son became angry over an expectation because he just wants his own way. At times the intentions are ambiguous and may reflect a person's ambivalence about a course of action. Acknowledging the ambivalence and trying to resolve it or encouraging the individuals to clearly state their intentions may initiate repair.

EXAMPLE

KEN: I decided not to go on the class trip.

DAD (Brent): Ken, you've been wanting to do this for weeks! How can you change your mind now?

KEN: I don't know, Dad. I just don't want to go.

DAD: It doesn't make any sense, son. I don't want you changing your mind again.

THERAPIST: Brent, I wonder if we can slow down a bit and try to understand Ken's reason for not wanting to go. [To Ken] So, it seems like you've come to a decision not to go and it's hard to know why.

KEN: Yeah, I don't know.

THERAPIST: Do you think maybe you had some reasons for going and some other reasons not to go? So it was hard to decide—you wanted to and you didn't.

KEN: I really want to see DC again. I haven't been there since I was really little. There's a lot that I wanted to see. But . . . Tracy is going . . . and I broke up with her last week. And . . . I don't know. It would be awkward.

THERAPIST: Ah! I see! You want to see DC but since you just broke up with Tracy, you're not so sure that you want to be that close to her for 3 days.

KEN: I know that there will be 50 other kids there too, so it's not like we'd have to eat together and walk through the museums together. But still . . .

THERAPIST: You would see her and she'd see you and maybe accidently be next to each other during some event.

KEN: Yeah. Maybe it's not such a big deal. I don't know.

THERAPIST: So you're not sure about it. Do you think it will bother her?

KEN: Actually she seemed fine about our breaking up. She said that she thought it was a good idea too. She was just afraid to bring it up. She still wants to be friends.

THERAPIST: And do you?

KEN: Yeah, that would be cool. I don't know. Maybe I could ask her if she'd be okay with my going. And tell her that if she'd rather that I not go, that's fine too.

THERAPIST: That makes sense, if you're not sure yourself.

KEN: I think that's what I'll do. Is that okay, Dad?

DAD: It's your call, son. You're giving this a lot of good thought and you can work out the best thing to do. I like how you're thinking this through. Sorry I wasn't more helpful.

KEN: No worries, Dad. I never told you about Tracy and me.

Comment: In this example, Brent, the dad, became annoyed with his son's decision before knowing why he had made the decision. It is best to maintain a curious, not-knowing stance toward the child's behaviors and choices before responding to them. Often conflicts can be prevented when the parent or child first becomes clear as to the motives of the other before reacting to the other's behavior. Or if the conflict remains, it tends not to be as intense, easier to resolve or to accept.

4. Breaks may be caused by themes of shame or other threats to the self. A child may not want to explore how he stole from his parent because he may perceive his action as representing his being bad or selfish. A parent may resist exploring how he threatened his child because he may think that it means that he is a bad parent. A child may resist recalling a traumatizing event because the distress caused by the memory of the event may be experienced almost as if he were again experiencing the trauma itself.

EXAMPLE

MOM [Jen]: Kate, I know that you took the money from my purse. Just admit that you did it and then we can work it out.

KATE: I didn't do it!

MOM: Kate, that's not helpful! If there was any doubt at all I'd let you explain that, but you and I both know that you did it!

KATE: You never believe me!

MOM: I will when you give me reason to believe you.

Comment: As is often the case, the therapist interrupts the parent-child dialogue when she sees that it is going toward attack/defend rather than intersubjectivity. She then turns the discussion away from whether or not the child stole from the mother to an equally important psychological reality, namely, what it is like when her mother does not believe her.

THERAPIST: I wonder, Kate, if we can set aside the money for a moment. What is it like when your mom does not believe you?

KATE: She never does!

THERAPIST: Ah! If that is so, that would be really hard! How come she never believes you?

KATE: Because she just thinks that I'm bad! She thinks that I do wrong things all the time!

THERAPIST: Ah! Kate! How hard that must be for you if you think that your mom thinks that you're bad. Have you told her that? Have you said, "Mom, when I do something wrong, it seems to me that you think that I'm a bad girl. You think that I'm bad and I hate that!"

KATE: No.

THERAPIST: Would you tell her that now, Kate? Or would you let me tell her for you?

KATE: You tell her.

THERAPIST: Thanks, Kate. [To Jen] I'll talk for Kate now. "Mom, sometimes when I do something wrong, I think that you think that I'm bad. And I hate that! And that's why I can't talk to you about what I do wrong. That's why! You think that I'm bad!

MOM: Oh, Kate, I'm sorry that you think that! It must be hard if you think that I think you're bad. So hard! I am sorry! I do get angry at what you do. And sometimes I don't know why you do it. But I don't think that you do it because you're bad.

THERAPIST [as Kate]: Are you sure, Mom? Are you sure that you don't think that I'm bad?

MOM: I don't, Kate. Even when I get really mad at what you do, I don't think that you're bad.

KATE: But I must be bad! Don't you know? No other girl would steal from her mom! A good mom! I must be bad!

MOM: Oh, Kate, I'm very sorry that you think that about yourself. Thanks so much for trusting me enough to tell me that you stole from me. Thanks so much. That took such courage. I know it did!

KATE: I don't want to, Mom. I don't want to! I don't know how to stop!

MOM: I know, honey, I know. I believe you. I really do.

Comment: When the shame is spoken about and receives empathy, the original issue—the child lying—tends to become more easily resolved, often with the child no longer denying what she did or no longer having an excuse for the behavior. Shame is often the dynamic behind the child's lying about her behavior.

5. Breaks may be caused by differences in experiences (thoughts, wishes, etc.) that are a threat to one or both members of the relationship. The parents may want their child to take music lessons while the child is more interested in playing sports. A child may enjoy playing video games that contain violence, while the parents may believe that playing them can undermine the child's development.

EXAMPLE

MOM: Dad and I are going Christmas caroling in the neighborhood. Would you like to come along?

LENNIE: No! I wouldn't be caught dead doing something like that. That's dumb! You never talk to those people anyway.

MOM: This will be a beginning then, and we'll feel good while we're doing it.

LENNIE: Great, I get stuck with parents who will be laughed at by everyone. And I'm sure my friends will find out.

Comment: In this example, the conflict might be predictable if a teenager has shown no interests in such activities with his parents in the past. Ideally, the parents will accept their son's desire not to go caroling in the neighborhood as reflecting his sense of what is cool or not, due to his age and friendships with his peers. Hopefully his mother would deliberately overlook his rude comments about her planned activity and see it as his exaggerated effort to justify his position. However, if Lennie habitually speaks rudely to his parents, then it might be wise to explore this pattern as to what it represents. He is more likely to speak politely if his parents clearly express how his tone impacts them and their relationship with him than if they react in anger and insist on his talking calmly. Helping him to become aware of why he might use that tone with his parents is also likely to reduce its use. A helpful response that accepts these differences and overlooks his rude comments might be something like: "Well, son, be sure that the windows are closed because we're going to be singing loudly! Also, if you mention it to your friends, asking for sympathy, you won't be teased. If anything, they might think more of you for being cool in spite of your parents."

6. Breaks may be caused by conflicting intentions and cross-purposes. The parent wants to clean the house on Saturday morning and the child wants to go shopping. One parent wants to spend money on a new couch and the other parent wants to save it toward a vacation.

EXAMPLE

MOM: How about we take the kids up to the lake this weekend and just relax?

DAD: I don't think that's a great idea. I can think of a lot we have to get done at home.

MOM: I know that. I just think that a bit of time together might reduce some of the tension that's existed between us and them lately.

DAD: It's likely to just cause more tension. I'd rather stay home!

MOM: Like every weekend. And we'll all just argue or go our separate ways.

DAD: And I guess you're saying it's my fault.

MOM: I'm saying that I have an idea to help the family and if you don't like it I wish that you'd come up with a better one!

Comment: In this example, the wife had a good intention to help the family. Her husband abruptly rejected her idea without seeing value in her intention and offering to explore other ways of achieving her goal. This led to her becoming annoyed with his lack of cooperation in working with her to achieve the goal and his greater annoyance and defensiveness. Such cycles of increasing conflict would be avoided if the first suggestion (a trip to the lake) were met with PACE and A-R dialogue rather than rejecting the idea without understanding its intention, and cooperating to find a joint solution to the difficulty.

III. INTERVENTIONS FOR RELATIONSHIP REPAIR

The intersubjective relationship is reestablished in various ways, depending on the reason for the break.

A. Simply accepting the break may be sufficient when it is a natural part of the ebb and flow process of the relationship. Acceptance is also quite sufficient once families have been able to accept the normality of breaks in all attachment relationships and even to see breaks as being opportunities to deepen and strengthen the attachment.

EXAMPLE

RON: So it looks like I'm not going to be able to spend the weekend with my friend, doesn't it?

MOM: It does, Ron. I'm sorry about that. I know that you were really looking forward to it.

RON: And I still don't get it, why it's that important for me to be at home when Uncle Bob and the family are here.

MOM: Yeah, I understand your thinking. I'm fine about your not being around the whole weekend, but not about your being gone all weekend.

RON: Any chance that Uncle Bob might decide to come next weekend instead?

MOM: So you're wishing for a miracle.

RON: Or that you'll take pity on your wonderful son.

MOM: Better put your money on the miracle.

Comment: The above dialogue may seem unrealistic to most family therapists, but it is quite normal for many families. It is a realistic goal to hold for families in AFFT. When the therapist holds the persistent goal of initiating and maintaining A-R dialogue and repair during treatment, families can develop the motivation and skills to have similar dialogues routinely.

B. Clarifying and addressing the reason for the break may reestablish intersubjectivity. Within the break, there is often little openness to the experience of the other. Each member of the conversation, in conflict, is attempting to give priority and value to their experience and to criticize or devalue the experience of the other. The intent is not to share experiences but to establish that "my experience is right and your experience is wrong." Examples involving the therapist assisting the family to explore the reasons for the break were given in the previous section.

Frequently, conflicts that lead to acts of discipline create a break in the relationship. Too often these are not discussed and the parent is content when the child does the behavioral consequence or follows the limit that was given. If the parent addresses the break afterwards, with empathy for the child's anger or distress over the discipline or limit, the child is more likely to accept the parent's directive without ongoing resentment. When the parent is able to communicate that the child's anger or disappointment as well as his conflicting thoughts or priorities are equally valid, the child often can accept the parent's authority and let it go. Relationship repair facilitates maintaining a secure attachment regardless of the conflict.

C. Address breaks as they occur between the therapist and one or more members of the family. One or more family members may misperceive the therapist's intentions. If someone believes that the therapist does not think that he is a good parent, because he is exploring a parenting behavior, the therapist might apologize for being unclear about her motive and state clearly that she does think that the parent is a good parent who is trying very hard to raise his child well. The therapist is simply saying that she thinks that one behavior may not have been as helpful as another might have been. If the parent states that he does not agree with the therapist's opinion, the therapist might simply acknowledge that they disagree.

The therapist might share her experience of the parent's honesty in stating his disagreement, as well as her curiosity over the parent's experience of the disagreement itself. The most important point is not about the content, but rather about the intersubjective process itself. When the therapist and parent are able to disagree and yet remain open to each other's experience, then the parent is more likely to be able to also remain open to his child's experience when they disagree.

EXAMPLE

THERAPIST: Thanks for coming in today. I thought that after our session last week with your son that it might be helpful if we met today without him.

TED [dad]: To give us a lecture about what we're doing wrong?

THERAPIST: If that's what you experienced last week, I am sorry. That was not my intent in asking for this meeting. But I was worried that you did not feel good about our last session.

TED: You kept correcting us when we wanted to make our point about why we need the rules that he hates.

GINA [mom]: And that bothers me, I just need to tell you and might as well tell you now. I think that you're giving him sympathy so much that it just makes him argue more when we set a limit. Like he's entitled to get what he wants.

THERAPIST: So that's been your experience. No wonder you and I really have not been on the same channel! I really am glad that I asked for just the three of us to meet.

Comment: When the parents clearly state to the therapist why they are annoyed with her interventions, she responds without defensiveness. Rather, she is glad that they now have an opportunity to repair their relationship.

TED: Does that mean that you'll support us rather than correct us?

THERAPIST: Again, I'm sorry that I came across as scolding you. I have to work harder to make it clear what my intentions are. I think where we might differ is that I see value in telling him I am sad when things in his life—including your limits—are so hard for him. My sense is that you don't agree. That you see my empathy as feeling sorry for him or even taking his side over yours.

GINA: Well, life is hard. I think that he's better off if he simply accepts that and does his job and does not dwell on how hard it is.

THERAPIST: Thanks, Gina. Is that what you do? Focus on what needs to be done and ignore any feelings about it.

GINA: Yeah! If I sat and felt sorry for myself, I would not get much done!

THERAPIST: If things are especially hard, do you rely on Ted at all?

GINA: Not really. I'm a pretty independent person. And I don't think he'd be too excited about it if I tried to cry on his shoulder.

TED: That's not really accurate. If you were having a hard time, I'd support you.

GINA: I know you would. It's just that I don't see the need for it.

Comment: The therapist has established a context in which the parents disagree with expressing empathy for their son when he becomes upset over their rules and consequences. The parents accept this exploration. If they had objected that it had nothing to do with their son, he would have clarified that he was not blaming them, but rather trying to understand whether or not they value empathy for themselves.

THERAPIST: So when I support Tim emotionally, and suggest that you both do the same, you question the value of that. I can understand better now.

I strongly believe that when we tell someone whom we are attached to how hard something is and then experience the distress with him, it is easier for the person to face what needs to be done, and the person usually finds more strength to get it done.

GINA: You've shown him that you get it for 3 weeks now and it does not seem to have made any difference, except maybe to make him more argumentative.

THERAPIST: Gina, I think that my empathy is not likely to have any impact if he sees that you and his dad don't experience empathy for him.

TED: Another lecture?

THERAPIST: Another discussion about an important area where we might disagree. If I may convey my thoughts about this a bit more. . . . Gina, you mentioned that you did not need comfort from your husband . . . and I'm not disagreeing with that. I'm wondering, though, if you let yourself ask for comfort around a hard time, and he gave it to you, if it would make it easier to manage the situation and if you would feel closer to him.

GINA: I don't know. I can't recall the last time that I did. We're just not that way.

TED: I'd love it if you did!

GINA: Why do you say that?

TED: Because sometimes I wish that you needed me more than you do. I wish that I felt more special to you, and if you turned to me for comfort once in awhile I think that I would know that I matter a lot to you.

GINA: But you do!

TED: Intellectually, I know that you do, but I just don't feel it that much.

Comment: The therapist might follow this discussion further as to its impact on their relationship. She decides to make the connection to Tim first and see if they agree with that.

THERAPIST: And I wonder if it is the same with Tim. He's a bright kid and your rules are fair. I know that at some level he knows that too. So why does he fuss so much about them? I think maybe because he wants you to comfort him a bit about his stress around them. I do believe that if he experienced at a deep level that you get it, you know his distress and feel it with him, that he would be more willing to accept your rules.

GINA: Why would it work that way? He'd want comfort from the people who made the rules? Who made his life difficult in the first place?

THERAPIST: Yes, he would! He knows at some level that you're not doing it to make his life difficult. . . . You're doing it because you love him and you want what is best for him. He just wants some acknowledgment that he's not happy about it, and you're okay about that. You're sad that it is hard.

GINA: Wouldn't it just seem fake? That we didn't mean it?

THERAPIST: It will be fake if you don't mean it. But if you see value in this and mean it, even if you are a bit awkward about showing it, he'll understand and really value it.

Maybe even more so because you're willing to do that for him even though it is hard for you.

GINA: Why wouldn't we, if we're convinced that it will be helpful to him? We do love him, you know.

Comment: Here Gina experiences criticism from the therapist when she did not intend to criticize her at all. The therapist repairs the relationship without defensiveness.

THERAPIST: I am very sorry if I've given any impression that I thought that you do not love him. You're here because you love him! You're willing to consider doing something that you are not used to. That is hard for you—giving him comfort when he is upset over your rules—because you love him. I do know that . . . and I know that if you choose to try this, it will be hard for you.

GINA: You don't really know how hard.

THERAPIST: Ah, you may be right! I don't know how hard. What makes it so hard?

GINA: You never met my mother!

TED: You never met her mother!

THERAPIST: So your mother taught you that comforting is not of value . . . that you better not ask her for it.

GINA: That's right. Or you were a baby. So I never did.

THERAPIST: And here I am saying that she was wrong. That if you allow your son to be comforted by you, he will accept the rules better, be stronger, and be closer to you.

GINA: That's hard to believe.

THERAPIST: And Ted does not agree with your mother either. He's telling you that if you let him comfort you, he will not turn away, he will not see you as a baby. Rather, he'll feel closer to you, and love supporting you.

GINA: Are you really saying that?

TED: With all my heart. I've wished that you were not quite so independent, that you would let me be strong for you at times.

GINA: You might not know what you would be getting in for.

TED: I know you. I know that it does not matter to me how much you rely on me. I want you to trust me. I will be strong enough to be there for you. As much as you want.

Comment: The therapist asked to see the parents alone because their verbal and nonverbal comments during the session with their son suggested that they did not agree with the course of therapy. While they did not express their reservations strongly, and most likely would have continued to meet with their son for awhile without bringing up their reservations about expressing empathy for their son's response to their rules, the therapy would not have been effective. In addressing their reservations, and encouraging their expression, the therapist was able to achieve some agreement on the intervention. The therapist was also able to understand the roots of their opposition and to initiate an intervention that would address that as well.

IV. OBSTACLES TO RELATIONSHIP REPAIR

A. When the therapist initiates relationship repair, he is taking a risk that the repair will be rejected. By initiating a repair, the therapist is indicating that the relationship is important to him and it is worth struggling to repair and deepen it. Since the client might refuse, the act of repair is inherently anxiety producing. The therapist may be tempted to avoid making the repair in favor of a defensive stance.

To address this obstacle, the therapist:

A. Recognizes his anxiety and accepts it as a normal part of any relationship that has special meaning and depth, that is, an attachment relationship.
B. Accepts the reality that in initiating repair he will become vulnerable, placing himself at risk to be rejected or misinterpreted by the family members.
C. Acknowledges that he may fear that the family will see him as incompetent and unable to offer effective treatment.
D. Addresses these fears and hopefully resolves them by
    1. Seeing the value in modeling repair for the family.
    2. Experiencing the value of repair for the deepening relationship.
    3. Being able to accept his mistakes and not need to be perfect.
    4. Reflecting on his fears and possible connections to his attachment history.
    5. Exploring his fears with a supervisor or therapist.

B. When a parent initiates relationship repair, she is also taking a risk that her child will reject her initiative. The parent may fear that the repair will be interpreted by the child as giving in or being weak and suggest a loss of authority.

To address this obstacle, the therapist:

A. Helps the parent to recognize and accept her anxiety and understand its possible meanings.
B. Helps the parent understand the value of modeling repair for her child.
C. Helps the parent understand the value of repair for deepening the attachment relationship.
D. Helps the parent to reflect on how her anxiety may connect to her attachment history.

EXERCISES

Questions

1. Attachment relationship repair:
   A. Always requires an apology.
   B. Requires an apology when one person was hurt by the actions of another, regardless of the reason.
   C. Never requires an apology.
   D. Requires an apology only when the one person deliberately hurts the other.

2. Attachment relationship repair:
   A. Is a sign that there is a serious problem in the relationship.
   B. In good attachment relationships occurs only about once a year.
   C. Is not related to the security of the attachment relationship.
   D. Is a natural ongoing part of a secure attachment relationship.

3. Attachment relationship repair:
   A. Is the responsibility of the person who caused the conflict.
   B. Is the responsibility of the parent.
   C. Is the responsibility of the child.
   D. Is the most effective when the two family members take turns initiating it.

4. Families in family treatment often find relationship repair to be difficult because:
   A. Differing experiences of events are not accepted and compliance is expected.
   B. Cycles of anger and defensiveness develop when repair efforts are made.
   C. Avoidance of conflicts is thought to be central to the good of the family.
   D. All of the above.

5. When a client in family treatment believes that the therapist was critical of him but the therapist was not being critical, the therapist would do best to:
   A. Apologize for not speaking clearly causing the client to perceive criticism when that was not the therapist's intention.
   B. Interpret the client's perception of criticism as being due to his relationship with his parent.
   C. Explore why the client is being oversensitive to feedback.
   D. First C, then B.

Exercise

The purpose of the following scripts is to experience either a repair or a defense and excuse following a mistake. Read the script presented and then add the sentence that represents either repair or defensiveness. After each, reflect briefly on the experience.

1. The therapist's mind wanders to something in his personal life and he does not notice that the client expressed sadness that he and his son were not close.

   CLIENT: It doesn't seem that important to you that I'm in a lot of pain about this.
   REPAIR: I am sorry that I was not listening for a minute. I truly am. Please tell me again what you said.
   DEFENSIVE: I guess I see too many clients.

2. A teenager tells his mother that he thinks that she is being unfair and she replies that he is just being selfish if he thinks that she is unfair.

   TEEN: Thanks for that, mom.
   REPAIR: I'm sorry, son. You were telling me what you think and I wasn't listening very well. I should not have said that.
   DEFENSIVE: If you weren't always negative about me, maybe I wouldn't become negative about you.

3. One partner says to the other that she wishes that they would spend more time talking, and her partner replies that she is never satisfied with what he does.

   FIRST PARTNER: That's not what I said at all.
   REPAIR: I am sorry for saying that. You tell me that you want to try to improve our relationship and I criticize you. I am sorry.
   DEFENSIVE: Well, you have to admit that you seem to focus more on what you don't like about our relationship than what you do like about it.

Experiential Exercises

1. Recall a recent conflict with a friend or family member where afterward you took the initiative to repair the relationship. Did you delay initiating the repair? Why? What did you say? How did you feel before, during, and after the repair? Were you open to the other's comments during the repair? Were you defensive? Would you engage in the repair differently now than you did then?
2. Recall a recent conflict with a friend or family member where afterward the other person took the initiative to repair the relationship. How did you experience those initiatives? Were you open or defensive during the act of repair? Did it change the relationship in any way? Why didn't you initiate the repair?

3. Recall a recent conflict with a friend or family member where afterward there was no effort to repair the relationship. You remained in the relationship as if the conflict had never happened. Why didn't you initiate the repair? Why do you think the other person did not? After not addressing the conflict and actively repairing the relationship, do you think it had an effect on the relationship in any way? Do you think that you will avoid repairing that relationship when it happens again?

ANSWERS

Questions

1. B
2. D
3. B
4. D
5. A

7 The Parent as Attachment Figure

When the relationship between parent and child is characterized by attachment security, children are then provided with the optimal environment to achieve their fullest potential. The responsibility of parents to be the primary attachment figures for their children may be the most important role that they have for ensuring their child's overall development. When parents provide attachment security for their children, the need for family treatment is greatly reduced.

In AFFT, the therapist has a complex relationship with the parent. The therapist must place expectations on the parents to provide attachment security for their children during the sessions, but at the same time the therapist needs to ensure that the parents themselves are safe during the sessions. If the parents are not experiencing safety, it is unlikely that they will be able to assist the child with his safety needs. Thus, the therapist's initial treatment goal is to become an attachment figure for the parents to ensure that they will be able to provide attachment security for their child. Once the therapist has become an attachment figure for the parents, then both parent and therapist function as attachment figures for the child.

The following represent the therapist's goals in his work with the parents prior to beginning joint sessions with the child.

IN THIS CHAPTER

I. The Therapist Becomes an Attachment Figure for the Parent
   A. The therapist utilizes the attitude of PACE in response to all of the parents' verbal and nonverbal expressions.
   B. The therapist is alert for and completely accepts any negative experience that the parent has toward the therapist and therapy.
   C. The therapist discovers each parent's strengths as a person and as a parent and actively communicates these discoveries to the parent.

II. The Therapist Explores the Parents' Attachment Histories
   A. While exploring the parents' attachment histories with them, the therapist is sensitive to defensive responses associated with particular themes and relationships.

B. As the parents explore stressful themes from their own histories, the therapist assists them in seeing how those themes are being activated by their interactions with their child and having an—often negative—influence on the interactions.

III. The Therapist Is Aware That Parenting Is Hard

IV. The Therapist Assists the Parents in Learning A-R Dialogue, PACE, and the Therapeutic Intention Prior to Joint Sessions

A. The therapist differentiates communications about experience, which is the focus of treatment, from communicating about behaviors and problem solving.

B. From the onset, the therapist demonstrates the reciprocal nature of A-R dialogue. Monologues—including venting and lectures—are interrupted with PACE.

V. The Therapist Assists the Parents in Developing an Attachment Perspective

VI. The Therapist Assists the Parents in Developing Attachment-Focused Interventions

A. Safety

B. Communication

C. Emotional Regulation

D. Structure

E. Signs of Affection

F. Comfort in Distress

G. Discipline

H. Praise

I. Relationship Repair

VII. If the Therapist Is Unable to Facilitate Safety for Parents and Child in the Treatment Session, AFFT Is Not Indicated

VIII. Obstacles to Establishing a Safe Alliance With the Parents

A. The therapist takes the child's perspective, seeing the parent as the problem.

B. The therapist takes the parents' perspective, seeing the child as the problem.

C. The therapist does not address the relevance of the parents' attachment histories to current family functioning.

D. The parents participate in treatment with angry lectures or defensiveness.

E. The parents want to avoid their own relationship conflicts and focus on their child instead.

F. The therapist addresses any of the above but the parents refuse to look beyond their child as the source of the problems.

G. The parents follow the therapist's leads in the sessions but do not follow through with anything that is explored, and may even criticize the child later for what he said.

Now I would like to focus on each of those areas of the work with the parents in greater detail, keeping in mind the dual goals of safety for the parents while at the same time asking the parents to provide safety for their child. From there, intersubjective exploration through A-R dialogue and the attitude of PACE is free to evolve and transform the family.

I. THE THERAPIST BECOMES AN ATTACHMENT FIGURE FOR THE PARENT

The therapist meets with the parents without the child at the onset of treatment to ensure that they are able to experience safety with the therapist before they are asked to provide safety for their child throughout the course of therapy. The therapist needs to establish an alliance with the parents so that they know that the therapist has confidence in them and that they have the same goals for their child. They need to know that they can speak honestly with the therapist about any differences that they may have or any anxiety that they experience during the course of therapy without harming their relationship with the therapist.

The first therapeutic goal is to help the parents feel safe with the therapist so that they can work together in facilitating the functioning of the family. If the parents do not experience safety, they are likely to feel judged and criticized when the therapist begins to initiate family interventions and make recommendations that will affect their parenting activities. To be safe with the therapist, the parents must experience the therapist's experience of them as:

1. Being good people.
2. Who are doing the best that they can for their children and family.
3. Who love their children and want to improve their relationships with them.

To facilitate this experience of him by the parents, the therapist carefully explores the parents' parenting history. This includes their experiences of self-as-parent from the moment they decided to become parents through the present and into the anticipated future. In the general sequence of this dialogue, the therapist:

1. Listens with PACE to the parents' reasons for seeking treatment. He takes these reasons seriously, asking about details of the concerns, including the history of the problems, whether they have been getting better or worse, what the parents have done to address their concerns and if that has been successful at all, and how these concerns have affected them.
2. Is curious about other aspects of the family that might be contributing to the stress that they are experiencing. This would include employment, whether they have moved or are intending to move, their marriage, and their individual functioning including health, mental health, and substance abuse, as well as their extended families.
3. Is curious about their perceptions of their child's strengths as well as their own. This

includes experiences of joy and pleasure that they and their children have had recently.

4. Is curious about their hopes and dreams when they decided to become parents. This helps them to recall their better days and to rekindle hope that they might be able to recapture them again.

5. Is curious about when they first started to doubt whether their hopes and dreams would come true. Often during this stage of the dialogue, the parents are covering some of the same concerns that they expressed in (1) above, without the angry tone that was most likely evident then.

6. Is curious about whether or not they have experienced grief over a sense that their hopes and dreams might never come true.

7. Is curious about any feelings of shame over a sense of failing as parents.

During this movement from (1) through (7), the parents may become increasingly vulnerable about the course of their family concerns. During this process, it is often easier for the therapist to experience empathy for them than it might have been when they began the session in anger. As the therapist expresses empathy for their family struggles, it is likely that the parents will experience an increasing sense of safety.

During this movement from (1) through (7), the therapist is receptive to openings for exploring with the parents their own attachment history. This theme is explored further in the next section.

Once the therapist has established within himself a positive, accepting experience of the parents and then believes that the parents are experiencing that, he can have some confidence that they sense that they are safe with him. At that point he can also have some confidence that if he gives them suggestions or makes interventions that encourage them to change some interaction patterns with their children, they will be more likely to respond cooperatively to his interventions, without defensiveness.

A. The therapist utilizes the attitude of PACE in response to all of the parents' verbal and nonverbal expressions. The therapist communicates that all themes and experiences are able to be safely explored. The experience of the parent is being understood—with empathy—and not evaluated.

EXAMPLE

LYNNE [mom]: Sometimes I think that I never should have been a parent!

THERAPIST: What a hard thought to have!

LYNNE: It just never stops! His demands seem endless. He seems so selfish! I know that he's only 6 but I just don't want to take care of him sometimes.

THERAPIST: When he goes on . . . and on . . .

LYNNE: And *on*! Over and over again! Do you think that I'm being selfish?

THERAPIST: Selfish! Ah, Lynne, that was not my experience at all. I was thinking how hard you work, how much you do for your son . . . and you seldom get a break. . . . And at his age he has no awareness of it . . . so he doesn't acknowledge it, or reduce his demands. I wonder, though if you think that you're being selfish.

Comment: The therapist begins by communicating his acceptance of her thoughts and his empathy for the distress that she experiences in having those thoughts. As she is becoming safe enough to focus on those thoughts, she asks the therapist for his experience of them. He directly answers her request, gives a reason, and then returns to her experience of her thoughts. He could have chosen to redirect her to her own thoughts without giving his thoughts, but this may well have increased her anxiety and may have led her to assume that the therapist did not approve of her thoughts. By responding, the therapist is giving priority to the value of intersubjective communications—and A-R dialogue—as providing a safe context in which self-exploration happens more easily.

LYNNE: Yes, I often feel that I'm being selfish. Like a good mom wouldn't feel these things toward her little boy. A good mom would just suck it up and do it, and love him every moment.

THERAPIST: Ah, you are hard on yourself sometimes. You think that the feelings that you have must not be felt by other moms. That your feelings make you into a poor mom.

LYNNE: Are you saying that other moms have these feelings too?

THERAPIST: I am. Do you believe me?

LYNNE: I want to.

THERAPIST: You do, don't you? But it is so hard to accept the part of you that just wants to rest, to have no demands. To just take care of yourself for a change.

LYNNE: Maybe only part of me, then, is a bad mom.

THERAPIST: Maybe every part of you is human! Maybe every mom has the loving parts and the angry parts and the wanting-to-be-left-alone parts. And what you do is keep taking care of him . . . telling those parts that they will have to wait. But I think that they are still healthy, assertive parts who just want to be heard . . . and accepted.

Comment: The therapist again gives his experience and then elicits her experience. Lynne is able to follow the therapist part way in saying that only a part of her feels annoyed with her son. But she is not yet there since she labels that part bad.

LYNNE: So I should accept those feelings too?

THERAPIST: I don't know about should. But if you did, what would happen?

LYNNE: Nothing, I guess.

THERAPIST: Maybe better than nothing. Now you might be annoyed at your son's 100 demands and also at part of yourself. Maybe if you accepted that part of yourself, your annoyance would be smaller and life would be easier.

LYNNE: Now you're saying I should be annoyed at my son and not myself?

THERAPIST: Again, I don't think I said should. Actually, I said you might be annoyed about his 100 demands, not him . . . and not yourself.

LYNNE: And that's okay?

THERAPIST [leaning forward, squeezing her hand, and smiling]: Any guess what I might say?

LYNNE: Yes [smiles].

Comment: The therapist lightly suggests that he is not telling Lynne what she should feel but is helping her to be aware of what she does feel as well as his experience of those feelings and thoughts. If she continues to indicate that she experiences the therapist as evaluating her thoughts and feelings, he will address that tendency in greater depth. When she seems to become open to the possibility of accepting her annoyance toward her son's demands—but not without some hesitation—the therapist acknowledges her courage to face these new experiences by squeezing her hand and affirming her efforts. He is communicating his pleasure in her efforts to face these difficult, shame-laden themes. The smile makes it a bit lighter and easier for her to accept. Lynne is now feeling safer, is experiencing the therapist as an attachment figure, and is allowing herself to be guided intersubjectively by his experience of her and her effort.

Throughout the dialogue, the therapist was communicating with PACE, which increased Lynne's experience of safety while this theme was being explored. In the process, new meanings were being cocreated.

B. The therapist is alert for and completely accepts any negative experience that the parent has toward the therapist and therapy. The clear message is that the relationship is strong and that they can address any differences or conflicts without threat to the relationship.

EXAMPLE

JAKE [father]: I'm not going to baby Sam. He's 9 years old!

THERAPIST: Jake! You think that I want you to treat your son like a baby?

JAKE: That's what it sounds like! Every time he is upset you want me to stop everything and go running to him and hug him and make him feel better. Well, I don't think that is what he needs and I'm not planning to do it.

THERAPIST: Thanks, Jake. If that's what you heard me say, I need to say what I'm thinking better. I can see why you're annoyed if you heard me say that.

JAKE: And it seems like every time we talk about something, you want me to do more. Like I'm never doing enough for Sam! You're always finding something wrong with how I'm handling things.

THERAPIST: Thanks, again, Jake. Thanks so much for saying that. I wasn't aware that you were experiencing that during our meetings. I didn't know that you sense that I'm disappointed in you as a father . . . that I think that you're not doing enough for Sam.

Comment: Jake's initial criticism of the therapist involved his perception of how the therapist wanted him to relate to his son. When the therapist gave Jake the opportunity to elaborate on his experience rather than arguing with him about it, Jake then revealed that his deeper criticism involved his perception that the therapist was not sensitive to him, to how hard it was to raise his son. He conveyed that the therapist seemed to be taking his inner life for granted and focusing only on his son's experience. The therapist responded with more acceptance and empathy over his experience, allowing Jake to deepen the experience even further.

JAKE: Well, it really does seem that way. I can't think of one meeting when you didn't tell me something new to do. I can only do so much! I have other responsibilities too.

THERAPIST: And I think that you're telling me—very clearly—that you're doing the best you can. And at times you're just worn out. And that I don't get that . . . like I think that you're a robot who should just give and give and give.

JAKE: And give some more. But I'm not a robot.

THERAPIST: I'm sorry, Jake, if that's what I conveyed to you. Like your own thoughts and feelings and wishes are not important . . . only Sam's are. I'm sorry that I gave you that impression.

JAKE: I think that I'm accurate. We are here for Sam, aren't we?

THERAPIST: Yes, we are. And we're here for your relationship with each other. And if I want to strengthen and deepen your relationship I can't forget you. And maybe I have . . . or at least I have not shown you enough that I haven't forgotten you.

Comment: The therapist's priority here was to repair the relationship with Jake before they could continue focusing on Sam's needs. With the therapist's acceptance of Jake's experience, he is able to go more fully into the experience and his anger is more apparent. The therapist is not defensive; he accepts Jake's experience of being seen as a robot without defending himself. When Jake points out the reality that the purpose of the treatment was primarily to help Sam, the therapist is able to point out that his goal is to facilitate their relationship and he most likely did not stress that enough.

JAKE: I know you haven't forgotten me. You always notice me when you want me to do something for Sam.

THERAPIST: I hear you saying that you don't trust my words right now. Like I might be trying to appease you to keep you motivated to do more for Sam.

Comment: Jake's sarcasm makes it evident that he is skeptical about what the therapist is saying. The therapist accepts that and tries to make it more clear.

JAKE: Maybe you're right. Like you'll repair the robot, but I'm still Sam's robot.

THERAPIST: Thanks for being honest, Jake. What would help you to trust that I know that you're a person too? That I'm interested in your experience too. That your experience is also important. What would help to build the trust?

JAKE: Just once in awhile . . . once in awhile . . . let me know that you get it. Parenting Sam is damn hard sometimes! Just get it . . . then maybe I won't seem so alone in this . . . in taking care of him.

THERAPIST: You just want me to get it . . . how hard it is to be there for your son so much. You just want me to get it.

JAKE: That's all.

THERAPIST: You're not asking for much, Jake. And I'm sorry that I've not shown you enough that I do get it. That took courage to tell me that. Thanks for trusting me enough to tell me that.

Comment: Again, the most important point is to not become defensive, but rather to respond with PACE. The therapist goes further and asks Jake's help to be able to win his trust. Jake essentially responds that he wants to experience the therapist's empathy for how hard it is to raise his son. The therapist then experiences and expresses empathy along with recognition for Jake's courage and honesty. Such responses are often central in relationship repair.

JAKE: I didn't think that we were going to go anywhere if I didn't.

THERAPIST: I agree with you. As long as you think that I see you as Sam's servant, we'd go nowhere. You're much more than that. And I haven't made that clear. I'm sorry.

JAKE: Okay, you made it clear! Now let's get back to Sam and your wanting me to baby him [smiles].

THERAPIST: Only after you baby yourself [smiles].

JAKE: Now that's real helpful!

THERAPIST: Okay, good point. Only after you take care of yourself . . . like you're doing now.

JAKE: That's better. . . . So what we just talked about . . . you'd call that babying myself.

THERAPIST: I'd call that taking care of yourself through being honest about your experience. I'd also call that making sure that I can be helpful to Sam by making sure that our relationship is strong enough to handle any differences that we might have . . . that you can trust me with your honesty about anything, including how you see our relationship.

C. The therapist discovers each parent's strengths as a person and as a parent and actively communicates these discoveries to the parent. When a parent is confident that the therapist perceives her as a good person who loves her child and who is doing the best that she can to be an excellent parent, the parent is much more likely to remain safe and be receptive to any questions or suggestions that he has about the parent's child-rearing beliefs and actions.

EXAMPLE

BRENDA [divorced mom of four children]: I don't get it. I tell her that if she'll just wait I'll help her out and she doesn't. She screams, and then we have a big fight and then she never gets me to help her. Why won't she just wait?

THERAPIST: It seems simple, doesn't it, just to wait 5 minutes? And she doesn't, so things get so much more difficult for you both.

BRENDA: And it's no good for the other ones either! I don't get to spend time with them when I'm fighting with her.

THERAPIST: And everyone is upset! Wow! And this happens a lot. How do you keep going day after day? You have a hard job, then you come home and you have four kids who want your time and attention and energy and you still have a dozen other things to do.

Comment: Brenda, a single mom with four kids, obviously has a very stressful life. She asks for ideas about a behavioral problem with one of her children. While the idea might be helpful, it will entail remembering to try something new, which is also adding one more responsibility. If the therapist steps back with her and reflects on how much she is already doing—her continuous commitment to her kids—she is likely to be more ready and able to take on something new. These comments cannot be a technique that is not genuine or they will not be effective. They must be heartfelt.

BRENDA: A dozen! I wish!

THERAPIST: And yet your spirits are up most of the time! Where do you find the strength?

BRENDA: Oh, I don't know. I guess it's just that I love the kids so much. And I know that while it's hard for me, it's harder for them. They didn't ask for the divorce, to move, to cut back on getting things that they want. They have it hard too . . . and they're kids.

THERAPIST: I should have known! Your strength comes from your love of your kids. From not forgetting their sadness and disappointments and anger about it all.

BRENDA: Yeah, I guess.

THERAPIST: And I think that those kids are lucky to have you as their mom.

BRENDA: I guess that's right.

THERAPIST: I know that's right, and I hope that you don't forget it often. You are one great mom.

BRENDA: I'm not perfect.

THERAPIST: I'm not saying that! They don't need a perfect mom. They need a mom who loves them, who worries about them, who notices them, who sweats for them and cries for them and who sometimes gets angry with them when they need it—and maybe even once in awhile when they don't need it.

Comment: The therapist is able to highlight her strengths to the degree that he can easily conclude that her kids are lucky to have her. Brenda is a bit anxious with that degree of praise and wants to ensure that the therapist understands that she is not perfect. That is an important point since if she felt that she had to live up to the therapist's unrealistic expectations, then she is likely to hide real problems that she is encountering. The therapist is able to reassure her that he is aware that she makes mistakes—and that is okay. The kids are still lucky to have her.

BRENDA: I do that well!

THERAPIST: Great! Oh, yeah, you wondered why your daughter doesn't just wait when you tell her to.

BRENDA: Yeah, why doesn't she?

THERAPIST: Maybe because of what you just said about how hard it is for her too. The unhappiness that she's experienced piling up and her wanting to be happy now.

BRENDA: But sometimes I can't do it now!

THERAPIST: True! You might if you could but you can't. And you love her so much you don't want to disappoint her when you know it will be hard for her. So it gets frustrating when she insists on it being now when it is impossible for you to do it immediately.

Comment: Brenda is now able to see a connection between her empathy for her daughter over the divorce and her impatience with her daughter's urgent demands on her. The therapist relates the anger to her desire to help her daughter to be happy, although sometimes it is impossible to do. This way of explaining her anger is likely to reduce any shame she may experience over her anger.

BRENDA: So what do I do?

THERAPIST: Accept her disappointment and experience empathy for her having to wait.

BRENDA: That empathy again? Is that all you ever say?

THERAPIST: You've noticed that I fuss about that a lot, don't I? I know you feel empathy. . . . I just think that you don't have the habit of expressing it. It's not how you were raised.

BRENDA: You can say that again.

THERAPIST: And why are you so patient with me when I nag you about it?

BRENDA: 'Cause I love the kids! [Laughs.] But it better work! [Laughs louder.]

Comment: The playfulness at the end enabled the parent to express some frustration with the lack of an easy fix to the difficulty with her daughter, while still accepting the recommendation. Laughing at the end was a joint acknowledgment that Brenda had some hard work ahead—which she would do because of her love for her kids—with no guarantees.

II. THE THERAPIST EXPLORES THE PARENTS' ATTACHMENT HISTORIES

The therapist explores with the parents any unresolved themes from their own attachment histories that are being activated within their relationship with their child. This is done in as natural a manner as possible, often when there are openings while exploring the parenting history or immediately after that. If the therapist adopts a very serious tone or delays this exploration to later sessions, the parents are likely to experience this line of questioning as suggesting that the therapist is blaming them for their child's problems. Instead, the therapist wants them to experience these questions as a natural part of the initial goal to get to know the family. The message being conveyed is something like: "Since often the way we raise our kids has been influenced by how we were raised ourselves, I wonder how you recall your own upbringing. What was it like for you growing up?"

As the dialogue continues, the therapist is likely to ask about:

1. The characteristics of the parents' relationships with their parents: sense of closeness, communication patterns, conflicts, joint activities, and interests.
2. The nature of discipline.
3. The nature of relationship repair.
4. The place of comfort and support in response to stress.
5. How various emotions (anger, sadness, fear, joy, love) were expressed or not in the family.
6. The presence of separations and loss through death, divorce, moves.
7. Their parents' marriage, cultural and religious practices, and values.

Throughout this exploration, the therapist is sensitive to the possibility that the parents may experience this dialogue as finding fault with them, blaming them for their child's problems. The therapist immediately addresses their verbal or nonverbal communications to that effect and works to repair the relationship. He would do so with a comment such as:

Oh, my, I wonder if you think that I'm blaming you for the concerns that you're expressing about your child. If that's what you heard in these questions, I am very sorry as that is not my intent and I am not blaming you at all. I am simply trying to understand what kind of a family life you learned when growing up to see if there might be connections with your family life now. Sometimes we find ourselves handling things the same way that our parents did regardless of whether or not we agree with how they raised us. Often our own strengths and weaknesses as parents grew out of how we learned about being parents through being raised by our parents. But, please believe me, I am trying to understand you better, not to blame you. Just to understand some possible tendencies in your responses, your perceptions, your thoughts and feelings that you developed over the years, even before becoming parents yourselves. If I can understand your strengths and weaknesses better, I can do a better job of being helpful to you and your kids.

A. While exploring the parents' attachment histories with them, the therapist is sensitive to defensive responses associated with particular themes and relationships. Instances of denial, minimizing, forgetfulness, and emerging emotional dysregulation all need to be explored and coregulated as needed. During this exploration, the therapist is also assessing whether ongoing individual treatment is necessary for the parent and, if so, if another therapist should provide that treatment rather than the parent's treatment being a component of the family treatment. As a rule of thumb, if the therapist believes that extensive treatment will be necessary, then the parent, or couple, should be referred to another therapist.

EXAMPLE 1

THERAPIST [for the past 10 minutes he has been exploring with John, the father of 13-year-old Nathan, the intense conflicts that he and his son have]: John, do these conflicts with Nathan remind you of anything from your relationship with your dad?

JOHN: This has nothing to do with me and my dad! It has to do with my son not acting in a more responsible manner.

THERAPIST: Wait a second, John! Do you think that I'm blaming you for these problems that you and Nathan are having?

JOHN: Of course you are! Otherwise you wouldn't be asking me about me and my dad.

THERAPIST: I'm sorry that I gave you that impression. I should have made clear my reasons for bringing up your relationship with your dad right then. Sorry I didn't.

Comment: The intensity of John's immediate response suggests that he experiences blame if the therapist asks him about his relationship with his father. That experience—that he is being blamed—needs to be addressed with empathy, and with the therapist apologizing if he said anything that might have suggested that he was blaming John for the conflicts with his son. The repair of such relationship breaks is always a top priority before continuing with A-R dialogue.

JOHN: Then why are you interested if it's not to blame me?

THERAPIST: Thanks for asking, John, because I have no intention to blame you. As I mentioned when we first met, I ask parents about their childhood because I want to understand the strengths and weaknesses of their family life growing up. All families are strong in certain areas and not so strong in other areas. If your son's behaviors touch on some of the struggles that you had with your dad, those old experiences will make it harder for you to respond to him than if he touches some of the strong areas of your childhood.

JOHN: It still sounds close to blaming me.

THERAPIST: John, I know that you're a good parent. Just being here, talking with me about this stuff is certainly one sign of that. I'm simply trying to understand if your son's challenging behaviors touch on any challenges that you had with your dad growing up. For example, was there much anger between you and your dad? If you two disagreed about something when you were a young adolescent, were you able to work it out easily or was it hard for you two? If anger was hard to handle between you and your dad, then it is likely to be hard for you to handle with your son.

Comment: John's question suggests that he is at least partially open to hearing the therapist's reason, which the therapist then gives. John is still not sold on the reason and the therapist first openly states his experience of John's strength and then asks a question about John's childhood to see if John will follow. This implies that the therapist is confident that now that John knows the reasons for the exploration, he is likely to be willing to do it. Such an assumption needs to be tested by John's response to the therapist's reasons. If John refuses, then the therapist follows his refusal by returning to his concerns with further acceptance, curiosity, and empathy for his refusal.

JOHN: I never fought with my dad! That's the difference between me and Nathan. I respected my father.

THERAPIST: What would your dad have done if you did argue with him when you were 13?

JOHN: I never did.

THERAPIST: How about when you were younger? When was one time when your dad got angry with you?

Comment: Often a parent indicates that they never had a certain childhood problem with their parent because they never engaged in the particular behavior. The therapist then simply has to go back further in time and ask about something that would be hard to deny and easier to acknowledge.

JOHN: Once, when I was about 8 . . . I got mad at Mom for not letting me play with my friends. I yelled at her . . . and he came running in from the other room, screaming at me, and slapped me hard and took me to my room. I spent the rest of the day there.

THERAPIST: That must have been a real hard thing to go through.

JOHN: But I never yelled at my mom again!

THERAPIST: And maybe never really got much practice in dealing with your anger. Thinking that anger itself was not okay. Not much practice in dealing with disagreements in the family without hurting the relationship.

Comment: The parent often expresses the positive about a difficult event. This serves to not criticize his parent and may also reflect how he has managed to integrate that event into a coherent narrative. The therapist needs to be cautious about questioning the positive slant on the event (e.g., "I never yelled at my mom again!") but can introduce some negative side effects of that event. Here, John then minimizes the side effects.

JOHN: My relationship with my father was fine. I just never disagreed with him.

THERAPIST: So there were some limits on what you could share with him. Probably made it hard to relax with him—in case he discovered something about you that he did not approve of. You might have respected him but had a harder time feeling close to him.

JOHN: My dad doesn't get close to anyone.

THERAPIST: Do you want to have a closer relationship with your son than you and your dad had?

JOHN: Yes, I really would.

THERAPIST: Then I think that you two have to learn how to disagree, how to handle angry feelings, how to get close after an argument. And all of those might be a bit of a challenge for you because your dad really didn't teach you those skills very well.

JOHN: I guess you're right. But I do my best.

THERAPIST: Yes, you certainly do. Just talking about this hard stuff with your dad shows how hard you are trying to be a good dad for your son.

Comment: If the therapist respects the parent's narrative about the positive qualities in his relationships with his parents, the parent is often able to acknowledge that he wishes he could have shared more with his parents (when he did not do so) and that he wants a closer relationship with his own child than he had with his parents. It is often easier to wish for a closer relationship with one's parent than it is to criticize that parent for being critical, distant, nonaffectionate, and so on.

EXAMPLE 2

CATHY [mom who has a 12-year-old daughter, Jenny]: Sometimes, I just want to scream, "Talk to me!" She completely shuts me out!

THERAPIST: What is the hardest about that for you?

CATHY: Wouldn't that bother you if someone in your family went days without hardly saying a word to you?

THERAPIST: Oh, my, I think that you think that I believe that it shouldn't bother you. I wasn't saying that at all! I'm sorry. I just want to know what about that makes it so hard for you.

CATHY: It's like I'm not important at all! Like I don't matter to her! I often felt that with my own mother and I swore I would never be in a relationship like that again.

Comment: Often when the therapist asks a parent what makes something hard for her, the parent assumes that the therapist is saying that it should not be hard. The parent assumes that the therapist thinks that the parent is overreacting. The therapist simply saying that she is sorry if the parent received that impression from something that she said often leads to much further exploration about why the parent thinks that her response is that intense. Often it is a short step to making a connection with the parent's own childhood.

THERAPIST: Ah, so it was like that with your mom.

CATHY: Yeah! Sometimes, I swear that she would ignore me for days or even weeks if there was one thing that I did that she didn't like. And often she wouldn't even tell me what it was!

THERAPIST: So you knew that she was angry with you about something, but she wouldn't tell you what it was. And there was no way you could find out. And you didn't know how long it would last before she talked to you again.

CATHY: No! Since she wouldn't talk to me, she never told me anything about what was going on and how long it would last. I was invisible! And there was nothing that I could do about it.

THERAPIST: And now when your daughter . . .

CATHY [interrupting]: My mother was just so mean! Once I just started crying and begging her to talk to me and she just walked out of the room. Another time I grabbed her hand and she froze and stared at me like she hated my existence until I took my hand away, and then she turned her back on me.

Comment: The therapist began to make a connection between what happened involving Cathy's mother and her relationship now with her daughter, but it was premature as Cathy now had a strong desire to tell more of the story with her mother.

THERAPIST: Oh, Cathy, how very, very painful that must have been for you . . . and still is!

CATHY: It's hard for me to think about. If I do I just hate her again! I hate her!

THERAPIST: So the memories bring it all back . . . the pain . . . and your hatred for what she did to you.

CATHY: And when Jenny doesn't talk to me . . . I almost feel the same hate come over me! I almost hate her! And I don't want to. I don't want to!

THERAPIST: You so much want a close relationship with Jenny . . . where you talk, and share . . . something that you never had with your mother . . . and when Jenny ignores you . . .

CATHY: It's like it's happening again! And I don't want that, but I don't know what to do about it!

Comment: Cathy's intense distress and her feeling that her relationship with her daughter is very similar to her relationship with her mother in many ways shows how much her past attachment history is active in her current relationship. The therapist helps Cathy to describe these connections and express her hopelessness, while looking for an opportunity to help

Cathy to begin to become aware of an important difference between the past and the present. The therapist cannot contradict Cathy's assumptions that things are hopeless, but by finding one difference the therapist may create a path through the sense of hopelessness.

THERAPIST: You couldn't stop your mother from ignoring you . . .

CATHY: And now I can't stop Jenny!

THERAPIST: Did you once think that you deserved your mother's treatment of you?

CATHY: What else could I think? I always felt that I just was not the daughter that she wanted.

THERAPIST: And now with Jenny . . .

CATHY: That I'm not the mom that she wanted. I'll never get it right! I can't be a daughter and I can't be a mother.

THERAPIST: Oh, Cathy! How hard this must be for you! I knew how much you've wanted to have a close relationship with your daughter . . . and now I understand better how much you want that.

CATHY: And she doesn't want it! She doesn't want me! Just like my mother!

THERAPIST: And if I say that I think that there's a big difference?

CATHY: What?

THERAPIST: You're the mother! You are not powerless like you were with your mother. You're trying and your mother did not. You can work with me to make sense of what's going on with Jenny and with you and Jenny and you can try new things, approach things differently. You have power now, Cathy!

CATHY: I can't make her talk to me!

THERAPIST: You're right! So we have to find a better goal. What you can do is work with me to make sense of why she doesn't talk and what we can do about it . . . what we can do in therapy and at home to make it more likely that she'll choose to talk with you again.

CATHY: How do you make sense of it?

THERAPIST: I know that you are not the mother to her that your mother was to you. I have no doubts about that. I also know that part of your daughter wants to be closer to you. . . . She just does not know how at times.

CATHY: Why—since I want to be close to her and if you're right that sometimes she wants to be close to me . . .

THERAPIST: What gets in the way? I wonder if part of it is how much you want to be close. And how little practice you got when you were growing up, about how to have an argument, a conflict, deal with it, and get back together again. I think that it's hard for you to repair the relationship after a break—because your mother never did—and your daughter isn't able to do it if you don't know how—and you start drifting apart even though much of the time neither one wants to.

CATHY: If that's all it is, then I'm going to learn.

THERAPIST: And you will. Because you want a good relationship with her and you know that a teenage girl gets so much out of a good relationship with her mother—something that you never had . . . that you'll learn how no matter how hard it is.

CATHY: Is it going to be that hard?

THERAPIST: It might be hard—like today's session is hard—but it might not take a long time because you want to get this right so badly. I don't see you slowing down anytime soon.

CATHY: No, I'm not going to slow down. You better not either! [Smiles.]

Comment: In pointing out a major difference between the past and the present, the therapist is able to help Cathy to see that there might then be hope, if they can just find a new way to approach the problem. As is often the case, if the therapist is able to help the parent look in the opposite direction, the solution often emerges. In this case, rather than search for how to improve closeness, the therapist suggested that they might address conflict—to learn how to have conflicts in a way that leads to relationship repair.

B. As parents explore stressful themes from their own histories, the therapist assists them in seeing how those themes are being activated by their interactions with their child and having an—often negative—influence on the interactions.

EXAMPLE

THERAPIST [to Steve, father of two boys and a girl, ages 9–16]: Steve, I'm not sure what you're thinking now. You seemed to be puzzled over what I said about how your relationships with your parents—and maybe your dad especially—might be affecting your relationships with your kids now.

STEVE: I'm not like my dad! I've worked hard to really be there for my kids.

THERAPIST: I am sorry, Steve, if you heard me say that you are like your dad. I truly am sorry. I meant nothing like that. I see you as being a committed and competent dad in so many ways.

STEVE: What do you mean then, about how my father is still in me and making it harder to to be the dad that I want to be?

THERAPIST: What I meant, Steve, is that he was your first model about how to be a father. And you've decided that you want to be a different kind of father.

STEVE: That's very true.

THERAPIST: And because of your dad, you probably still have some blank spots. He so often did not notice things about you that you needed him to notice that at times it might not occur to you that your kid is doing something and could use your help, or your ear, or an idea, or a nod of your head. Your dad did none of those and at times you might just not notice.

STEVE: I hate thinking that. I want to be the dad that I never had. I want it so much that I can taste it! And you're saying that because of him—still—I might not be able to do it.

Comment: Steve is defensive about the possibility that he has some of his father's parenting traits because he wants so much to be a different father to his kids than his father was to him. For Steve, it is all-or-nothing thinking. In rejecting ways in which his father might still be influencing him, he will be unwilling and unable to reduce that influence. The therapist's goal is to help him to see and accept the presence of those influences so that he can then explore more successfully ways to change them. Steve also has the unrealistic view that if he does not get it right with his kids every time, he is hurting them. The therapist addresses that belief too, again working to help Steve to accept himself as a parent so that he then can improve in realistic ways.

THERAPIST: I'm saying that you want to do it 100% right. I'm saying that most dads who had great dads themselves might do it 80% right. You, because of your dad, might do it 70% right.

STEVE: But my kids need more than that.

THERAPIST: That's where we might differ, Steve. No parent can get it right all the time. And that's okay. Kids need to know that their parents will get the big things right, and will try to take care of most of the small stuff. And if they don't always get it right, that's okay. Even better than okay, in a way, because the kids then develop more of their own skills to take care of the stuff you don't get right.

STEVE: Then why do I feel so crappy when I don't get it right? If the kids will still be okay?

THERAPIST: I think, for a couple of reasons. First, you don't have confidence that the kids will be okay. Also, I think that you are terrified that if you don't respond well in a certain situation that your kids will see you the same way that you saw your dad.

STEVE: I just want to be able to say good-bye to my past and be confident that I am getting it right.

THERAPIST: And we will say good-bye as soon as we have confidence that it doesn't affect you in any significant ways anymore. And we're getting there.

STEVE: What do we still have to do? What am I missing?

THERAPIST: Again, Steve, I want to say that you get the big stuff real well. Things that I'd like to focus on are like an interaction that you had with Seth last session. Seth mentioned that he really liked working on his model planes by himself and you suggested that he could get it done better and faster if he let you help him.

STEVE: That was to show how much I want to do things with him.

THERAPIST: Yes, though at the same time saying that you had a better idea than his. I noticed that he seemed disappointed but felt that he did not want to hurt your feelings by saying that he'd rather work on it alone.

STEVE: Did he?

THERAPIST: That was my sense . . . from the way that he got quiet and more subdued.

STEVE: I missed that.

THERAPIST: That's what I'm getting at. You want so much to show the kids how important that they are to you that you might miss the times that they might want to do independent things. I thought that in this case it might also reflect how you said that your father always used to tell you what you should feel and think. That what he thought was better than what you thought.

STEVE: Do you think that I did that?

THERAPIST: Not nearly to the degree that your dad did. But I think that when you want something so much—like doing things with your kids and showing them your love—you might just not notice that they want something different from what you want so much.

STEVE: So what's the take-home message from this?

THERAPIST: I think, Steve, that when the kids see that you recognize and value what they think and feel and want, even if they want more independence from you, then they will feel closer to you because they will see how much you notice what they want and that you value what they want, in part because they want it.

STEVE: So it's more than doing things with them. It's seeing them as individuals, apart from me, and celebrating who they are. You're right, I never had that experience from my father and I don't think I've seen before how important that would be for them and was for me. I always wanted more time with my dad because I seldom got it. When my kids don't want more time with me, I've been thinking I've been doing something wrong, when actually, I guess, I've been doing something right—they have so much time with me they now also want some independent time. Wow!

Comment: When parents strive very hard to be better parents than they had, they often overlook that accepting and encouraging their child's independent strivings is what the child sometimes needs the most from them. The parents are at times threatened by this, fearing that their child does not want to be close to them. The therapist focuses on the importance of the balance between emotional intimacy and autonomy. Not having emotional intimacy with their parents, they often focus on that almost exclusively and do not notice what they can do to promote autonomy, namely accepting and enjoying the child's emerging self-reliance as well.

III. THE THERAPIST IS AWARE THAT PARENTING IS HARD

The therapist is aware of how hard it often is being a parent who serves as a source of attachment security for her child. The therapist communicates this with PACE. As the parent experiences the therapist's empathy regarding the stress of parenting, the parent is also more likely to experience the therapist's hope for the future and confidence in the parent's ability and commitment to provide good care for her child.

Parenting is a complex psychobiological activity that involves the integrated activity of five neurological systems in the brain (Baylin & Hughes, 2010). Caregiving behaviors require the activation of these five systems, which involve approach behaviors, reward experiences, child-reading skills, meaning making including the attachment narrative, and executive functioning. In an unpublished article, Baylin and Hughes introduced the concept of blocked care to refer to the psychobiological process whereby caregiving behaviors are shut down on either a chronic or acute basis. Blocked care may be chronic when the parent had very poor care as a child. It may be acute when the parent is experiencing intense current stress such as divorce, unemployment, illness, or other losses. Blocked care may also apply to the parent's ability to care for all of her children or it may be specific to only one child. It may be specific to one child if that child activates unresolved issues from the parent's own childhood while the parent's other children do not. Or it may be specific to one child if that child has difficulty engaging in attachment behaviors toward the parent due to prior abuse or neglect or if the child has a specific disorder such as autism.

Concepts such as blocked care make it easier for the therapist to experience empathy for the parent who may be facing extreme challenges from the past or present in attempting to raise her child. The parent may be very motivated to be the best parent possible, but the complex psychobiological systems required to parent well may simply have difficulty functioning adequately. Extended, quality parenting requires high degrees of engagement across all systems. Thinking that the parent simply must try harder is not helpful to the parent or her child.

A concept such as blocked care is also likely to help parents to have greater empathy for themselves. Parents who make frequent parenting mistakes often are their own worst critics. They are very vulnerable to shame. When they become aware that their heart is not engaged in the parenting process to the degree that it once was, their shame is likely to become greater. When parents understand that it takes more than willpower to parent well over an extended period of time, they are likely to have greater patience with their mistakes and discouragement. Knowing that complex psychobiological systems are in play and that the activity of these systems is necessary for good caregiving behavior, they are likely to have greater empathy for themselves at those times when they cannot find the energy to parent well.

IV. THE THERAPIST ASSISTS THE PARENTS IN LEARNING A-R DIALOGUE, PACE, AND THE THERAPEUTIC INTENTION PRIOR TO JOINT SESSIONS

Once the parents have established a sense of safety with the therapist, in part from exploring their parenting and attachment histories with him, then the therapist is ready to present to the parents how AFFT works. He will make explicit now what he had been demonstrating in the A-R dialogue that he had with them as well as in the attitude of PACE that he held with them.

A. The therapist differentiates communications about experience, which is the focus of treatment, from communicating about behaviors and problem solving. The therapeutic intersubjective stance is committed to the safe sharing of experience much more than the description of facts or arguing over what really happened. In most social-emotional realities, the primary reality is subjective and experiential, not objective. Conflicts occur when the parent and child or two partners have different experiences of an event and they quickly assume the stance that if one is right, the other must be wrong. As a result, each tries to convince the other that the other's experience is wrong by presenting his or her own experience as if it were an objective reality. Not only does that devalue the other's experience, it prevents the other from being able to describe the experience in any depth or detail, which causes each never to truly understand the other's experience and why he had that experience.

Often the parents or the child want to focus on the event itself and try to determine what was true or right. Such a focus tends to overlook or dismiss the experience of the event, or to assume that there is no difference between the experience and the event itself. The child may attempt to give his experience of the event, for example, "You were so mad that I was scared that you were going to make me go to bed without dinner!" The parent may respond that such an experience was wrong or exaggerated or a lie, for example, "How could you say that? You know I'd never do that! You just want the therapist to feel sorry for you."

In the intersubjective stance, the therapist consistently experiences the family members' experiences with acceptance, curiosity, and empathy (and sometimes with playfulness). The therapist also works to ensure that the family members begin to respond to each other in the same manner. By so doing, the family members are more able and willing to share their experiences with the other family members and the therapist. Family members begin to know each other more deeply, have greater empathy for their experiences, are less threatened if the other's experience is different from their own, and begin to influence each other, not through power or consequences, but more from understanding and reciprocal compassion.

The intersubjective stance is a radical shift from common communications and arguments whose function is to change the other's thoughts, feelings, and behaviors. The following is an example of how this stance would work in early therapeutic sessions, trying to shift family members into participating in the intersubjective manner of knowing, relating with, and influencing each other. This might be typical of early dialogues in the treatment of some families.

EXAMPLE

ABE [dad]: We had a big argument two nights ago. Jackie got a poor grade in her history class and we told her that she would not be having the car until she brought the grade up.

JACKIE [age 16]: That is so unfair! One lousy grade and now they think I'm going to be a dropout!

ABE: We didn't say that! We just reminded you of the rules that we set up when you got your license last year. And if I remember right, you agreed to them.

JACKIE: But that's just one grade. And there are reasons! All my other grades are fine.

ABE: You know the rules!

THERAPIST: Thanks, guys, I have a thumbnail sketch now of the argument, so why don't we start making sense of it?

Comment: The therapist implies quickly that there is little value in restating the details of the argument without an open, intersubjective stance to each other's experience.

ABE: There is nothing to make sense of except why she feels entitled to be outraged when she got the bad grade and now doesn't want to accept the consequence.

THERAPIST: Okay, Abe, let's start with your daughter's anger at losing the car. But if I ask her to help us to understand it, you're going to have to listen and not argue about what she tells us.

ABE: Okay, but it won't change my mind!

Comment: When Abe says that nothing his daughter can say will change his mind, he essentially is saying that he will not engage intersubjectively, which requires a reciprocal openness to the other. The therapist then develops an intersubjective dialogue with Abe and his experience—his decision to not be open to his daughter's experience.

THERAPIST: Because . . .

ABE: A rule's a rule.

THERAPIST: Sounds like I have to make sense of your strong belief that there are no exceptions to the rule that a poor grade means no car. Why no exceptions?

ABE: That's all we need! A little anger and I cave in. Is that what you're suggesting?

THERAPIST: I'm sorry if I gave you that impression. No, I wasn't suggesting that at all. I was just wondering if there might ever be a reason why you would change the no-car rule because of a poor grade.

ABE: I can't think of one.

THERAPIST: Suppose Jackie had a teacher who had been very unfair to her. Suppose she made an honest mistake about the day of a big test and had not studied for it.

ABE: She didn't tell me either of those.

THERAPIST: So there might be possible reasons. I wonder if the anger between the two of you prevented you both from ever getting to Jackie's experience about the situation and really understanding it.

ABE: She got angry first!

THERAPIST: Let's set that aside for now. Abe, what do you worry might happen if you allowed Jackie to drive the car if her experience of the poor grade made some sense to you?

ABE: She probably wouldn't believe that I stick to what I say. I'd lose my authority.

THERAPIST: I see. Now it makes sense why it would have to be a really exceptional reason to change that rule. You fear losing your authority as a parent. You fear that Jackie might lose her respect for you. Maybe even that you would lose all influence that you might have over her.

ABE: She'd think that I'm easy. And she'd start to try to get away with more and more.

JACKIE: That is so unfair! What have I ever done that was trying to get away with more and more?

THERAPIST: Slow down, Jackie. Right now I need to understand your dad's experience. Sounds like yours is different, but I need to understand his first.

Comment: The therapist is making it clear that the experience of each family member is important and needs to be fully understood before exploring another family member's different experience. If Abe's experience is that he thinks that his daughter would "try to get away with more and more," then his reasons for that thought need to be understood. That experience is not wrong. Whether or not his daughter would do what he thinks she might do is not the point at all. Later, her experience associated with his thoughts about her may need to be explored and understood, but to do so now would be premature and not productive. It would just move the argument to a larger stage.

JACKIE: But I've never tried to spend my life getting away with stuff!

THERAPIST: I hear you, but I have to ask you to hold it for now. I need to understand your dad now and I'm not there yet. Also, if you can delay your response until you understand more about his thought, your response might be different.

JACKIE: Okay.

THERAPIST: Abe, it sounds like you believe that your authority with your daughter is based on your being consistent in enforcing the rules that you have given her.

ABE: Isn't that a reasonable assumption?

Comment: Since individuals are not used to having someone truly try to understand their experience, they often assume that such efforts are an implied criticism of that aspect of their inner life.

THERAPIST: I'm not judging that. I'm trying to understand what your assumption is.

ABE: I guess that's right.

THERAPIST: And if you lose your authority, Jackie might start making decisions that would really place her at risk or interfere with her future?

ABE: I'm not saying that. She is responsible. It's just something that might come up in the future.

Comment: When the therapist accepts and explores Abe's comment that his daughter would "try to get away with more and more," Abe corrects himself by saying that she is responsible, implying that she would not do that.

THERAPIST: When she might need your guidance.

ABE: Yeah, and she would need to trust my word.

THERAPIST: Do you worry that your daughter will not value your word, value your opinion?

ABE: If I give in because she gets upset, that might happen.

THERAPIST: And what would that be like for you if your daughter someday thinks less of you, less of your judgment and guidance?

ABE: I wouldn't like it.

THERAPIST: Because . . .

ABE: I'm her dad. And that's not going to stop when she's 18. I want her to always be able to come to me.

THERAPIST: And that would break your heart if your daughter, as a young adult, had no confidence in you, did not rely on you for anything.

ABE: Yes, it would.

THERAPIST: Because . . .

ABE: Because she's my daughter and always will be. And I'll always love her and hope that she loves me.

THERAPIST: So we're talking about a lot more than a grade and the use of a car. You seem to experience this conflict as a test of whether or not you will be able to have an important relationship with your daughter for years to come. And you really, really want such a relationship.

Comment: The therapist is able to bring out that the specific conflict relates to a much larger issue. This is often the case, but the family members are often not aware of the larger issues, or if they are aware of them, they remain unspoken.

ABE: Yes, I do.

THERAPIST: I hear you, Abe. And I can tell how much Jackie means to you by the way you talk and the way you struggle with this important theme. She is so important to you. Your relationship with her is so important to you, and you fear that you might lose it . . . or begin to lose it . . . if you let her use the car after getting that grade.

ABE: Maybe it's not that big.

Comment: Often when the therapist has been successful in making the connections between the conflict and underlying factors, the family members start to think that the issues that seemed so important just a few minutes before may actually be not that important.

THERAPIST: But it might be and you don't want to take the chance.

ABE: I guess that's right.

THERAPIST: I wonder if you would just listen to Jackie's experience now, like I think she just heard yours—and seemed to be touched by it—if you would really listen to her experience of this, and allow yourself just to be open to what it means to her, to you, and to your relationship, now and in the future. Just listen and understand. After that you might be in a better position to know what might be best for her and for your authority, and for your relationship with her in the future. I don't know where it will lead and I won't tell you what is right, since there is no right. I think if you know your daughter's experience, the best course to take will be obvious for you. If you don't know it, then I think that your decision is based more on your doubts and fears about losing authority, but not on a conviction that you will.

ABE: Okay. I get that. I'll listen with an open mind.

JACKIE: That's not necessary, Dad. I didn't know how much that meant to you. It's okay. I'll bring up my grade and then I'll get the car.

Comment: Jackie's comment, while seeming to come out of the blue, is actually not that uncommon when a family member truly listens to—and experiences—the other's experience intersubjectively. If the experience is met with acceptance, curiosity, and empathy, then the issue about which there was a conflict tends to be less important to both.

THERAPIST: Slow down, Jackie! I'm saying that a lot to you, aren't I? Where did that come from?

JACKIE: I don't want my dad to doubt how important he is to me. Of course he's important. He and Mom are the most important people in the world to me. I want him to know that, and that's more important to me than driving the car.

ABE: Honey, you can have the car.

JACKIE: Dad, I don't want the car.

THERAPIST: Both of you, cut it out! I'm getting all mixed up here. This stuff about how accepting and understanding each other's experience will bring closeness and cut down on conflicts is not supposed to work this fast. Jackie, you haven't even told your experience yet.

ABE: I don't have to hear it. What she just said makes me know that she's not going to try to get away with things. That was a nutty thing to even think!

THERAPIST: Where did it come from?

ABE: My dad, I guess.

THERAPIST: You think?

ABE: Yeah. It certainly didn't come from Jackie. She's never done anything like that before, just like she said, and I can understand why she'd be mad at me for not knowing that. And whatever the reason, the grade was a fluke. I know that if she keeps the car that grade will still go up. I know Jackie.

THERAPIST: A special person to you.

ABE: She and her mom are the most special people in my life.

JACKIE: You too, Dad. And you'll always be important to me. More than any car.

THERAPIST: More than a Porsche?

JACKIE: Well . . .

Comment: This example demonstrates the need to slow down family members' habit of reacting to the other's experience before they know what the experience is. If they are able to delay such reactions—defensive responses to assumptions about the other's experience—and simply join the other's experience with acceptance, curiosity, and empathy, their subsequent response is likely to be very different. This relates to the fact that our assumptions often change when we truly know the other's experience. Possibly more importantly, the other's experience is likely to change through joining someone in an experience intersubjectively. His accepting, curious, and empathic presence is likely to help the family member to reexperience an event, often with changed assumptions himself.

Family stress and relationship breaks are often based on the difficulty that the family members have with accepting that each other's experience may well be different and that no experience is right or wrong. If parents restrict their evaluations and limits to behaviors, not experiences, many family problems would become easier to resolve and communication within the family would be much richer. Since this is at the core of A-R dialogue, the therapist is quite explicit about this process before beginning joint sessions. Then when the therapist leads the discussions about experiences with PACE, and discourages the evaluation of experiences, the parents are likely to be more receptive to interventions.

B. From the onset, the therapist demonstrates the reciprocal nature of A-R dialogue. Monologues—including venting and lectures—are interrupted with PACE. The therapist presents this process to the parent prior to the onset of the joint sessions. Many parents will see the value in such an approach and be receptive to the therapist interrupting them when they begin to lecture the child during a joint session. Other parents may intellectually understand but resist implementing the practice out of fear of loss of control, being seen as being permissive, etc. Such factors, when intense, most likely relate to an unintegrated feature of the parent's own attachment history.

EXAMPLE

THERAPIST [to Jake, the father]: So, at some point in the discussion Rob might say something like, "Dad, I really don't like Stan [his younger brother]!" At that point it would be great if you responded with PACE.

JAKE: What I'd rather do is tell him that he shouldn't feel that way toward Stan.

THERAPIST: Thanks for letting me know now. What makes you want to say that to Rob?

JAKE: Well, he is 11 now and his brother is only 7. I mean, it would be nice if he started to take on a little more responsibility.

THERAPIST: And how is his telling you that he does not like his brother making him less responsible?

JAKE: Well, he needs to just accept that he has to look out for his brother more. He's old enough now to help his brother out sometimes. If he could accept that, then he wouldn't be saying that he doesn't like him.

Comment: Jake's argument reflects a common assumption by parents that if they can control how a child thinks and feels about something, then they can be confident that they will get the behavior that they want from the child. This assumption often is just the opposite of what actually happens. When the child becomes aware that the parent is trying to control his thoughts, emotions, or wishes, the child often resists such control and resists doing the behaviors that the parents want. Children are actually more likely to accept parents' behavioral expectations when parents do not evaluate and try to control their inner life. If the therapist does not inform Jake about the need for PACE in exploring the conflict, Jake is very likely to give his son a lecture about the problem, telling him what he should think, feel, and do regarding his younger brother.

THERAPIST: I wonder if I could separate his behavior—looking out for his brother more—and his experience of not liking him. You think that the two are connected and I'm suggesting that they're not, or at least not in the way that you're suggesting.

JAKE: I don't see how Rob's not liking Stan is going to make him want to help him out more.

THERAPIST: Good point, and if you're right—that it won't—then I can certainly see how you would think that responding with PACE is not going to be helpful.

JAKE: So why are you recommending it?

THERAPIST: Because in this example I didn't say that Rob truly did not like his brother. I said that he told you that he did not like his brother. The two may be totally different. Also, if he knows that you accept him regardless of what he thinks of his brother, he may well like his brother more.

JAKE: How do you mean?

THERAPIST: We don't know why he said that to you. Let's assume that you accepted his telling you that—and you were curious about why he said it, and you said something like, "Gee, Rob, I wasn't aware that you felt that way. Thanks for telling me. Help me to understand it better. How come you don't like Stan now?" Then he might say, "Because it seems like I have to do all the hard stuff and he doesn't have to do anything." Or "Because you always want to do things with him and you never have time for me." Then you could respond with empathy for his experience that you favor Stan over him. If that's where the conversation went, my guess is you two would be closer. And when he knows that whether or not he likes his brother will not affect his relationship with you, he might simply start liking him more.

JAKE: Do you think that he might think something like that?

THERAPIST: I don't know, Jake. That's where PACE comes in after he tells you something about an experience. We get to know him much better then, rather than his being secretive about what he is thinking or feeling or wishing. If he stops sharing his inner life with you, you won't know what's going on with your son until maybe a problem develops.

JAKE: I'm going to need some help with this.

THERAPIST: I'll be happy to give you a hand whenever you get stuck. My guess is that when you see how helpful PACE is to get your son talking with you—really talking about what's going on with him—that you'll catch on fairly quickly.

JAKE: I'd like that.

Comment: In this example, the therapist is trying to convey the value of parents always approaching their child's inner life with PACE. When the child's inner life is accepted and not evaluated, the child is likely to have much less resistance to any related behavioral expectations.

V. THE THERAPIST ASSISTS THE PARENTS IN DEVELOPING AN ATTACHMENT PERSPECTIVE

The therapist assists the parents in developing an attachment perspective that informs and guides their parenting stance. This perspective includes the utilization of PACE and A-R dialogue in their daily lives with their children in order to improve psychological safety, intersubjective exploration, and discovery, as well as the nature and quality of their parent-child communication. The therapist's discussions, modeling and coaching in this perspective, may be seen by some therapists as infantilizing the parents when, in fact, parents often report being empowered by new ways of successfully communicating with their children, addressing and repairing conflicts, and being able to facilitate greater family harmony without sacrificing autonomy.

For many parents—and therapists—an attachment perspective is a new way of understanding how parents might best raise and influence their children in meeting their developmental challenges. For a long time the primary parenting perspective has involved learning and reinforcement theory which stresses that how parents correct their children following the child's behaviors will determine whether or not those behaviors will increase or decrease. As parents begin to develop an attachment perspective, they are often likely to drift back into assumptions of rewards and consequences as representing the main way of influencing their child's development.

The following represent basic differences in understanding or emphasis between the attachment and reinforcement perspectives:

- Attachment stresses connection more than correction. Focusing on the quality of the ongoing relationship between parent and child is seen as being much more important than focusing on specific reinforcement contingencies.
- Attachment stresses the reciprocal nature of the relationship—the intersubjective nature of the attachment relationship. The parent is more able to have a positive impact on the child's sense of self and subsequent behavior when the child is able to have a positive impact on the parent.
- Intersubjective learning about oneself and the world is seen as more basic and comprehensive than is learning based on association and reinforcement.
- Attachment stresses the importance of children's need for psychological safety if they are to utilize their psychobiological abilities for comprehensive learning.
- Attachment security facilitates a child's identification with his parents, which is central to his readiness and ability to engage in behaviors that are similar to the parents' values and beliefs.
- The parents' primary intention in interacting with their child is for reciprocal enjoyment as well as sharing ideas, activities, and interests. The primary intention in the interaction is not to impact the child's future behaviors. When such reciprocity is present, the behaviors usually take care of themselves.
- While both theories stress that parents focus on specific behaviors that they want to influence or change, attachment theory stresses the importance of getting to know the child's inner life of thoughts, feelings, and wishes. The inner life is not evaluated, but rather is understood and accepted.

An attachment perspective helps parents not to take for granted the importance of the relationship between parent and child. By taking this perspective, it is much easier for parents to remember the value of PACE, A-R dialogue, relationship repair, safety, and intersubjective exploration in their efforts to raise their children.

VI. THE THERAPIST ASSISTS THE PARENTS TO DEVELOP ATTACHMENT-FOCUSED INTERVENTIONS

The therapist explores practical interventions that will bring attachment-focused parenting into the day-to-day life of the family. The psychoeducational aspect of day-to-day parenting from an attachment perspective often has a place in treatment once basic relational skills of A-R dialogue and PACE are in place.

The following represent core intervention themes for attachment-focused parenting.

A. Safety

Safety follows naturally when children are confident that their parents will always meet their needs and often satisfy their wants. The attitude of PACE and A-R dialogue generates a background sense of safety that permeates daily living. Safety is also facilitated when eight themes, listed below, are consistently in place.

When a child's behavior is becoming dysregulated or manifesting what might be called misbehavior, the first question that a parent might ask is whether the child is not feeling safe. The following might cause the child to experience less safety:

1. An environmental change, threat, or uncertainty about the future.
2. Misperception or misunderstanding of an attachment figure's behavior.
3. A parent is in distress and less available psychologically or physically.
4. Discipline at home or school has involved seclusion or relationship withdrawal.
5. Developmental changes are producing anxiety and self-doubt.
6. A recent loss due to death, divorce, moving, or a peer conflict.
7. Change in the makeup of the family.

B. Communication

Parents are both interested in and nonjudgmental about the inner life of the child. The child is encouraged to express thoughts, emotions, wishes, and intentions. The parents make clear their inner life as well. The inner lives of family members are welcomed with A-R dialogue, not evaluations, criticisms, or indifference. This facilitates their child's reflective functioning.

C. Emotional Regulation

Children are encouraged to identify, regulate, and communicate their emotional states. Such encouragement comes not from lectures, but when parents are willing and able to accept their children's negative emotions just as they accept positive emotions. Parents coregulate their children's emotional state by matching the affective expression of the children's emotions.

D. Structure

The main activities and events in a child's life have a predictable sequence. Such predictability creates a sense of safety for the child. The structure is not rigid but is able to flexibly respond to varying needs of family members and periodic changes in routine.

E. Signs of Affection

Parents frequently demonstrate their love for their children through nonverbal signs that they enjoy, take delight in, and treasure them in their lives. They communicate this through touch, eye contact, and facial expressions in their initiatives and responses to the children's initiatives. Verbal affirmations that are congruent with the nonverbal expressions are also present.

F. Comfort in Distress

Parents convey to their children and to each other that when a person is in distress, other family members comfort and soothe each other. They do not face distress alone.

G. Discipline

Discipline is directed toward children's behavior, not their inner life. Efforts are made to understand the meaning of the behavior, but the parent decides how to respond to it. Any anger is brief and the relationship is repaired shortly afterward. Forced isolation or relationship withdrawal are not part of discipline. Corrections are directed toward behavior alone, not guesses about children's motivation, thoughts, or emotions. Routine discipline with empathy tends to be much more effective than discipline with anger.

H. Praise

Praise is expressed as a spontaneous demonstration of the parents' pride in a child's behavior, not for the purpose of creating behavior change.

I. Relationship Repair

The parent is aware of the importance of initiating relationship repair following conflicts, separations, or misunderstandings. The parent communicates clearly that the relationship is more important than conflicts or other interests.

These themes are general guidelines for creating a home environment that generates attachment security. They need to be modified for children who are in foster care or who have been adopted and demonstrate significant attachment difficulties due to prior histories of abuse, neglect, or loss. They also may need to be modified if the child's attachment difficulties are due to intense distress in the current placement due to divorce, illness, or a parent's history of substance abuse or mental health problems that have affected the child. These modifications are addressed in some detail in Chapter 8.

VII. IF THE THERAPIST IS UNABLE TO FACILITATE SAFETY FOR PARENTS AND CHILD IN THE TREATMENT SESSION, AFFT IS NOT INDICATED

Since the sense of safety is the foundation of attachment, AFFT is not the treatment of choice when the therapist is unable to establish a sense of safety for the parents, who in turn are not able to ensure that their child is safe during the treatment session. The first three sections of this chapter are intended to facilitate the parents' sense of safety and the final three are intended to assist their child to also experience safety. When the therapist is not successful in attaining this initial therapeutic goal prior to the onset of joint treatment, then AFFT that involves joint sessions with parent and child is not indicated. Or if the joint sessions are initiated and then the therapist discovers that he did not establish safety as he thought he did, then the joint sessions are stopped and he returns to seeing the parents alone again.

Parents do not need to be "perfect" before starting joint sessions. Rather, the therapist needs to know:

- The parents are willing to explore the issues mentioned in the first three sections of this chapter whenever they appear to be having an effect on their relationship with their child.
- The parents are willing to work with the therapist over areas of differences.
- The parents are willing to repair their relationship with their child when they relate to him in a manner that jeopardizes his sense of safety.
- The parents are motivated to address any challenges that are impairing their ability to become secure attachment figures for their child. This includes being willing to seek therapy for themselves as individuals or as a couple if their challenges cannot be successfully addressed during the initial meetings.
- The parents have given the therapist permission to interrupt what they are saying or doing during the session if the therapist believes that their words or actions are hurting their relationship with their child. The therapist will recommend another way to relate to the child around that theme and the parents are willing to attempt that or to work with the therapist to resolve their differences.

If the therapist does not believe that the above factors are present, then he needs to see the parents alone until those issues are addressed before starting joint sessions. He might recommend individual therapy for the child if he believes that the parents' challenges are significant and they are unable or unwilling to address them in a timely manner. The therapist is willing to continue to work with the parents alone, addressing their challenges and their differences with the therapist, as long as they are willing and the therapist believes that there is hope for progress.

Some professionals may think that this attitude might be overprotective for the child. They believe that whatever the child might experience in therapy about which the therapist is concerned (angry criticisms, threats, shame-inducing comments, negating experiences) is certainly already happening at home, if not more intensely. Their goals would be to try to join such interactions in the session and introduce changes from within.

AFFT takes the position that safety is crucial for the treatment sessions to generate A-R dialogue, which is central to change. The therapy office needs to be a sanctuary for all family members, and especially for the child. At home the child has established a set of defenses that protect him from any of his parents' comments or behaviors that generate fear or shame. These defenses are adaptive when attachment security is not present. In therapy, the therapist essentially says to the child, "You are safe here. You can relax your defenses and relate openly and honestly with your parents to resolve struggles that the family is having." If the child does relax his defenses and his parents then make the same comments or do the same behaviors that they do at home that require his defenses, then there is the risk that the child will be traumatized by the therapy sessions. There is also the risk that the child will be less willing to trust his parents, to be vulnerable with them again. In these situations, individual treatment for the child is likely to be the better option.

VIII. OBSTACLES TO ESTABLISHING A SAFE ALLIANCE WITH THE PARENTS

A. **The therapist takes the child's perspective, seeing the parent as the problem.** Probable causes and means to address them:

1. a. The parents may have begun treatment with a punitive and angry attitude that made it hard for the therapist to have empathy for them.

   b. Their discipline interventions may have been harsh and authoritarian.

   c. They may be defensive and unwilling to explore their own histories.

   d. The child may have adopted a victim role and the therapist is rescuing the child.

   e. The parents may be acting in a way that the therapist believes to be emotionally, verbally, or physically abusive or neglectful.

2. a. The therapist needs to get to know and like the parents better. He might do this by trying to experience empathy for how hard it is for them to raise their child,

discover what is under their behavior, and sense their shame and why they are reluctant to explore their histories. (Deepen PACE with parents.)

b. Explore their original hopes and dreams.

c. Experience empathy for them when they were children if they were not raised well. Resistance to exploring is met with empathy and relationship repair.

d. The therapist reflects that rescuing the child is not in the child's best interest and if the impulse continues, reflect on a possible connection with the therapist's own attachment history.

e. If the therapist perceives the possibility of abuse or neglect, she needs to address it, including following mandated reporting laws. The therapist then needs to repair his relationship with the parents if possible.

f. The therapist might reflect if the parents activate something from her own attachment history. This could make it difficult to experience empathy for them, to be open to understanding them without judgment, or to address areas of differences.

B. **The therapist takes the parents' perspective, seeing the child as the problem.** Probable causes and means to address them:

1. a. The child's behaviors may be especially challenging.

   b. The child may express a sense of entitlement that is hard to experience empathy for.

   c. The child may be very resistant, critical, and not motivated in therapy.

   d. The child may be verbally abusive (swearing, name calling) to the parents in therapy.

   e. The parents may have adopted a victim role and the therapist is rescuing them.

2. a. The therapist needs to discover the meaning of the child's behaviors and experience empathy (PACE).

   b. The therapist needs to assist the child to experience and communicate vulnerability.

   c. The therapist accepts resistance, including low motivation, and explores it with PACE.

   d. The therapist considers verbal abuse as behavior that is addressed with PACE until there is agreement that it will stop. Refusal to agree is addressed with PACE.

   e. The therapist reflects that rescuing the parents is not helpful and if she still does, to reflect on a possible connection with her own attachment history.

   f. The therapist might reflect on whether the child activates something from her own attachment history. This could make it difficult to experience empathy for the child, to be open to understanding him without judgment, or to address differences with PACE.

C. **The therapist does not address the relevance of the parents' attachment histories to current family functioning.** Probable causes and means to address them:

1. a. The parents feel blamed by such an exploration.
   b. The parents become anxious when they think about their attachment history.
   c. The child is in a crisis and the parents are impatient to begin the joint sessions.
   d. The therapist does not address with firm empathy the need to explore the attachment histories.

2. a. The therapist needs to repair the relationship and present the need to do so with PACE.
   b. The therapist focuses with PACE on the history, providing brief treatment to the parents regarding their histories.
   c. The therapist expresses empathy for the crisis and the parents' wish to attend to it immediately, while remaining firm on the need to establish the treatment foundation of safety for all before proceeding—and knowing the histories is crucial to that.
   d. The therapist needs to be convinced of the vital importance of knowing the histories in order to proceed with confidence that the necessary safety for all is ensured before beginning AFFT.
   e. The therapist needs to reflect on what prevents him from ensuring that the parents' attachment histories will be addressed. He needs to explore his own attachment history if necessary.

D. **The parents participate in treatment with angry lectures or defensiveness.** Probable causes and means to address them:

1. a. The parents are not safe; they are experiencing fear or shame.
   b. The parents habitually communicate in that manner.
   c. There is an immediate crisis that they are unable to communicate with A-R dialogue.
   d. The therapist is not addressing their manner of participation.

2. a. The therapist responds to their fear or anxiety with PACE; she engages in relationship repair as needed.
   b. The therapist addresses their manner of relating with PACE and engages in relationship repair as needed. Making connections with their attachment history may be necessary.
   c. The therapist addresses this change in their participation with PACE, focusing on the recent events in their lives.
   d. The therapist reflects on not having addressed their manner of participation. She determines if this avoidance is a pattern and then corrects it, exploring her own attachment history if necessary.

E. **The parents want to avoid their own relationship conflicts and focus on their child instead.** Probable causes and means to address them:
   1. a. The parents habitually avoid their own relationship problems.
      b. The parents have ongoing intense conflicts that they have not resolved.
      c. The parents minimize the connection between their problems and their child's behaviors.
   2. a. The therapist addresses their relationship in the first session. Incongruities between what they report and their manner of relating with each other in the sessions are addressed with PACE.
      b. The therapist addresses the conflicts with PACE and indicates that they need to be addressed either before beginning joint sessions or along with them, depending upon their severity. The therapist engages in relationship repair as needed.
      c. The therapist makes clear her belief in the connections between the parents' relationship problems and the child's problems—if not the onset then at least the resolution of them. The therapist engages in relationship repair as needed.

F. **The therapist addresses any of the above but the parents refuse to look beyond their child as the source of the problems.**
   1. a. The parents have been criticized or blamed by other professionals.
      b. One or both parents have unresolved trauma that is being rigidly avoided.
      c. The parents do not sufficiently engage in reflective functioning.
      d. The parents have rigid child-rearing beliefs based on compliance.
   2. a. The therapist addresses the source of the parents' reluctance to consider their parenting, including their experiences with other professionals.
      b. The therapist is alert for signs of distress, which are addressed with PACE.
      c. The therapist explores their readiness and ability to explore their inner lives and to be curious about the inner life of their child.
      d. The therapist gently addresses whether or not there is any chance of flexibility and openness to other beliefs about child rearing.
      e. The therapist addresses their rigid resistance with PACE, with curiosity about what they fear would happen if they were to raise their child differently. He also is ready to repair their relationship frequently, to discover their strengths including their commitment to being good parents and doing what they think is best for their child, and to invite them to express their doubts about the therapist and also to explore whether they might find common ground.

G. **The parents follow the therapist's leads in the sessions but do not follow through with anything that is explored, and may even criticize the child later for what he said.**
   1. a. The parents may be concealing their lack of agreement with the therapist's approach.

b. The parents may be finding it hard to implement the therapist's approach, but are concealing the difficulty from the therapist.

c. The parents may have minimized their shame, discouragement, or anger over their child's problems.

d. The parents may not be motivated sufficiently to do the necessary work to change their own relationship patterns.

2. a. The therapist addresses the lack of follow through at home as well as their criticism of what the child says in therapy. He follows their response, seeking resolution.

b. The therapist explores with PACE their apparent lack of trust in discussing their difficulties in therapy.

c. The therapist explores their emotional response to their child's problems, including possible connections to their attachment histories.

d. The therapist explores their lack of motivation with PACE. If there is no improvement, he explores the possibility that AFFT is not an appropriate treatment for that family. The child's safety is jeopardized if the parents criticize him for speaking in therapy when the therapist has made it clear to him that he is safe to do so.

EXERCISES

Questions

1. The therapist does not have to assess the parents' functioning as attachment figures for their child prior to joint sessions because:
   A. The family treatment itself will determine that.
   B. The children are used to whatever difficulties the parents present, so there is no reason to try to avoid these difficulties during the course of treatment.
   C. In family treatment, the parents should not be seen alone.
   D. It is important to assess the parents' functioning as attachment figures prior to the beginning of joint sessions.

2. Attachment-focused family therapy practitioners believe that:
   A. Psychological safety for all participants facilitates therapeutic conversations and change.
   B. Intersubjective exploration facilitates affect regulation and cocreation of new meanings.
   C. The family setting is the only context for adequately addressing attachment-related problems.
   D. Both A and B.

3. In becoming an attachment figure for the parent, the therapist:
   A. Strives not to evaluate the parent's experience.
   B. Communicates to the parent her positive experience of him.
   C. Accepts and encourages the parent to communicate his negative experience of the therapist.
   D. All of the above.

4. In recognizing and communicating her experience of the parent's strengths, the therapist needs to be aware of the following:
   A. The parent may develop a false sense of pride.
   B. The parent may begin to conceal mistakes or problems from the therapist.
   C. The parent may not believe the therapist.
   D. Both B and C.

5. In exploring the parenting history, the therapist:
   A. Minimizes the parent's focus on the child's problems.
   B. Enables the parent to discover her vulnerability embedded in her parental doubts.
   C. Assures the parent that she has every right to be angry with her child.
   D. Convinces the parent that the problems do not lie within the child.

6. To generate safety within the parent, the therapist needs to experience the parent as:
   A. Being a good person.
   B. Doing the best that she can.
   C. Having nothing to do with the child's problems.
   D. A and B.

7. The parent's own attachment history:
   A. Only has an impact on caregiving behaviors if the parent was abused.
   B. Is the primary therapeutic issue that needs to be addressed.
   C. Needs to be explored for its relevance to the current family difficulties.
   D. Is not relevant to the family relationship patterns in the present.

8. Parents are often reluctant to explore their own attachment histories because:
   A. They experience such exploration as blaming them.
   B. Their history may be stressful to remember.
   C. They do not see its relevance to their present problems.
   D. All of the above.

9. Which of the following is not a central parenting intervention within an attachment focus?
   A. Reinforcement of good behavior.
   B. Providing a predictable daily structure.

    C. Repairing the relationship following a conflict.

    D. Accepting the child's negative emotions.

10. Acute blocked care is a term that refers to:

    A. When one parent interferes with the other parent's ability to care for the child.

    B. Difficulties in providing caregiving relating to impaired functioning of one or more of five psychobiological factors in the parent.

    C. Difficulties in providing caregiving due to current stresses in the parent's life.

    D. B and C.

Experiential Exercises

1. Reflect on your own attachment history.

    A. Are there aspects of your history that are still stressful to think about? Are there aspects that are confusing and hard to remember? What do you think makes those aspects of your history hard to reflect on?

    B. In answering A, are you aware of any impact that those aspects have on your current functioning, either in your professional life or your personal life?

    C. Do you notice any patterns in your professional life as a therapist, social worker, and so on that prove to be difficult for you? This might include working with parents, particular symptoms, particular traumas or losses, or a particular age or gender of child. Do you see any possible connection between that area of difficulty and your unique attachment history?

2. Reflect upon a particular parent or parents that you have had difficulty experiencing PACE for. List various features about that parent or your relationship with that parent that prove to be the most difficult.

    A. Are there any parts of your own attachment history that are activated?

    B. What would you be able to do to increase your acceptance, curiosity, and empathy for that parent?

3. Reflect upon whether you have difficulty addressing your concerns about parents' experience or behavior toward their children as well as their relationship with you.

    A. If you have difficulty initiating a discussion of those issues, what makes it difficult?

    B. What might you do to make it less difficult?

    C. If the parent expresses anger or disappointment about your treatment interventions, do you respond with defensiveness? If so, why? How can you reduce your defensiveness?

Answers

1. D. In family treatment the child needs to experience safety just as the parent does. If the parent is not able to serve as an attachment figure for safety during the session, then the child should not be asked to relax his defenses and allow himself to become vulnerable. Habitual defenses at home may help to protect him from harsh criticisms, but if the same criticisms occur during treatment, they may be experienced as traumatic.

2. D. C is incorrect because while the family setting might be the preferred place to address attachment-related problems, it is not the only one. Individual therapy may still be beneficial when family sessions are not possible.

3. D.

4. D.

5. B. The exploration of the parenting history often assists parents in letting go of some anger over their child's behaviors and in experiencing the vulnerability associated with not being able to resolve the problems that the child is manifesting. Often, as a result of this, parents are able to see that the problems go beyond the child, but the therapist is not working to convince the parents of this. They also may be able to see the child's strengths more, without total focus on the problems. But the therapist does not minimize the problems.

6. D. The relationship between the parent and child may well be contributing to the child's symptoms, and the therapist needs to help the parents feel safe enough to be able to explore that.

7. C.

8. D.

9. A.

10. D. Blocked care refers to impaired functioning of one or more of the psychobiological factors related to caregiving. Acute blocked care refers to the impact of current stresses on those factors.

8 Attachment-Focused Family Therapy for Foster-Adoptive Families: Dyadic Developmental Psychotherapy

Attachment-focused family therapy was initially developed for the treatment of traumatized children and youth with serious attachment problems. Often when traditional treatments were provided, little progress was evident, despite providing for their care, for an extended period of time. These children and youth were having difficulty functioning in their foster or adoptive homes as well as in group or residential treatment centers. This treatment was developed not only for these traumatized children but also for their parents and caregivers who were having difficulty facilitating their children's attachment at home. This treatment became known as dyadic developmental psychotherapy (DDP). It is based on the premise that the parent-child attachment relationship will be the central factor in the child's subsequent healthy development.

This chapter focuses on DDP, which represents the ways that AFFT is adapted to address the unique needs of foster and adoptive families, including children who have experienced abuse, neglect, and abandonment. While the elements of AFFT that are utilized for all families are present, the particular themes and challenges of this population need to be presented in detail. At the same time, themes and interventions stressed in this chapter may well be relevant to other families as well. When families have experienced significant distress over a period of time, or when the parents have attachment histories characterized by abuse or neglect, there may be definite similarities with the themes described here.

A. Before beginning to provide treatment for the child, the therapist needs to develop an alliance with the foster or adoptive (f/a) parents.

B. Given the severity and nature of the symptoms, treatment is likely to be a longer and more gradual process cycling through the various themes in more numerous, increasingly large steps.

C. Even though safety and intersubjective experience are the first goals, still the therapist will introduce stressful—minor, not major—themes in the first session.

D. The child is likely to show a pervasive need to control everything that occurs in the treatment session.

E. As the child begins to let go of control a bit and move into themes of trauma and loss, she is very likely to begin to experience associated emotions.

F. As the child begins to experience the past traumas and attachment problems as well as new attachment experiences with his f/a parents, he may show a lack of emotion.

G. The child is likely to manifest an intense, lifelong sense of shame that makes treatment very difficult for him.

H. Two general themes tend to dominate the treatment.

I. The child is very likely to mistrust the foster or adoptive parents.

J. The child is likely to maintain a strong, possibly rigid, attachment (loyalty) to his biological parents that may well make it difficult for him to develop a secure attachment with the foster or adoptive parents.

V. Intersubjective Exploration and Cocreating a Coherent Narrative

VI. Obstacles to Treatment

    A. Intense Emotional Dysregulation

    B. The Absence of an Attachment Figure

    C. The Lack of Comprehensive Services and Support

I. FOSTER AND ADOPTIVE FAMILIES

Children and teens living in foster and adoptive homes have all experienced separation and loss of their birth family. They have also typically experienced early dysfunctional parenting, including abuse, neglect, or exposure to inappropriate adult behavior. Notable for this group of young people is the lack of early intersubjective experience. They frequently enter their adoptive or foster homes unable and unwilling to enter intersubjective relationships. They do not want to discover their parents in a reciprocal relationship, which will also reveal who they are. Feeling shamed and unwanted, they are unlikely to expose themselves readily to such experience. They also do not want to use these relationships to look outward and share the world, exploring its impact on each other. Instead they focus all their attention on staying safe, using coercive or self-reliant behaviors to stay in control within their relationship with their parents. These controlling behaviors avoid intersubjective experience.

Parents who foster and adopt enter the parenting relationship with optimism and confidence. What happens when their hopes and dreams are not fulfilled? Sadly, living with a child who avoids intersubjective experience can impact negatively on the parents' own beliefs about themselves as parents. They can start to experience themselves as failing. They too start to feel unsafe in the relationship and like their child they withdraw from the intersubjective experience.

This relationship has an additional level of complexity in that the behavior of the child can activate aspects of the parent's own attachment history, especially relationships that are unresolved and poorly integrated. As part of a controlling pattern of relating, the child actively searches for these vulnerabilities; finding the right buttons to press provides a sense of predictability that leads to a fragile if temporary security. The parent's dysregulation to such triggers leads to anger, fear, and discouragement that further compromises safety for both of them. Parent and child redouble their efforts to avoid intersubjective experience.

DDP is a form of AFFT that specifically addresses these complexities. The interventions described throughout this workbook are the same interventions that are also the basis of DDP: establishing safety and intersubjective exploration, A-R dialogue, PACE, relationship repair, and working toward the parent providing attachment security for the child. DDP is a specialized form of AFFT.

There are specific reasons for applying AFFT differently to foster and adoptive families which relate to the complexity of symptoms presented, as well as relationships with birth, foster, and adoptive parents, or the lack of stable attachment figures:

1. **Complexity of symptoms.** These children and teens are likely to manifest symptoms secondary to complex or developmental trauma due to abuse, neglect, abandonment, or multiple placements. Additionally, they are likely to manifest symptoms secondary to severe attachment disruptions or violations leading to features characteristic of attachment disorganization.

2. **Relationship with birth family.** Most, if not all, of the child's symptoms had their onset prior to the child living with the current parents or caregivers. While the child is likely to continue to experience an intense and complex relationship with his original parents, these parents are very often not present and not available for relationship repair.

3. **Relationship with current foster or adoptive parents.** Many of the child's symptoms are directed at the foster or adoptive parents. This tends to create frustration and resentment, since these parents were not the source of the symptoms and may actually be providing the child with the best care that he has ever received. To add insult to injury, many foster and adoptive parents have been unfairly criticized as being the source of

the child's symptoms. Additionally, they may not have been given the information and support that they needed to be able to parent the child as well as possible. As a result, they may be reluctant to engage in treatment. Of course, some of the current problems and conflicts may relate to the nature of the current placement, including the foster/adoptive parent-child relationship. For the above reasons and others, parents and caregivers may be reluctant to acknowledge their part, though it may be small, in the child's current difficulties.

4. **Lack of stable attachment figures.** Sadly, many children in foster homes as well as group and residential centers have no attachment figures who have a stable, ongoing commitment to them. This makes it difficult for them to experience sufficient safety and motivation to resolve past traumas and work toward their psychological development. It also makes it very difficult for them to have the opportunity to develop a relationship with someone that is characterized by attachment security.

II. COMPLEX OR DEVELOPMENTAL TRAUMA OF CHILDHOOD

Complex trauma occurs when an individual has been exposed to multiple traumatic events with an impact on immediate and long-term outcomes. When complex trauma occurs through childhood with early onset within the family, is chronic and prolonged, and impacts on development, it is called developmental trauma.

When children have been abused and neglected by their parents, they are very likely to manifest a range and severity of symptoms much greater than if they experienced a simple trauma that might have been caused by an accident, dog bite, or surgery. Developmental traumas caused by a child's attachment figures, either through their own actions or through failing to protect them from the actions of others, have more comprehensive and severe consequences, including the following:

1. Attachment (e.g., distrust, isolation, poor boundaries)
2. Biological (e.g., sensorimotor, somatic, and various medical problems)
3. Affect regulation (difficulty identifying, regulating, and expressing one's emotional life)
4. Dissociation (e.g., distinct alterations in states of consciousness, impaired memory)
5. Behavioral controls (e.g., impulsive, aggressive, oppositional, compliant, reenactments, sleep, eating, substance abuse)
6. Cognition (e.g., attention, learning and language, focusing and object constancy)
7. Self-concept (e.g., negative, shameful, or poorly defined) (Cook et al., 2005).

Given the comprehensive and serious nature of these symptoms, very often DDP cannot be the sole treatment provided. While facilitating attachment security between the child and the parents may be the most crucial intervention for long-term success, other services may be crucial as well, including:

1. Psychiatric
2. Specialized educational services
3. Specialized neuropsychological or psychoeducational assessments
4. Occupational therapy, especially sensory integration
5. Speech and language services
6. Social services, especially adoption and foster care
7. Parent treatment, education, support services

A. Shame

All children experience shame, but supported by parents they learn to limit shame-inducing behaviors. Children learn what acceptable behavior is, experience guilt when they "misbehave," and develop a sense that the self is worthwhile. This early experience of shame is integrative. For children who experience developmental trauma, the experience of shame is disintegrative. Their parents do not support the regulation of shame, nor do they reestablish safety through relationship repair. Such experiences of shame repeated many times become disintegrative and the shame becomes part of the child's core identity. As the child experiences himself as shameful, never quite good enough to belong, he becomes chronically angry and controlling of others. Trapped in shame, he feels abandoned and the shame becomes toxic to him. This leads to a state of development within which the child experiences difficulty regulating emotion and thinking reflectively. He is left unable to respond flexibly or to control impulses.

Within DDP, the therapist must actively facilitate the experience of safety that is necessary if the child is to remain engaged in exploring and resolving experiences of shame. The therapist uses empathy and curiosity, accepting the child's resistance and helping him to stay engaged. As the therapist accepts and is curious about the child—including the shame of his past—without being judgmental, a new, non-shame-based meaning is cocreated. The child is helped to stop hiding from the foster or adoptive parents and to begin to trust in and elicit the care they can offer. As the child experiences the parents' empathy, curiosity, and acceptance of the full range of experiences being explored, the child is helped to take this shame-reducing therapeutic experience into his daily life.

B. Precarious Sense of Safety

When a child has been exposed to severe trauma, by his parents or with the passive acknowledgment and acceptance of the parents, she is going to have great difficulty establishing and maintaining safety. She does not turn to her current caregivers for safety. In fact, she may view her parents and therapist with suspicion since she was abused by "caregivers" and not by strangers. She is likely to be hypervigilant, hypersensitive, and hyperreactive, all of which will make it difficult for her to trust the intentions of the adults who are caring for her or providing treatment. She will have little confidence that they want what is best for her.

The therapist and parents can never take for granted that a child who experienced a pervasive lack of safety early in life is now experiencing safety just because no obviously stressful event is occurring. There may be many threats to the child's safety from moment to moment, including:

1. Misperception of the parent or therapist's intentions.
2. Routine conversation or events that have become associated with a trauma in the mind of the child.
3. Emotional variations that would be experienced as routine by others are experienced by the child as severe and lead to dysregulation.
4. What we think is a stressful theme is experienced by the child as a traumatic theme.
5. The child makes nonverbal cues that she is becoming uncomfortable. These are missed or ignored by the adults, and the child begins to feel trapped.
6. An explored event elicits shame within the child, which triggers dissociation or rage.
7. The child experiences therapy as an effort to fix her so that she can stay in the placement. Her shame makes it very difficult to address her challenges.
8. Due to the pervasive nature of her symptoms, the therapy begins to focus only on the symptoms, leading to anxiety, hopelessness, and greater shame. The person of the child is lost and she becomes a victim, a problem, or damaged goods.

C. Reestablishing Safety

The therapist needs to continuously monitor whether the child's verbal and nonverbal communications reflect safety or its absence. When the child may not be experiencing safety, the therapist needs to:

1. Accept and acknowledge the child's distress with PACE.
2. Change the focus to a less threatening theme.
3. Take a break by talking with the parents for a time with no expectation on the child to respond or participate if he would rather not.
4. Engage in some joint activities that will help the child regulate his affective state.
5. Before exploring that theme again, develop a safety plan with the child to ensure his safety while he is exploring the trauma. This will include communication and attachment as well as cognitive (imagination, visualization, maintaining specific thoughts) and behavioral (exercises, movement, activities) strategies.

Some therapists and parents fear that if the child shows distress and the therapist then moves away from the topic, the child is likely to learn to manipulate the adults by pretending that his distress is greater than it is. The temptation is then to expect the child to work harder or the therapist becomes frustrated with his lack of motivation. It is best to err on the side of assuming the need for safety rather than that he is manipulating to avoid a difficult theme. It is also important to remember that often a child who does not trust adults will use manipulation as a survival skill. He may well be manipulating because he does not feel safe in the first place. By ensuring greater safety, there may well be less perceived need for manipulation. If the therapist does believe that the child is now habitually avoiding any difficult theme by manipulating, then it is likely to be more productive to gently address that tendency with PACE rather than confronting it with frustration, disappointment, or annoyance.

Other therapists believe that since the client is a traumatized child, it is crucial to give the child total control of the session by assuming a strongly nondirective stance. That stance, while providing an experience of immediate safety, is not likely to generalize to the child's experiencing safety throughout his life. His habitual avoidance patterns of anything that might be stressful or that might remind him of something in the past greatly constricts the options in his life. He becomes less and less confident that he can manage stress and more and more vigilant about anything new or out of the ordinary in his environment. This child will never be safe because he is terrified by his inner life—by the perceptions, emotions, thoughts, and memories that exist within his own mind—and which could be activated by numerous things throughout the day.

It is the middle way between being directive and nondirective where the therapist must take a stand with traumatized children. This stance is known as follow-lead-follow. The therapist follows the child's initiatives—which are based on the child's interests and immediate focus of attention—and then the therapist gently but clearly directs the child to attend to stressful themes—beginning with the smaller stresses—and then follows the response of the child to the therapist's initiative. Throughout the dialogue there is no frustration, no "should," no insistence that the child maintain the dialogue. If the child is not able to directly focus on the traumatic memories then the therapist meanders forward, slowly, moving toward the avoided themes, approaching them from other directions, accepting the child's need to set the pace and decide the best way to take the next step. With each cycle, the child is likely to experience some increased safety, with the process as well as with the content that he has been so strongly avoiding.

III. DISORGANIZED ATTACHMENT PATTERNS OF CHILDHOOD

When a child is traumatized by her parents or not protected by them when she is in distress, her biological tendencies to turn to her parents for safety become disorganized.

Innate behavioral patterns that involve seeking attention and response from the parents to ensure safety tend to become unpredictable, inhibited, or dysregulated and dysfunctional. These children do not develop—through reliance on their parents' regulation, anticipation, and coping skills—their own self-regulation, planning, or organized responses to stressful events.

As a result, routine stress often becomes unmanageable and major stress becomes completely overwhelming. The children become very dysregulated in their cognition (attention and focusing difficulties), emotion (extreme or labile emotional reactions or the absence of such in dissociative features), and behavior (hyperactivity, impulsivity, explosiveness). They are at risk for problems of externalization and internalization. Given that self-blame is the only possible meaning that they can create from being abused by their parents, this permeates their limited self-awareness. It is therefore likely to be their first assumption about why they misbehave. They therefore habitually experience or cover over the experience of shame.

To try to create safety, without relying on their parents, these children have a strong tendency to want to control every person, thing, and event that they are faced with throughout the day. They resist allowing others to decide for them, so they may become quite oppositional with their parents. Other children tend to try to control events by being very secretive and avoidant, complying with expectations when being observed while doing what they want if they think that they will not be detected.

When children resist relying on parents, they also tend to resist engaging them and others in reciprocal relationships. Sharing and taking turns is too anxiety provoking for them. Given this tendency to go it alone, they are also likely to have little readiness for intersubjective experiences that require this reciprocal stance. As a result, they avoid engaging with others in a way that might help them to experience themselves in a more positive manner than they were able to experience with their abusers. They are also less able to discover who their adoptive or foster parents are—what are their thoughts, feelings, intentions, and beliefs—and less able to be influenced by the guidance about life that their parents would be able to give them. By avoiding intersubjective experiences, they are avoiding a central way that they might create a new meaning for the abuse and neglect of their past, along with the shame and fears that accompany them. Without intersubjective experiences with their new parents, they often fail to develop genuine interests in the events of their life. Rather, their focus is mostly on trying to ensure their own safety.

IV. ESTABLISHING ATTACHMENT SECURITY WHILE RESOLVING TRAUMA

Since the primary function of attachment is to generate safety, an intervention that facilitates the development of attachment behaviors toward attachment figures is also likely to be the therapy of choice for the treatment of childhood trauma. While facilitating attachment, the therapist is helping the child to feel safe enough to begin to resolve the trauma. While resolving the trauma, the therapist is helping the child to turn toward the attachment figure under times of stress, which deepens the attachment. The therapeutic work on both themes is complementary. One does not have to be completed before beginning the other. One helps the other.

DDP with foster and adoptive families is a specialized application of AFFT and as such utilizes the same basic interventions of A-R dialogue for the coregulation of affect and the cocreation of meaning, intersubjectivity, PACE, relationship repair, and working toward the parent or primary caregiver being the primary attachment figure. There are unique factors that apply to foster and adoptive children and their parents because of their symptoms secondary to severe trauma and attachment challenge.

A. Before beginning to provide treatment for the child, the therapist needs to develop an alliance with the foster or adoptive (f/a) parents. Chapter 7 is even more important in working with foster and adoptive parents than it is in working with more traditional families. There are a number of reasons why establishing the alliance between the therapist and parent is often crucial if the treatment is to be successful.

1. The child is at risk to manifest significant attachment problems, including attachment disorganization. Following abuse or neglect by his first attachment figures, along with one or more losses of attachment figures, the child is likely to have significant difficulty experiencing his f/a parents as the source of safety and new intersubjective learning. The f/a parents need to work closely with the therapist to understand their child's significant challenges as well as the parenting interventions that have the best chance of aiding his development.

2. The child is likely to manifest many challenging, controlling behaviors that represent his lack of trust of his parents, his preference for negative responses rather than positive interactions, his efforts to reject his f/a parents before they reject him, and his great difficulty engaging in reciprocal, intersubjective activity. The f/a parents are at risk to develop acute/specific blocked care syndrome, mentioned in Chapter 7. Ongoing counseling, support, and guidance of the parents by the therapist is often crucial if, together, they are to successfully help the child. The parent must be reminded not to forget the importance of self-care if she is to consistently care for her child, who may constantly resist her care. The parent's own attachment history is likely to be activated by the child's oppositional or avoidant behaviors. She must be encouraged to address and resolve any areas that are activated.

3. Parenting a child with characteristics of developmental trauma and attachment disorganization requires more comprehensive, specialized caregiving interventions. These interventions are congruent with those presented in Chapter 7. However, the interven-

tions are likely to need to be applied more consistently and persistently. There are also likely to be additional themes that require a specialized response.

a. The need to establish and maintain the child's sense of safety must always be in the mind of the parent. Changes, separations, surprises, discipline, even affection, often are experienced as threats to the child's sense of safety.

b. Structure and supervision are crucial for creating a sense of safety as well as for increasing the child's ability to regulate and organize his emotional, cognitive, and behavioral functioning. The ongoing presence of a caregiver who is able to consistently demonstrate the attitude of PACE will facilitate the child's sense of safety and new learning. It is important that structure and supervision be presented as a gift, not a punishment.

c. While the child is desperate for comfort, affection, and praise, these experiences are often difficult for him to integrate and often lead to resistance and dysregulation. The parent needs to communicate these positive experiences in small, persistent, and gentle ways, while showing empathy for the child's difficulty receiving them.

d. Discipline is often experienced by the child as being punitive, even abusive. The parent needs to discipline with empathy, not anger, and to patiently assist the child to understand the parent's motives for discipline.

e. The child's reflective functioning is likely to be weak. The parent needs to convey nonjudgmental curiosity about the child's thoughts, emotions, and intentions, while clearly expressing her own thoughts, emotions, and intentions.

f. The child's emotional regulation skills are also likely to be weak. The parent needs to match the child's affect expression and also to remain regulated herself to avoid contagion and escalation.

g. The child's shame is pervasive. The parent needs to clearly differentiate the child's behaviors from his inner life of thoughts, emotions, and intentions. Only the behavior is evaluated. Shame is met with empathy, not efforts to verbally convince the child that he is really good.

h. Relationship repair is difficult as the child is likely to have an intense reaction to conflict and limits, as well as the parent's mistakes or unavailability. The parent needs to initiate repair quickly after a relationship break and not employ relationship withdrawal as a discipline technique.

4. The child is likely to have great difficulty engaging in reciprocal, joyful, intersubjective activities. The parent needs assistance to remember to perceive the child who is beneath the symptoms. Her persistent positive perceptions of her child—without denying the symptoms—are necessary if the child is to begin to perceive his strengths and vulnerabilities that are much more than his symptoms.

B. Given the severity and nature of the symptoms, treatment is likely to be a longer and more gradual process cycling through the various themes in more numerous, increasingly large steps. Early in treatment the primary focus is on establishing and maintaining safety while enabling children to experience intersubjectivity through A-R dialogue and PACE. These factors represent both the context where treatment can occur and the central psychological abilities that will enable the treatment to be successful. Safety and intersubjective exploration must be present throughout treatment, but early on, the therapist has less confidence that the child is presently experiencing safety and is able to interact intersubjectively. The child is first learning the process of treatment—as well as the larger process of close, attachment-focused relationships—and from there will apply these new skills to trauma resolution and narrative creation. Each time, the cyclical process of safety and intersubjective exploration deepens them both.

Therapy is likely to last for months or even a few years if the child's comprehensive trauma and shame-related symptoms are to be addressed and she is to develop the readiness to be in a secure attachment relationship. Therapy is also likely to last at least 90 minutes in order for the therapist to have time to meet with the parents first, and then to develop the A-R dialogue, address and begin the integration process for themes of shame and trauma, and end with a period of reflection and quiet togetherness between the child and the parents.

Treatment termination is not determined simply by a reduction of the presenting symptoms. The therapist needs to ensure that there has been a significant reduction of the child's sense of shame, and that she is demonstrating a readiness to turn to her parents for comfort. She also needs to show that she can resolve conflicts and accept relationship repair. Finally she needs to demonstrate a significant improvement in affect regulation as well as reflective functioning. She is now able to use words rather than impulsive actions to manage stress and turn to her parents for assistance.

EXAMPLE

THERAPIST: So, Johnny, I hear that you got a great Lego set for your birthday—how did you like that?

JOHNNY [age 8]: I did! It's great!

THERAPIST: Wow! It sounds like it. What's so great about it?

JOHNNY: You can build all these neat things!

THERAPIST: Wow! And what have you built already?

JOHNNY: I built this big truck that picks up dirt and stuff.

THERAPIST: All right! Sounds like a lot of fun. Seems like your mom and dad made the right pick in getting you that Lego set.

JOHNNY: Yeah, they did.

THERAPIST: What's that mean anyway—that they made the right pick?

JOHNNY: I don't know.

THERAPIST: How did they know that you'd like it so much?

JOHNNY: I don't know.

THERAPIST: I wonder. Maybe . . . maybe they're getting to know you.

JOHNNY: I guess.

THERAPIST: Maybe they notice you so much, they can tell now what you like and don't like and they just knew that you'd like that Lego set.

JOHNNY: Yeah.

THERAPIST: Does it also mean that they like you a lot and want you to have a lot of fun when you play?

JOHNNY: I guess.

THERAPIST: And why do you think they like you so much?

JOHNNY: I don't know.

THERAPIST: I didn't think that you did. That might be something new for you. Wait! Maybe we can ask them why. That's it. We'll ask them why. Do you want to or do you want me to?

Comment: The therapist is activating Johnny's mind so that he might develop the habit of wondering about things that are central in his life, of being more aware of what he thinks and feels and what others think and feel. The therapist can focus on anything that is happening in the child's life in the present and wonder about its place in the child's life and mind. The therapist begins with routine things and only gradually introduces more stressful themes. Throughout, the child will discover that no matter what they discover together about his inner life, it will never be judged but will be responded to with PACE.

C. Even though safety and intersubjective experience are the first goals, still the therapist will introduce stressful—minor, not major—themes in the first session. The therapist must be clear that she wants to discover all aspects of the child, including parts of the child that elicit fear or shame, anger or sadness. She will help the child to discover that he is safe when those themes are focused on, that he is still completely accepted. She will demonstrate that as he makes sense of those themes, their associated emotions become smaller and do not need to be avoided.

Whenever the therapist leads the dialogue into an area of the child's inner life, or into another theme, she is immediately alert to the child's response to her lead, and she then follows that response. If the child goes more deeply still into the theme that the therapist initiated, then the therapist joins with the child in exploring the theme further. If the child moves toward a related theme, the therapist follows the new theme. If the child makes it clear that he does not want to pursue that theme, the therapist accepts the decision with empathy and possibly curiosity about the child's desire not to explore it.

EXAMPLE 1

THERAPIST [first session]: That really sounds neat! You were able to show your mom how to send photos over her cell phone?

JENNY [age 11]: Yeah, she never knew how to do it.

THERAPIST: And you've probably known since you were 3.

JENNY: Almost!

THERAPIST: That's great! Oh, yeah, that reminds me. I hear that you are in a bit of trouble for using your mom's phone to call your friends without asking.

JENNY: I guess.

THERAPIST: Yeah, that's what I heard. Oh, your voice got really quiet all of a sudden. Is it hard to talk about stuff that you might be in some trouble about?

JENNY: I guess.

THERAPIST: Yeah, that's what I thought. Well, we'll be talking about all kinds of stuff here. Things that you feel good about and things that you feel not so good about. Things that are fun and things that are hard. For you and your mom and dad too! That's how I get to know you guys. I'm interested in everything.! That okay?

JENNY: I guess.

THERAPIST: Probably some parts are more okay than other parts [laughs].

JENNY [laughs]: I guess.

Comment: As the therapist moves from the strengths and enjoyable events to vulnerabilities and difficult events and back again, her overall voice tone, facial expressions, and rhythm of the dialogue are about the same. PACE is evident throughout, gradually showing that all aspects of the child's life are safe to be explored. The therapist is not simply interested in problems, and when they are explored it is not in a serious, lecture-style tone. All are part of the A-R dialogue. The therapist is interested in the child, not the problem.

EXAMPLE 2

THERAPIST: So you guys came back early yesterday. I thought that you would be gone all day.

RON [dad]: We were planning on taking in a movie after we did some shopping, but there was nothing good on at the cinema. So we stopped for a snack and then decided to head home.

THERAPIST: Well, at least did you get an ice cream out of it?

JAKE [age 9]: Yeah, a sundae with nuts and whipped cream.

THERAPIST: And you didn't save any?

JAKE: No!

THERAPIST: You too, Dad?

RON: I actually had one too—first one in a couple of years.

THERAPIST: So your son is a good influence on you.

RON: That's for sure. I'm going to have sundaes more often now. Together with Jake!

JAKE: Let's go every day, Dad.

RON: Well, every day might be a bit much. I think I'd gain too much weight.

JAKE: Okay, three times a week.

THERAPIST: That's great, you two. You'll probably get to taste all the flavors there are in the next few months. Oh, that reminds me, Jake, of how different it was when you were a little kid. I remember that your first dad often would eat and make you wait until he was done and if there wasn't any left over you didn't get any.

JAKE: Yeah, and sometimes if he was mad about something he would throw away the left-overs and I couldn't have them.

THERAPIST: Throw the food away . . . when you were hungry!

JAKE: Yeah, he said that I was bad and didn't deserve any.

THERAPIST: Oh, my, Jake, and he was your dad. That is hard to understand.

RON: I'm so sorry, son. You didn't deserve that! And you're not bad.

JAKE: Sometimes I feel that I am, Dad.

RON: I know, son. I know. I hope someday you will see the great kid that I see.

Comment: The therapist followed a natural connection between his enjoyable ice cream treat with his adoptive dad and being deprived of food by his birth father. He did so in the same rhythmic voice tone, and Jake responded without hesitation or stress. If the therapist had adopted a tense, serious tone, Jake would have been more likely not to respond or to do so reluctantly with only a few words.

EXAMPLE 3

THERAPIST: So you guys had a pretty good vacation.

SEAN [age 15]: I guess.

THERAPIST: What did you like the best?

SEAN: I don't know. Water skiing, I guess.

THERAPIST: You water ski? Been doing it long?

SEAN: Yeah. About 6 years, I guess.

THERAPIST: Okay, about as long as you've been with your parents. Guess you started the first summer.

SARAH [mom]: Yeah, it was. He liked it right off and was really good at it.

THERAPIST: That's great, Sean. You had so many hard times when you were younger. I'm glad that you got a chance to just enjoy life a bit when you met your parents. Are you?

SEAN: I guess.

THERAPIST: What was the hardest—during those early years before you met your mom and dad?

SEAN: Everything!

THERAPIST: What would be one of the things that bothered you a lot?

SEAN: Getting beat every day, okay?

THERAPIST: I'm sorry, Sean. I get it that you do not want to talk about that now. It all was so hard and just thinking about it must be hard.

SEAN: It doesn't serve any purpose.

THERAPIST: So, why put yourself through those hard memories if there is no value to it?

SEAN: That's right.

THERAPIST: Sean, you decide how and when we talk about that stuff. Things like that are so hard to remember. You have to feel ready to and it has to make sense to you.

SEAN: What sense does it make to talk about it?

THERAPIST: Great question to think about. I guess so that at some point the memories won't be so hard and if something that happens in your life now reminds you of something from the past, when you think of it, it won't bother you. And you won't have to avoid things or get knocked off balance if you run into something that triggers a memory from the past.

SEAN: I've thought about that stuff a lot and it never seems to get easier. That's why I don't think about it.

THERAPIST: Remembering that stuff with someone like your mom who loves you and helps you to feel safe with it is a big part about what would be different about talking about it here and thinking about it in the past when you were alone so much.

SEAN: I guess.

THERAPIST: So we'll let it go for now and I'll bring it up in the future. You can trust me and your mom that we'll never try to trap you so that you have to talk about this stuff.

SEAN: Good.

Comment: Through this follow-lead-follow process there tends to be a rhythm to the dialogue and a natural, reciprocal quality in the discussion that often does not occur in dialogues with children in therapy. Stressful themes are not avoided by the therapist. As safety and the experience of intersubjective exploration deepen, these themes tend to be addressed rather than avoided by the child.

D. The child is likely to show a pervasive need to control everything that occurs in the treatment session. A nondirective approach is unlikely to lead to therapeutic progress. A directive approach is likely to lead to increasingly intense power struggles. Instead the therapist needs to note the child's "resistance" and then respond to it with PACE. This often rigid pattern of defense needs to be understood for its past survival value, accepted, explored with curiosity, and then experienced with empathy. Gradually it is likely to decrease as the child is able to trust and join the intersubjective dance more easily.

EXAMPLE

TRACY [adopted, age 8]: I want to draw a picture like I did last week! [She makes this statement shortly after she sits down with her parents at the beginning of the session.]

THERAPIST: Thanks for letting me know what you'd like to do, Tracy. That was fun. We'll have some time to draw again a little later.

TRACY: No! I want to do it now!

THERAPIST: Wow! You really want to draw! And you don't want to wait.

TRACY: No! Now!

THERAPIST: Thanks for telling me how much you want to draw. Thanks, Tracy! Looks like it is hard to wait. How can I help you, because we're not going to draw right away?

TRACY [stomps her foot]: Now! I want to do it now!

Comment: A nondirective stance would allow Tracy to color at that point, thinking that her strong desire to control the situation results from her pervasive experience of a lack of control when she was abused in the past. The belief is that through giving her control she will feel safer, which in turn will enable her to relinquish control. I believe that this may be the case when the child expresses desire and can accept the adult's decision, though possibly with some anger and disappointment. When the child insists on control, often with a harsh demand, I do not believe that the child feels safer if the adult agrees to the demand. More often the child has a sense that the adult is intimidated by her power and is accepting her demand out of fear, not empathy or reciprocity—and if that is the child's perception, the therapist accepting the demand will not increase the child's sense of safety.

THERAPIST: It really is hard to wait. What makes it so hard?

TRACY: I want to do it now!

THERAPIST: I know, Tracy, I know! Why do you think it is so hard to wait?

TRACY: I don't want to wait. I want to draw now!

THERAPIST: I just thought of something, Tracy. Do you think it's hard to wait because you want to decide what to do? That you really don't like it if I decide?

TRACY: I don't want to wait!

THERAPIST: I think that might be it. It is really important for you to decide what we're going to do and when we're going to do it. And when I say that I'll decide, or we'll decide together . . . you get really angry at me. Really angry!

TRACY: You're mean!

THERAPIST: Yes, that's it, isn't it? You really are angry that I won't let you decide. And you think that I'm being mean to you. Now I see why you are so angry! You think that you have a mean therapist and that it's not fair.

TRACY: It's not fair! You are mean!

THERAPIST: Thanks for telling me. If you think that I'm mean to you, no wonder you get angry with me. No wonder! If I don't let you do what you want to do—right now—you think that's because I am being mean. And you don't like that. Of course you wouldn't! Why would a therapist be mean to you?

TRACY: You don't like me!

Comment: The therapist has helped Tracy to understand more about why she wants to make the decision so strongly: the therapist saying no elicits anger because she thinks that he is being mean to her because he does not like her. Given her abusive history, her assumption that he has a negative motive in saying no is certainly understandable.

THERAPIST: Ah, Tracy, no wonder you are angry. You think that I don't like you! How hard that would be if your therapist didn't like you. I am so sorry that's what it seems like to you. That it seems to you that I don't like you.

TRACY: That's why you won't let me draw now.

THERAPIST: That's what you think, isn't it? That's what you think!

TRACY: Why don't you then?

THERAPIST: Great question, Tracy. If it's not because I'm being mean, you want to know what is the reason. Great question!

TRACY: Why don't you?

Comment: Now that Tracy is engaged in a reciprocal conversation about their conflict, it is much more likely that she will be open to understanding a different motive for the therapist's saying no to her. Not only will this help to resolve the current conflict, it is also likely to be a step toward Tracy engaging in such reciprocal conversations in the future as her negative assumptions about the motives of her attachment figures are reduced.

THERAPIST: Oh, Tracy, one reason is that I think that we should decide those things together. If I think that one thing is good for you to do here and you think another . . . I like to figure out what is best together rather than just have one of us boss the other. And one reason I think that it is best to wait, Tracy . . . one reason, and this might be hard to hear . . . and if it's hard, I'm sorry . . . one reason that I want you to wait is that I hear that you often want to decide things like this at home and at school and that you get angry a lot when your parents or teacher says no and then sometimes things seem to get worse. So I think that if we could figure that out what makes it so hard to wait . . . that might be better than drawing right now. That's my reason, Tracy, not to be mean to you. I'm sorry if that's what you feel.

TRACY: I don't like to wait!

THERAPIST: Ah, Tracy, thanks for telling me that. Thanks! I feel better now that maybe you believe me about my reasons for asking you to wait. Let's talk about that a bit. What do you think makes it so hard for you to wait?

Comment: The therapist has taken Tracy's strong need to control the situation and used that as the beginning of an A-R dialogue. This will enable her to reflect more about her inner life, which developed in an abusive environment. This is likely to help her to gradually differentiate that environment from her new safe environment and develop a new narrative whose foundation is this new environment, not the previous one. Significant change begins to occur when the child's default position about reality is her new environment rather than her old one.

E. As the child begins to let go of control a bit and move into themes of trauma and loss, she is very likely to begin to experience associated emotions. These include fear, sadness, anger, shame, general anxiety, and possibly excitement, joy, love, or gratitude. Her ability to regulate her emotions is likely to be poor and movement into these emotional states is likely to lead her toward dysregulation. The therapist needs to be continuously aware of this process, coregulating the emotion by matching the emerging affect expressions as well as setting a pace of exploration that matches the child's ability to regulate the emerging emotions.

EXAMPLE

[Continuing the above example where the therapist asks Tracy what makes it hard for her to wait.]

TRACY: I don't know!

THERAPIST: Ah, let's wonder about that a bit, then. Let's wonder, what might it be?

TRACY: I don't like to wait!

THERAPIST: Yeah, you don't like to, you don't like to. I wonder. I wonder. Do you think that it's so hard . . . I know that when you lived with your birth parents you so often had to wait . . . so long for food, and for someone to play with you, and for someone to help you do things. . . . You had to wait so long, so often, that maybe, now, you might be feeling, "No more! No more waiting!" Do you think so?

TRACY: I didn't have to wait with my mommy! She took good care of me!

Comment: Often at the core of the child's resistance to exploring symptoms is a reluctance to connect the symptoms to the original abuse and neglect. This may well relate to attempts to avoid the pain of those memories. Closely related to recalling the pain is a loyalty to the birth parents—a reluctance to acknowledge that they abused the child. Shame toward the self is often closely related to this loyalty to the abusive parents.

THERAPIST: Ah, Tracy! You are upset that I said that your mommy made you wait too long and too much. You're upset with me now for saying that!

TRACY: She did take good care of me! She did! [Tracy jumps up from the couch and runs to the opposite wall. She turns and looks at the therapist.] You're being mean again! You're being mean!

THERAPIST: Oh, Tracy! This is so hard. Now you think I'm saying mean things about your mom. And you're mad at me again. You love your mom and you don't want me to say that she made you wait too long. You don't want me to say that.

Comment: Tracy is reluctant to acknowledge her mother's neglect of her. The therapist does not argue with her, but rather focuses on a possible motive about why she might not admit to the neglect—she loves her mother. Such acknowledgments—without arguing—often enable the child to begin to face what actually happened and to begin the long process of trying to make sense of it. At this moment, the therapist's acceptance and empathy, conveyed with matched affective expressions in voice and facial expressions, enables Tracy to be able to regulate the emerging intense emotions.

TRACY: Why did you say that? Why did you?

THERAPIST: What do you think, Tracy?

TRACY: Why didn't she give me anything to eat? Why didn't she? Sometimes she ate everything and didn't let me have anything! Why did she do that?

THERAPIST: Oh, Tracy, that must have been so hard for you! And you don't know why she did not feed you when she had food. You don't know why. And I don't know why either. I don't know why a mom wouldn't feed her little girl. I don't know!

TRACY: She was mean to me! She was mean!

THERAPIST: How hard! How hard, Tracy, to think that your mom was mean to you! Your own mom! And not knowing why.

TRACY: Didn't she love me? She didn't love me!

Comment: After suddenly facing the fact that her mother neglected her, Tracy quickly concludes that her mother was mean to her because maybe her mother did not love her. Some professionals will discourage such conclusions, explaining that the mother did love the child but simply had a lot of her own problems that were not the child's fault. Such efforts are not in the best interest of the child, just as it would not be helpful to tell the child that the mother did not love her. The professional cannot evaluate the mother's motives for the neglect. He simply must stay with what he knows. The child needs to struggle with how it makes sense to her. The professional can help with the process with PACE, but not by telling the child what to think, feel, and believe about it.

THERAPIST: Oh, my! How hard is that to wonder if your mom loved you or not. How hard! And I don't know, Tracy. I don't know if your mom loved you or not. I don't know why she did not feed you when she had food. All I know is that it was very hard for a little girl. Very hard for you, Tracy!

TRACY: I don't want to talk about this anymore!

THERAPIST: Of course not, Tracy. Of course not. I understand. This is so hard! Why not go over and sit with your new mom? Sit with her while I get a book for you two to read.

[Tracy goes to her adoptive mother, sits close to her on the couch, and lets her adoptive mom put her arm around her and pull her close. Tracy puts her thumb in her mouth and leans against her while her adoptive mom reads her a children's story.]

Comment: When the child is exploring a traumatic theme and suddenly concludes that the discussion is over, it is important for the therapist to accept the child's decision. Efforts to elicit a bit more information or a deeper experience of the trauma may make the child feel trapped in the exploration. This reduces her sense of safety while facing these frightening themes. It increases her reluctance to go there again. Later in the session the therapist might reflect a bit on the discussion of the neglect, but not in detail. Such reflection communicates that it is safe to recall the conversation and to understand it from a more reflective, less affective, stance.

F. As the child begins to experience both the past traumas and attachment problems as well as new attachment relationships with his f/a parents, he may show a lack of emotion. This lack of expressed emotion may be misinterpreted as meaning that the past trauma and attachment breaks really don't bother him. In a similar manner, the lack of expressions of joy and love while relating with his f/a parents may be misinterpreted as meaning that he is faking it or giving the therapist what he thinks he wants. When the absence of the expression of emotion is interpreted that way, there is great danger that the child will not receive the intersubjective experiences from the therapist or f/a parent that he needs to resolve past events and deepen his ability to experience new relationships.

The lack of expressed emotion with regard to the past represents the child's need to dissociate from his emotions in order to attempt to survive events that elicited terror and shame. He defended against the extreme pain by not feeling anything. Such pain for a child is overwhelming unless he is with a comforting attachment figure who can coregulate the emotions that are being evoked. Even then it is difficult. Alone, it is impossible for a child to manage. He will either dissociate from the emotion or become very dysregulated with rage outbursts, terror, or despair.

Thus, the lack of emotion does not show that it doesn't bother him. Rather, it was his way to try to cope with an unbearable situation. The child needs to be affirmed in his defense against the pain. He needs help to make sense of why he does not feel the impact of those events. He needs to experience the comfort and understanding of an attachment figure to help him to begin to feel again, remain regulated within the emotion, and integrate the event into his narrative.

The lack of expressed emotion with regard to the present attachment relationship may reflect his fear of the experience, rather than meaning that he is faking it. He may fear that the attachment will not last. He may fear the associated emotions of being dependent and vulnerable that the attachment evokes. He may fear that as the f/a parents get to know him better they will withdraw their love. Because of his shame he is often convinced that he is unlovable.

The lack of expressed emotion with regard to the present attachment relationship may also reflect his lack of experience with such relationships. He may not know how to experience love, joy, affection, or comfort. He needs to learn how by having such experiences and he needs help from his therapist and caregiver to do so. If it is superficial or giving the therapist what he wants, then he needs help to deepen the experience. This help best comes through PACE and an adult communicating fully his experiences and patiently waiting as the child begins to have the experience intersubjectively. When a therapist communicates nonverbally and verbally what it is like to miss his mother, the child is likely to gradually begin to have the experience of missing his mother. The child intersubjectively experiences the therapist's experience and then gradually begins to have a similar experience himself. Any new skill—and experiencing emotional intimacy is a skill just as riding a bike is—seems superficial or artificial at first. With time, as it is integrated, it gradually takes on a more natural, spontaneous, and real quality. Empathy, shared experience, repetition, and patience are crucial for this skill to develop.

G. The child is likely to manifest an intense, lifelong sense of shame that makes treatment very difficult for him. The traumas are embedded in shame, so to explore them for the purpose of achieving resolution and cocreating new meanings requires the child to experience his sense that he deserved them. His current symptoms are likely to be experienced as being due to his being worthless, bad, and unlovable. Also, shame tends to create hiding, withdrawing behaviors rather than the intersubjective openness that creates therapeutic effectiveness. The therapist's patient but persistent curiosity often leads to the emergence of this underlying state of shame.

EXAMPLE

THERAPIST: Seems like you guys had quite an adventure. That's really great! I was wondering too, Seth about your taking your sister's game and throwing it in the lake. What was that about, do you think?

SETH [age 12]: Dad said that we could go back there next month too. It was a lot of fun!

THERAPIST: Go again, great! Lucky you! How about your sister's game?

SETH: I don't want to talk about it!

THERAPIST: Because?

SETH: It's over with! What's that thing you got on your desk?

THERAPIST: Oh, just a fancy type of puzzle. I'll show you later. I'd like to understand what was going on with you at the lake with your sister.

SETH: I don't want to talk about it.

THERAPIST: Because it's over, you said. So I guess that means that you and your parents and maybe your sister already dealt with it.

SETH: Yeah, we did.

THERAPIST: I'm glad you guys did. What did you figure out about it?

Comment: The therapist is not saying that Seth should talk about the incident at the lake. He simply wants to know why Seth doesn't want to. When Seth says that it is over and they dealt with it, that sounds reasonable to the therapist, and the natural question then is what did they figure out. The therapist remains curious—wanting to know how the event was resolved.

SETH: I won't do it again!

THERAPIST: Because . . .

SETH: Because I get in trouble when I do stuff like that to her, that's why!

THERAPIST: Does it make sense that your parents would say that you're in trouble for destroying something of hers?

SETH: Why do we have to keep talking about this? It's over!

THERAPIST: I hear you, Seth. You really don't want to talk about it. What I'm trying to understand—if it's over and dealt with—is why you really don't want to talk about it. Since you have broken a number of things of your sister's and you get in trouble each time, I thought maybe I could help you to figure it out, so you wouldn't get in trouble so much.

Comment: The therapist's questions continue because he still does not understand how the problem has been dealt with. As it seems clear that it hasn't been dealt with, he is curious about that. As the resistance to the discussion becomes stronger, the therapist's curiosity persists as he tries to understand that. He goes deeper and deeper into Seth's motives to avoid exploring what he did wrong, which leads to a pattern of avoidance of conflict and rejection fears for Seth. The therapist also clarifies his motives for this questioning when Seth asks.

SETH: I want to just forget it! I don't want my parents to think about it again.

THERAPIST: Because . . .

SETH: Because they'll just get mad again and give me a lecture again!

THERAPIST: I don't think they will now, Seth. . . . They know I'd fuss if they did and they also know that's not what therapy is about. It's just about making sense of things.

SETH: I don't need to!

THERAPIST: If we could make sense of it, then maybe you wouldn't do that stuff anymore and not get into trouble so much.

SETH: I just don't like her! Okay? Happy now?

Comment: Seth is finally able to express his underlying motive for his behavior toward his sister. Most likely he was not clear about the motive himself until the dialogue kept moving him in that direction. When he does give the motive—with anger but also vulnerability now that it is known—the therapist acknowledges how difficult it was for him to express it.

THERAPIST: Oh, Seth! Thanks for telling me that. That must have been hard to say . . but you did! And now it's easier to make sense of throwing her game in the lake. And some of the other stuff. Thanks, Seth, for being brave and telling us.

SETH: You just won't leave it alone! You want me to be unhappy!

Comment: Seth—in discomfort over the disclosure—now expresses his assumption that the therapist had negative motives for the discussion—a common assumption that children with trauma or attachment problems have during such stressful dialogues. The therapist does not defend himself but expresses empathy and understanding. Seth's resistance to the discussion makes sense if he thinks that the therapist is asking the questions for the purpose of making him unhappy.

THERAPIST: Ah! Seth, I'm sorry if that's what you think. No wonder you don't like to talk with me about some of this stuff! You think that I want you to be unhappy. If I did want you to be unhappy, of course you wouldn't trust me. You wouldn't want to talk with me. Of course you wouldn't!

SETH: Well, why do you then?

THERAPIST: Just to make sense of it, Seth. So I can help you and your parents to make sense of stuff too. Because I really believe that if we make sense of things that in the long run you'll be happier. If you weren't in trouble so much for breaking your sister's stuff, I think you'd be happier.

SETH: Well, it doesn't make me happier.

THERAPIST: I get that, Seth, I really do. What is it about talking about something you do wrong that makes you unhappy?

SETH: How would you like having your face rubbed into something that you did wrong?

THERAPIST: That's what it is like for you? Having your face rubbed in it? No wonder you really don't like talking about things you do wrong. And my wish is simply to help you make sense of it and help you not get into trouble so much. But that's not how you experience it. It's really hard for you to think about what you do wrong. Really hard! [Seth is quiet and seems discouraged.] I wonder, Seth, if, when you do something wrong, you're really hard on yourself. Like you think that it means that you're just a bad kid. . . . Maybe that's it. And you worry that when your parents think about this again, they'll think that you're just a bad kid, too.

SETH: Well, I'm always in trouble!

THERAPIST: Ah! I think that I'm right. When you do something wrong . . . you do worry that it's a sign that you're a bad kid. You do worry. How hard that must be for you . . . if you think that you're just . . . a bad kid.

SETH: Well, I am.

Comment: For foster and adopted children with a history of abuse and neglect, the deepest psychological truth is often that they were abused and now they do bad things because they are bad kids. Shame most often underlies their behavioral difficulties and especially their strong resistance to addressing these difficulties. When the child is finally able to acknowledge the shame, it is crucial not to try to talk him out of the experience of shame but rather to respond to it with acceptance, curiosity, and especially empathy.

THERAPIST: Ah! No wonder you don't want me to try to make sense of it. You think that if I make sense of it, I'll decide that you're just a bad kid. And maybe your parents will decide that too.

Seth: Why else would I do that stuff so much?

THERAPIST: Great question, Seth. I know that there are reasons that we just don't know about yet. And I want to help us all to make sense of it. I have a lot of guesses why you do that stuff a lot. None of my guesses have to do with your being bad. None of them. But you think you are. . . and that's more important than what I think. And it must be hard to think that. That's why I thought that if we could make sense of it, maybe try out some of my guesses . . . you might think that there are different reasons for what you do rather than being a bad kid . . . different reasons.

SETH: Like what?

THERAPIST: I didn't think you'd ever ask [smiles]. Thanks, Seth, for trusting me a bit to be willing to try to make sense of it with me and your parents. Let's go back then to what you said about not liking your sister. That's a good place to begin. What do you think causes you not to like her?

Comment: Now that the shame has been experienced, acknowledged, and accepted, the child is often motivated to explore what other motives might lead him to repetitive misbehaviors. The possibility that he might not be bad is likely to activate Seth's curiosity—and improve his reflective functioning—about who he is and might be.

H. Two general themes tend to dominate the treatment. The first consists of the traumas—and their effects—that occurred prior to the child's placement in her present home. The second consists of the child's experiences and behavior in her current home. Some children have more fear and shame associated with the first theme, while others have greater difficulty with the second theme. In the first session, the therapist lightly touches on each area and assesses the child's responses to determine which of the two themes appears to be easier for the child to address. The therapist would then focus on that theme first.

I. The child is very likely to mistrust the foster or adoptive parents. His mistrust of his primary caregivers is likely to be pervasive. He has a history of abuse, neglect, rejection, and abandonment that may well have involved a series of parent figures. Why should these parents be different? As a result, the child needs assistance in learning whether or not he should trust them, how to trust them, what attachment and caregiving behaviors actually are, seeking and accepting comfort, and learning to give and receive affection. He also needs to learn the function of discipline as well as how to engage someone intersubjectively. Eye contact and touch may both be difficult for him, and these behaviors will have to be gently encouraged. These factors need to be experienced in treatment first before it is likely that the child will be able to safely begin to explore new ways of relating with his caregivers at home.

J. The child is likely to maintain a strong, possibly rigid, attachment (loyalty) to his biological parents that may well make it difficult for him to develop a secure attachment with the foster or adoptive parents. He shows loyalty to his parents by finding fault with his new parents and by not relying on them. Also, if he develops an attachment to his f/a parents, he is beginning to give up hope that he will ever reunify with his biological parents. His loyalty is likely to be intense for the following reasons:

- He experiences shame over the abuse because his parent's experience of abusing him was that he was bad and deserved it. The parent's experience became the child's intersubjective experience of the reason for the abuse. His shame is embedded in this early parental justification for the abuse. Within shame, he is unlikely to develop a new perspective on his relationship with his biological parents.

- If he faces the abuse, he is pulled into the traumatic memories. Loyalty minimizes the impact of the abuse on him.

- By minimizing the abuse, it is easier for the child to maintain a belief that his parents loved him while maintaining his desire to love his parents and believe that they were good people. It is important that the therapist make it clear to the child that while the birth parents' abusive or neglectful behaviors hurt him and his development in many ways, this reality does not imply that the parents were bad people. Nor does it suggest whether or not they loved the child or whether he should love them. The child needs to struggle with those themes in developing a coherent narrative. But denying the abuse will not make those issues easier to integrate. Denying the abuse only leaves the child in shame.

V. INTERSUBJECTIVE EXPLORATION AND COCREATING A COHERENT NARRATIVE

These children face extremely difficult and challenging tasks. They need to resolve past traumas while at the same time responding to and integrating the numerous opportunities presented to them to have a new life—in a new world extremely unlike the original world of abuse and neglect. Certainly their pervasive symptoms make this difficult. But so do the features of their inner life—their thoughts, emotions, perceptions, wishes, beliefs, and memories that developed in the past life. It is not helpful to tell these children, "Get over it" or "Get on with your new life." That would essentially be telling them not to use their mind in their efforts to learn how to live in this new world. Their mind is embedded in the past. The sense of self—the narrative as it moves and develops through time—is embedded there also. The solution is not to split off the past, although many children, with the hopeful blessing of their new parents and even professionals, attempt to never think about the old life. That solution is unrealistic since the new world will hold many experiences that activate memories from the old world. It is also not therapeutic since the child will always have a part of the self that is covered with dark clouds, always threatening to pull the child into shame and nameless fears, rage, and despair.

The task for these children is to create a coherent narrative that can make sense of the events of the more distant past along with the radically different events of the recent past, present, and anticipated future. Just as an infant needs much assistance from his parents to make sense of his developing life, so too does the foster and adopted child. This child cannot create a narrative alone. It must be cocreated with the active participation of the new parents and therapist primarily, and with the secondary help of other relatives, professionals, and peers.

This process of making sense of the events of his life requires that the child be open to the events that are present to him. He needs to take those events and organize them into his narrative in a manner that is coherent with the rest of his narrative. To do so he needs to be open to the event in a way that does not deny or distort the meaning of the event. Rather, he is receptive to the emerging experience and works to integrate it with past experiences already a part of the narrative.

A momentous shift in this process occurs when the child begins to consistently make sense of the past events of abuse and neglect from the perspective of the new events of safety and love. He leaves behind his rigid tendency to make sense of new events (seen as manipulation, tricks, deceptions, or early stages of abuse and neglect) from the perspective of the old events of abuse and neglect.

A key component of this shift will consist of the child's openness and ability to engage in intersubjective experiences with his primary attachment figures. In his life characterized by abuse and neglect the child had few intersubjective experiences. His parents gave much greater priority to their own experience of events and little to that of their child. The child's experience was not noticed or valued very often. For the most part the child was an object to the parent. He was not able to influence the parent's experience as would occur naturally in intersubjective experiences. The child was likely to become an object of aggression, sexual gratification, disgust, or ridicule with little worth other than to meet the perceived needs of the parent. The child's narrative became founded on the experience of self as object to the parent's desires. The perception of self as intersubjective partner was barely present. As the f/a parents and therapist present this intersubjective experience to the child, he needs to perceive it, recognize it, want it, and then develop the ability to participate in it. As he takes this journey, he becomes open to an entirely new interpersonal world. He now has the central tools needed to cocreate a new narrative that gradually becomes coherent.

EXAMPLE

JUDY [age 13, shouting at adoptive mom]: You don't care! You don't! You like it when I'm unhappy! You really do!

THERAPIST [with animation and a sense of urgency]: Judy! So that's what you think about why your mom won't let you go on that trip. That's what you think! No wonder that you're angry with her! You think that she deliberately wants to make you unhappy!

JUDY: She does! She always does!

THERAPIST: So when she says no to you, you think that's the reason. And you think it's always the reason. To make you unhappy!

JUDY: That's right!

THERAPIST: Oh, my, I get it! Would you tell your mom that . . . would you tell her, Judy, that when she says no to you, you think that's because she wants you to be unhappy?

JUDY: That's right. You do. You just want me to be unhappy!

BETH: Oh, Judy, I'm sorry that you believe that! Of course you'd be angry with me if you thought that! Of course. And I am sorry that I'm not more clear about why I say no sometimes.

Comment: Both the therapist and Beth respond with empathy for Judy's experience without trying to give her an alternative reason for her mother's behavior. Empathy is almost always the best first response before being curious or presenting an alternative way to experience an event. Most parents do not naturally begin with empathy. The therapist has discussed the value of beginning discussions with empathy and also has modeled and coached them in such interactions.

JUDY: You're not sorry! You're not sorry or you'd stop doing it!

BETH: If that was why I say no to you, of course you'd be right. But that's not why I say no to you.

JUDY: I don't believe you!

THERAPIST: You don't, do you? You think that your mom is lying to you now, don't you?

JUDY: She is! She's only saying it because you're here. She doesn't mean it!

THERAPIST: What makes you so sure, Judy? When I look at your mom, she seems to me to be really sad that you become so unhappy when she says no to you.

JUDY: I don't see it! She's probably faking that she's sad.

Comment: Responses like this are common. The child has had so few experiences of compassion and empathy from others that when they are present, she does not experience them. This is more than being afraid to admit it; she truly does not know how to perceive the parent's empathy. She needs help to begin to develop the experience of perceiving and receiving her mother's empathy. It will help if the child will consider the possibility that she did not have the experience very often in the past.

THERAPIST: Do you know what she would look like if she really did feel sad for you that you become unhappy when she says no?

JUDY: What do you mean?

THERAPIST: I wonder if you've never felt a mom feel sad for your unhappiness. I think that your first mom—and you were with her for 6 years—often did things that hurt you and she didn't seem to care, or at least she didn't stop doing it. Maybe you just started expecting that . . . only seeing that . . . so if this mom really felt sad for you . . . you might not know what it looks like.

JUDY: She's not sad for me.

THERAPIST: Look at her now. To me, she looks sad for you. How would she look differently if she really were sad for you?

JUDY: I don't know. Maybe this way. But she's still probably faking it. That's what I said before.

THERAPIST: Would you look at her and tell her that? "Mom, I think that you're faking it. I don't think that you're sad for me."

JUDY: I don't think you're sad for me. You're just faking it.

BETH: I'm sorry that you don't feel what's in my heart for you.

JUDY: There can't be anything in your heart for me!

THERAPIST: Because . . .

JUDY: It just can't be! My first mom never had anything in her heart for me. She laughed when I cried! She laughed!

THERAPIST: Ah! How hard that would be! Tell this mom that. Tell her that you think she'll probably just laugh at you if you're so unhappy that you cry.

JUDY: I think that you'll laugh if I cry. . . . Why are you crying? Why are you crying?

BETH: Because of the pain you must have felt when your mom laughed when you cried.

JUDY [begins to cry]: Don't cry!

Comment: The nonverbal expressions on Beth's face along with her tears are being experienced by Judy, which conflicts with her concept of being a self who does not deserve tears due to her previous very different experiences with her biological mother. The extreme contrast between her current, powerful, nonverbal experience of her mother's empathy and her preconceptions startle and frighten Judy and she tries to resolve it by stopping her mother's tears. Children are also sometimes afraid of the parents' tears because they believe that they are now a burden to their parents or that they have to now take care of their parents.

THERAPIST: Look at your mom, Judy. Why can't she have tears for you?

JUDY: She shouldn't! They make me nervous! I don't know!

THERAPIST: Look at your mom. Look at her. Those tears in her eyes are for you.

JUDY: I don't deserve them.

THERAPIST: Why don't you, Judy?

JUDY: Because my first mom didn't have tears! Why didn't she have tears for me?

THERAPIST: I don't know, Judy, I don't know. But I wish she did. Why does this mom have tears for you?

JUDY: Why do you?

BETH: Because you're unhappy. You've been unhappy too much in your life. Because you're my daughter. Because when I say no to you, you become unhappy some more. And I wish . . . I wish I could help you to be happy . . . not unhappy . . . and often I can't. . . . And that's why . . . all of those reasons . . . I do cry for you.

JUDY [staring at Beth, tears rolling down her cheeks]: When I see your tears for me, I get scared.

THERAPIST: Why, Judy, why?

JUDY: Because I don't know why . . . I don't know . . . who I am.

Comment: Statements like "I don't know who I am" often emerge when a child is face to face with an intersubjective experience with her new attachment figure that contradicts an equally important experience with a prior attachment figure. This vivid contrast creates confusion and anxiety and, when regulated, often leads to a radical shift of perception of self. The new attachment figure's experience of the self of the child starts to be the template from which the child contrasts other intersubjective experiences—but often only after periods of confusion and doubt.

THERAPIST: Ah! Look at Beth, Judy. Look at your mom. She will help you to know who you are. Look in her eyes. You will find who you are.

JUDY: I don't want to.

THERAPIST: Because . . . why, Judy, why don't you want to?

JUDY: I can't. I'm scared.

THERAPIST: You are. You are scared. And you need your mom now, Judy. [Judy looks into Beth's eyes again and begins to cry more. Beth moves toward her and embraces her. Judy begins to cry deeply.]

Comment: Dramatic moments like these are most often embedded in many moments of smaller challenges to a client's preconceptions that were based on an earlier template of self and other embedded in abuse and neglect. The gentle persistence of the adoptive parent and therapist in presenting alternative intersubjective experiences of self for Judy over and over again is what gradually opens the door to a new self-experience of worth and of being lovable.

VI. OBSTACLES TO TREATMENT

A. Intense Emotional Dysregulation

Children with developmental trauma and attachment disorganization frequently have extreme difficulty managing routine frustrations or limits. When the therapist gently and slowly addresses issues related to past traumas or current stresses, the child may be at risk to react with fight, flight, or freeze. Thus he may become aggressive, run out of the office, or dissociate. The therapist's slow, gentle approach may not be sufficient to assist the child in remaining regulated while exploring stressful themes.

The therapist should become aware of the child's regulation skills during the frustrations and demands of daily life before beginning treatment. If the child becomes aggressive or runs out of the home in response to small frustrations, then he is at risk to have a similar response to therapy.

The therapist should consider the following:

1. Initiate treatment by trying to establish reciprocal interactions with A-R dialogue around casual, light, enjoyable themes and activities. He should embed minor stressful themes within the dialogue. If the dialogue already has momentum, the child may continue with it around the stressful theme. However, it is not wise to totally avoid the stressful themes with the hope that the child will initiate discussion of them on his own once he feels safe. His pervasive tendencies of avoidance and control are likely to prevent him from ever feeling safe enough to introduce those themes.
2. Express PACE around the difficulty of exploring stressful themes.
3. Provide many breaks around these stressful discussions. The child must not feel trapped in the discussion.
4. Bring puppets or stuffed animals into the treatment, having them talk for the child or for other children in similar situations.
5. Talk quietly with PACE with the f/a parent, allowing the child to engage in another activity at the same time. Most children will also listen to what is being said and be able to reflect on what they are hearing as long as they are not expected to acknowledge it or respond.
6. Provide the child with cues or words that guarantee him that the discussion will stop when he needs a break.

7. If a child often needs to be restrained for the sake of safety at home, it may be necessary in therapy as well. The therapist should expect that the parents will restrain their child as they do at home when necessary. The therapist should assess whether the child is psychologically and physically safe during the restraint. The therapist should never provoke a restraint, but rather plan the session to reduce the likelihood that it will occur. If the child is never so dysregulated at home that he needs to be restrained, then it should not be necessary in the therapy session either.

B. The Absence of an Attachment Figure

Many foster children do not live with an attachment figure. These children may reside in group homes, residential facilities, emergency shelters, or short-term or marginal foster homes. Many programs do not value attachment as a guide to developing the adult-child relationship. There are still foster care programs where foster parents are encouraged not to facilitate their foster child's attachment with them.

When a foster child does not reside with an attachment figure, any treatment provided would be individual psychotherapy. However, the therapist could still use DDP principles. A-R dialogue, PACE, and relationship repair all would still have a place in treatment. The treatment goals might still involve assisting the child to develop affect regulation and reflective functioning. An intersubjective stance rather than the traditional therapeutic stance would still be indicated. When the child does not reside with an attachment figure, the individual therapist would then assume the role of the child's attachment figure.

When the individual therapist, using DDP, is functioning as an attachment figure for the child, he needs to ensure that he is able and willing to provide treatment for a sufficient length of time, most likely a minimum of 9–12 months. Ideally, he would be available as long as the child requires treatment, but when this is not the case, he should make clear the duration and the reasons for the limit.

When the therapist is the child's only attachment figure, he still must be clear as to the need for professional boundaries, though these boundaries might be broader than is traditionally the case. I would recommend that the therapist consider remembering the child's birthday or other special event with a card and possibly a small gift. When treatment ends, he might give the child a gift as well as allowing him to mail or e-mail him about how things are going. The therapist should also be free to give the child a hug, if he is confident that both the child and he remain safe. If there is danger that the child might misperceive the therapist's intentions, then giving a hug would not be appropriate. I do not believe that children understand a professional therapeutic relationship as an adult would. Without signs of interest, caring, and concern, children are likely to believe that it's just a job.

The intersubjective stance is very beneficial for a child without another attachment figure. Such a child especially needs the intersubjective experience of knowing a good person who takes delight in her and perceives her strengths, courage, persistence, and worth.

If she is to discover those features in herself, she needs to experience an adult who discovers those features in her. This does not make her chronically dependent upon the therapist for her sense of worth any more than a child who is securely attached to her parent remains dependent upon her when she is an adult. Also, when a child has been abused and neglected by her parents, she desperately needs to experience an attachment figure whose experience of her is different than was the case with those who abused her.

However, it is crucial that the therapist not forget that the child is only with him an hour a week and that the relationship will not be permanent. As a result, therapy needs to go slower than if the child resides with a secure attachment figure. If the child becomes dysregulated during the week by themes that emerged in therapy, she is likely to have to manage these strong emotions and disturbing thoughts alone. The therapist needs to have confidence that he is exploring themes that the child will be able to manage alone until the next session.

I should note that some residential programs are successful in providing attachment figures for children living in them. These programs make a commitment to selecting residential workers with the ability and commitment to function as attachment figures and they provide them with sufficient training, support, and supervision so that they can perform their responsibilities well. It is crucial that the staff are adequately selected, reimbursed, and given the range of support services that they need to reduce the frequency of turnover.

Foster parents, teachers, and residential workers, among others, can function well as attachment figures for foster children and other at-risk children who do not have a permanent, secure attachment figure. They need to make the child aware of the temporary nature of the commitment if there is any uncertainty. They also need to be prepared to support the child in his experience of grief and loss at the end of the relationship. They also need to receive support themselves from other professionals so that they can manage their own grief, especially when the child remains in a very difficult life situation.

C. The Lack of Comprehensive Services and Support

As indicated at the beginning of the chapter, children with developmental trauma and attachment disorganization often have multiple, complex developmental difficulties that require a full team of adults to be able to adequately meet their needs. Parenting these children may be very difficult, and parenting them without knowledgeable professional help may be next to impossible. Even with psychological treatment that addresses their trauma and attachment difficulties, they still are likely to need a variety of services.

Their educational needs are likely to be significant. They may have learning disabilities and low achievement due to poor attendance, multiple schools, inability to concentrate, and difficult relationships with teachers and peers. Often these children do not respond well to traditional behavioral management programs based on reinforcement theory. Typical reinforcers have little lasting value and they often do not generalize to attachment relationships. Often their developmental age—including social, emotional, and reflective functioning—is significantly lower than their chronological age. Because their academic performance is periodically adequate, their spotty performance is often attributed to motivational issues. "They can do it if they want" is often unfairly said about them. Their shame also often prevents them from learning from mistakes and they are placed in situations where they fail again and again. They will not learn from their mistakes when they do not acknowledge making any—their shame prevents them from facing mistakes.

Family support services for f/a parents are often lacking or do not address the severity of the child's problems, nor the nature of the problems. Too often, the prediction "He just needs a loving family" proves to be woefully inadequate. These families need understanding and empathy, information and practical ideas. They also need to have professionals see them for the good people they are, who are doing the best that they can, and who care deeply for the child. Foster children are often moved rather than providing the foster parents with adequate support. Adopted children are often placed with adoptive parents who are not given adequate information, training, or support. Children often have multiple placements without the adults who are responsible for their development acknowledging that each failed placement is another trauma and each failed placement reduces the likelihood that the child will ever be ready and able to develop a secure attachment with the next caregiver.

Finally, the legal system often does not adequately address the psychological needs of these children. Children may be denied treatment when they have to testify in court against the abuser, out of fear that their testimony might be compromised. That can last for months or more than a year. Children are returned to parents who have been found to have abused or neglected their child when the only thing that has happened since they were placed in foster care is the passage of time, some visitation, and maybe a parent education class. None of those three has been shown to be effective in addressing the reasons for abuse and neglect.

The therapist's role is often to provide psychological treatment to the child, to provide counseling, information, and guidance to the f/a parents, and to facilitate the child's attachment with the f/a parents. If reunification is being pursued the therapist needs to assess if the child is safe with the parents who abused/neglected him before beginning DDP with those parents. Family treatment in reunification programs places the child under great risk to not experience safety when the parents are in denial about their behaviors that led to the child being removed from their care. The therapist, who may be the professional who knows the child's developmental needs and challenges best, must also consider being an advocate for appropriate services with the social service, educational, and legal systems. He may need to request evaluations by other professionals regarding the child's complex needs. Throughout it all, he needs to educate others on the importance of attachment security in facilitating the child's overall developmental needs.

EXERCISES

Questions

1. Employing AFFT with foster and adopted children is likely to be different for which of the following reasons:
   A. These children and teens are likely to manifest symptoms secondary to complex or developmental trauma due to abuse, neglect, abandonment, or multiple placements.
   B. Most, if not all, of the child's symptoms were present prior to the child living with the current parents or caregivers.
   C. While the child is likely to still experience intense and complex relationships with his original parents, those parents are very often not present and not available for relationship repair.
   D. All of the above.

2. The child is more likely to experience safety during the course of treatment if:
   A. The therapist avoids exploring traumatic themes for weeks or months.
   B. The therapist calmly insists that the child follow a gradual schedule for exploring traumatic themes.
   C. The therapist initiates exploration of a stressful theme in the first sessions and follows the child's cues as to how far to explore it.
   D. The therapist adopts a nondirective stance in which the child decides when traumatic themes will be explored.

3. The child's efforts to control the course of the treatment session and many other experiences in his life is due to:
   A. His belief that he is responsible for keeping himself safe.
   B. His experience that when another is in control, he is at risk of being abused.
   C. His lack of ease with reciprocity.
   D. All of the above.

4. Children often experience shame following the events of abuse and neglect that occurred with their biological parents because:
   A. They have not had any psychotherapy.
   B. They have not been told by others that it was their parents' fault.
   C. They seldom experience shame because of their young age at the time.
   D. They experienced their parent's experience of the abuse intersubjectively.

5. The foster or adopted child's efforts toward developing a coherent narrative are greatly aided when:

A. The intersubjective experience that he has with his adoptive parent becomes his template for his identity.

B. He forgets the abuse and neglect from the past.

C. He begins to comply with his adoptive parents' expectations.

D. More time has passed after the abuse stopped than the length of time when he was actually being abused.

Vignette Exercise

How might you respond? Read the following vignettes and then offer possible responses the therapist might make.

1. A child tells you that she doesn't feel anything.

   _____
   _____
   _____

2. A child tells you that he doesn't need a relationship with an adult, so why not stop trying to make him want one?

   _____
   _____
   _____

3. The child tells the foster mother that whenever she scolds her, the child experiences it as being screamed at. The foster mom is both disbelieving and shocked that the child might experience her that way.

   _____
   _____
   _____

4. A child ignores what you have said to him and starts talking to the foster parent about whether they can do an activity on the weekend. The foster parent gets drawn into the conversation.

   _____
   _____
   _____

Experiential Exercise

1. Imagine that two separate children lived with their respective parents for 5 years and are now living with families that they never met before—strangers to them.

A. One child was abused and neglected by his parents. Imagine your first few sessions. Imagine how his foster parents are likely to relate with him.

B. The second child's parents died in a car accident and she has no relatives. Imagine how you and the foster parents are likely to treat and relate to her.

Do you think there would be any differences in your treatment of the two children? Do you think that the foster parents would relate to the two children differently? If you think there would be differences, do you believe that they would be indicated by their different histories? Do you think any differences would be due to differences in assumptions about the child's experience? Do you think such assumptions are valid?

ANSWERS

Questions

1. D.
2. C. This middle way avoids the problems associated with both the directive and the nondirective approaches.
3. D.
4. D. Children are very much influenced by the meaning that their parents attribute to events. When the abusive parent believes that the child deserves the abuse, it is very difficult for the child to think and believe differently.
5. A. When the child begins to make sense of the world the way his f/a parents do, he is increasingly likely to be able to develop a perspective of his past that differs from the perspective presented by his abusive or neglecting parents.

Vignette Exercise: Suggested Responses

1. A child tells you that she doesn't feel anything.

   Empathy for what it might be like not to feel. Curiosity about how she might have come to not feel; when she first noticed that she did not feel.

   Wonder if she did not feel because no one was willing and able to help her handle hard feelings. Experience and communicate her bravery to face hard times alone as well as her wisdom to stop feeling when it was likely to be too hard to bear.

2. A child tells you that he doesn't need a relationship with an adult, so why not stop trying to make him want one?

   Curiosity about how he learned that he did not need such a relationship. Curiosity if it related to frightening relationships with adults in the past. Empathy for those hard past relationships. Experience and communicate his wisdom in avoiding relationships that might be hurtful. Curiosity if there might be other relationships that the child might enjoy even though he doesn't need them. What might they be like? Any downside to having no relationships? Sadness, loneliness, doubts.

3. The child tells the foster mother that whenever she scolds her, the child experiences it as being screamed at. The foster mom is both disbelieving and shocked that the child might experience her that way.

   Empathy for the foster mother who is now learning about the child's experience. Guidance for the foster mother to respond to the child's experience with PACE. Empathy for the child who experiences corrections as shouting. Curiosity about the source of the child's experience, wondering if scolding reminds her of screaming from her past.

4. A child ignores you and starts talking to the foster parent about whether they can do an activity on the weekend. The foster parent gets drawn into the conversation.

   Playfulness about being left out, about the lovely sharing between foster parent and child that does not involve the therapist. Curiosity about how the child turns to the foster parent for another discussion when the therapist mentions something a bit difficult. Talking to the foster parent about how hard it is for the child to explore stressful themes. Curiosity about whether the child might explore the stressful theme with the foster parent. Encouragement to the foster parent to relate to the stressful theme with PACE.

A Demonstration Session of Attachment-Focused Family Therapy

Included in this Workbook is a DVD of a simulated treatment session that demonstrates central features of AFFT. In this session the author is the therapist while the mother, Karen, and her adopted daughter, Tina, are actors. I chose to use actors because of the importance of confidentiality in psychological treatment. Even if all members of the family give permission to have a recording of a treatment session released, it is impossible to predict who might view the recording in the future, especially since its sale is not restricted to professional audiences.

This demonstration session represents the first session in which Tina and Karen were seen together. Tina's parents were seen the week before to obtain a history and to present the nature of AFFT to them. Tina, now 17 years of age, was adopted when she was nine after entering foster care at 3 years of age following early abuse and neglect. In the following 6 years prior to adoption she lived in 7 foster homes. Her parents sought treatment because of Tina's distant and angry attitude toward them, which had been present for the past several years. She also was somewhat defiant, expressed little remorse for misbehavior, and seemed to be looking forward to the day that she would leave home. Karen has two biological children in their early 20s. They were the "good kids" in the family, and Tina has always felt less loved by her adoptive parents than they appeared to be. While some of the content of this session is specific to adoptive families, the treatment process is the same and there are themes that are similar to those that occur in all families.

In this demonstration session I am quite verbal, active, and take responsibility for moving the dialogue along in ways that will hopefully evoke a deeper level of reciprocal communication and understanding. The particular content is much less important than is establishing and maintaining the affective-reflective dialogue. In such a dialogue the experiences of the members of the family are met with PACE in order to generate the intersubjective experiences that are crucial for both safety and new psychological learning about both self and other. When Tina experiences PACE regarding her experiences, she is able to go more deeply into them, helping her to make sense of them, regulate any fear or shame associated with them, and communicate them more fully to Karen. Her expressions are constantly met with acceptance, curiosity, and empathy (and a few times with playfulness). Not being evaluated, criticized, or told what she should think, feel, wish, or do, she is increasingly able to be aware of and express her vulnerabilities. My initial focus is to ensure that Tina experiences safety with both me and with her mother, while then facilitating her ability to engage in A-R dialogue.

Because of my commitment to the dialogue, I will relate with the family in whatever manner is necessary to ensure that the ongoing intersubjective experiences are facilitated and protected. I relate differently depending upon the family members' self-expressions, attitudes, and stage of treatment. As the therapy progresses and the family members are more comfortable with A-R dialogue, I am likely to assume a more receptive stance as they take more initiative for it. Since the parent is the attachment figure for the child, not vice versa, initially I focus on the child's safety and need to be able to explore his or her own experiences. The child's "presenting problems" are normalized, any associated emotions of shame, fear, anger, or discouragement are co-regulated, and the meanings of these behaviors become understood and expressed. As the parents are able to understand their child and their child's behaviors from the perspective of his or her experience, often the parents then respond to these behaviors with much greater empathy and much less judgment.

THE DEMONSTRATION SESSION

The treatment begins with Tina being quite clear that she does not want to improve her relationship with her parents and that she sees little interest in therapy, which she believes had not helped in the past. I completely accept Tina's initial stance, explore how it relates to her past, including her uncertainty about why her parents adopted her, leading to her saying that she is "the problem child," the "odd man out" relative to her adoptive parents' other two children, and ending with "they are not my brother and sister, they are her kids." As her expressions of anger and resignation were met with PACE, she was able to go more deeply into her experiences to express the reasons for not wanting to be close to her parents. This eventually led to her saying that she often felt like her adoptive parents were like her foster parents and they were not going to keep her either.

When Karen tried to reassure Tina that she most certainly would keep her, I interrupted her in order to stress that Tina's experience was what was important in the dialogue and that Karen was not going to talk her into Karen's experience. Karen needed to understand and have empathy for Tina's experience.

During this early discussion I was able to express my experience of Tina's strength in being able to get through and deal with all of the hard experiences that she has had since her birth. Since she had to rely on herself so much it was understandable why she would not have the habit of relying on her parents, and even prefer not to rely on them. This normalizes her reluctance to become emotionally closer to them, while seeing her independence as a strength rather than a weakness.

After exploring her life with her peers for a few minutes, I redirect the dialogue back to her relationships with her parents. Tina says clearly that she does not talk with them and does not care either. I wonder if her early self-reliance when she did not have parents to turn to made her not see the value in turning to her adoptive parents. Tina says that she does not think about her past but when she says, "I don't know how to talk to her!" that comment gave me an opportunity to connect her not knowing how to talk with her mother now, to not having any "practice" chattering with a parent when she was a child. It seemed to be important to help her to see more clearly how her very difficult first nine years when she had no parent to rely on relate to the difficulties that she now has relying on parents who are available.

At this point Karen spoke of how—when her biological children left home—she went from having three children to having none. Such a comment could easily be experienced by Tina as a rejection, so I helped Karen to clarify that she meant that because she is not close to Tina, it does not feel like she has a child at home. Worrying that Karen may also be becoming somewhat defensive over the negative experiences that Tina was describing about their relationship, I acknowledged how hard it must be for her to hear Tina's experiences and how well she was listening. Karen then said that Tina "shuts me out" and I brought out the reasons that Tina said that she did that, hoping to increase Karen's empathy for Tina.

When Karen seemed to be receptive to my comments about Tina's reasons, I thought that it was safe for Tina to tell her mother directly what was behind her distance from her mother. I gave Tina phrases to say to her mother—phrases that seemed congruent with what Tina had so far been expressing in the session. This deepened Tina's experience of her distance from her mother, her fear of abandonment, and of not being good enough for Karen. Tina's expression of her experience was so deep and clear that both became very vulnerable and Karen experienced a much deeper empathy for her daughter.

Giving children words to say to their parents about their inner lives often facilitates a deepening of the parent-child intersubjective experiences. Children—and their parents as well—who participate in AFFT often do not have the experience of communicating about the thoughts, feelings, and wishes that underlie their behaviors. When I provide words that are not congruent with the child's inner life, the dialogue will become barren and ineffective.

The dialogue now was increasingly safe and intersubjective, with both aware of more positive features in the other and being able to communicate that to the other. Karen was able to say that she appreciates Tina more than her biological children because "they had it easy," whereas Tina had to really work to develop a good life for herself. This led to Tina saying that she did experience her mother caring for her but she still has doubts about the strength of her caring. Tina then expressed the very powerful image of worrying when she went to bed at night if her parents would "have my bags packed" when she got up in the morning. Again, asking her to tell her mother that directly deepened the experience for both of them.

In the final 10 minutes I reflected on my experience of both of them during the session, giving expression to changes that I saw—both seemed more hopeful about the relationship and more able to see the other's experience of it. This reflection enabled them to step back and experience the session again from a more distant stance than was present in the immediacy of the earlier interactions. Suggesting that they tell Tina's father about the session was another way to reflect on it again while telling him as well as stressing the need to have him be involved in the ongoing treatment. A bit of playfulness at the end of the session also enabled the intense emotions that they experienced to become lighter and integrated. Finally, there was mention that they will still make mistakes, anticipating that they might get discouraged or dismiss the value of this session the first time that some of their prior difficulties re-emerge.

I would anticipate that in future sessions these same themes would be explored again since they have been dominant for Tina all of her life. Her anxiety about finally developing emotionally meaningful relationships with her parents would most likely cause her to find ways to avoid such a relationship—anticipating that it would only lead to pain. I would work to help her and her parents make sense of the process and be patient with it. I would also try to lead Tina into a more in-depth exploration of her past. If she were able to explore the shame, despair, rage, and terror that she must have experienced in years past over the events of her life, she would most likely be able to integrate those events into her narrative while relying on her adoptive parents for comfort. While resolving the past traumas, she would be deepening her attachments with her adoptive parents.

B Certification Program for Dyadic Developmental Psychotherapy and Attachment-Focused Family Therapy

A certification program for DDP has been developed that is applicable for all those who wish to practice AFFT. Chapter 8 in this workbook details the specific themes and interventions that are relevant for the specialized treatment of foster and adoptive families with children who have experienced developmental trauma and attachment disturbances. DDP was developed for that specific population.

For information regarding the certification program, the therapist should visit www.dyadicdevelopmentalpsychotherapy.org.

The following books and articles also serve as resources for DDP and AFFT:

Becker-Weidman, A., & Hughes, D. (2008). Dyadic developmental psychotherapy: An evidence-based treatment for children with complex trauma and disorders of attachment. *Child and Family Social Work, 13*, 329–337.

Becker-Weidman, A., & Shell, D. (Eds.). (2005). *Creating capacity for attachment.* Oklahoma City: Wood 'N' Barnes.

Becker-Weidman, A., & Shell, D. (Eds.). (2010). *Attachment parenting: developing connections and healing children.* Lanham, MD: Jason Aronson.

Golding, K. (2008). *Nurturing attachments: Supporting children who are fostered or adopted.* London: Jessica Kingsley.

Hughes, D. (2004). An attachment-based treatment of maltreated children and young people. *Attachment and Human Development, 6*, 263–278.

Hughes, D. (2006). *Building the bonds of attachment: Awakening love in deeply troubled children* (2nd ed.). Lanham, MD: Jason Aronson.

Hughes, D. (2007). *Attachment-focused family therapy.* New York: Norton.

Hughes, D. (2009). *Attachment-focused parenting.* New York: Norton.

Hughes, D. (2009). "Attachment-focused treatment for children." In *Clinical pearls of wisdom.* (M. Kerman, Ed.). New York: Norton, pp. 169–181.

Hughes, D. (2009). "Principles of attachment and intersubjectivity: Still relevant in relating with adolescents." In *Teenagers and attachment: Helping adolescents engage with life and learning.* (A. Perry, Ed.). London: Worth Publishing, pp. 123–140.

Hughes, D. (2009). "The communication of emotions and the growth of autonomy and intimacy within family therapy. In *The healing power of emotion: affective neuroscience, development, and clinical practice.* (D. Fosha, D. Siegel, & M. Solomon, Eds.) New York: Norton, pp. 280–303.

References

Baylin, J., & Hughes, D. (2010). *Parenting in connection: A psychobiological model of caregiving and blocked care.* Unpublished manuscript.

Cassidy, J., & Shaver, P. R. (Eds.). (2008). *Handbook of attachment,* 2nd ed. New York: Guilford.

Cicchetti, D., Toth, S., & Lynch, M. (1995). Bowlby's dream comes full circle: The application of attachment theory to risk and psychopathology. *Advances in Clinical Child Psychology, 17,* 1–75.

Cook, A., Spinazzola, J., Ford, J., et al. (2005). Complex trauma in children and adolescents. *Psychiatric Annals, 35*(5), 390–398.

Fosha, D., Siegel, D., & Solomon, M. (Eds.). (2009). *The healing power of emotion.* New York: Norton.

Marvin, R., Cooper, G., Hoffman, K., & Powell, B. (2002). The circle of security project: Attachment-based intervention with caregiver-pre-school child dyads. *Attachment and Human Development, 4,* 107–124.

Schore, A. N. (2001). Effects of a secure attachment on right brain development, affect regulation, and infant mental health. *Infant Mental Health Journal, 22,* 7–67.

Siegel, D. J. (2001). Toward an interpersonal neurobiology of the developing mind: Attachment relationships, "mindsight," and neural integration. *Infant Mental Health Journal, 22,* 67–94.

Sroufe, L. A., Egeland, B., Carlson, E., & Collins, W. A. (2005). *The development of the person.* New York: Guilford.

Stern, D. (1985). *The interpersonal world of the infant.* New York: Basic Books.

Tangney, J., & Dearing, R. (2002). *Shame and guilt.* New York: Guilford.

Trevarthen, C. (2001). Intrinsic motives for companionship in understanding: Their origin, development, and significance for infant mental health. *Infant Mental Health Journal, 22,* 95–131.

Index